The Repertory Movement

A History of Regional Theatre in Britain

GEORGE ROWELL AND ANTHONY JACKSON

D1328709

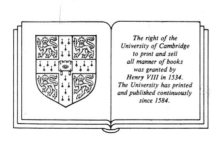

The right of the
University of Cambridge
to print and sell
all manner of books
was granted by
Henry VIII in 1534.
The University has printed
and published continuously
since 1584.

CAMBRIDGE UNIVERSITY PRESS

Cambridge
London   New York   New Rochelle
Melbourne   Sydney

Published by the Press Syndicate of the University of Cambridge
The Pitt Building, Trumpington Street, Cambridge CB2 1RP
32 East 57th Street, New York, NY 10022, USA
296 Beaconsfield Parade, Middle Park, Melbourne 3206, Australia

© Cambridge University Press 1984

First published 1984

Printed in Great Britain at the University Press, Cambridge

Library of Congress catalogue card number: 84–9522

British Library Cataloguing in Publication Data
Rowell, George
The repertory movement.
1. Repertory theatre – Great Britain –
History
I. Title II. Jackson, Anthony, 1943–
792'.0941   PN2595.3
ISBN 0 521 23739 4 hardcovers
ISBN 0 521 31919 6 paperback

LIVERPOOL POLYTECHNIC
C.F. MOTT CAMPUS
LIBRARY

202192

WD

Contents

v

Illustrations

Note: Photographs of theatres and productions are the copyright of the individual theatres unless otherwise stated in the captions.

Acknowledgements

A book such as this could hardly be written without the generous help and advice of a large number of individuals and institutions. Particular debts are acknowledged in the text where appropriate, but of the many who have assisted us in one way or another – too numerous to list here in full – we wish especially to record our gratitude to the following. Their views and the information which they have given us have been invaluable – though they must not be held responsible for any of the opinions we express or the interpretations and conclusions we reach in the course of the book, which are, of course, our own.

We would like to thank: John Bailey, Tim Baker, Peter Cheeseman, Alan Durband, Michael Elliott, Richard Eyre, John Faulkner, Giles Havergal, Jo Hodgkinson, Phyllis Leggett, Vivian Nixson, Clive Perry, Geoffrey Rowe, Ronald Russell, Reginald Salberg, Barry Sheppard, Clare Venables, Hazel Vincent-Wallace, Richard Williams, Peggy Ann Wood, and the various staffs of the Citizens' Theatre, Glasgow, the Everyman Theatre, Liverpool, the Nottingham Playhouse, the Royal Exchange Theatre, Manchester, the Salisbury Playhouse, the Victoria Theatre, Stoke-on-Trent, the Local Studies Department of the Nottinghamshire County Library, the British Theatre Association Library and the Research Library of the Arts Council of Great Britain.

1 Introduction

GEORGE ROWELL AND ANTHONY JACKSON

IT IS SURPRISING that until now there has been no sustained account published of the British repertory movement. It is surprising because that movement, beginning to all intents and purposes in 1907 with Miss Horniman's company in Manchester, but with roots in ideas and experiments stretching back into the previous century, has played a vital – often a dominant – role in the British twentieth-century theatre. In the two most recent decades indeed it has come to provide both the basic energy of the nation's theatre and much of its very life-blood too. Its history has hitherto been recorded by or been about participants in the movement, or has focussed on individual theatres and particular periods. To such as J.C. Trewin on Birmingham, Rex Pogson on Manchester, Grace Wyndham Goldie on Liverpool, and the books of influential figures such as Basil Dean, Iden Payne, Tyrone Guthrie and Norman Marshall, and of more recent commentators such as John Elsom, the student of the subject is deeply indebted. But a survey of the movement as a whole has until now been lacking. Some seventy-five years on, it seems appropriate to take stock of its development, its achievements, its contribution to the British theatre's sense of itself – and this the present study strives to do.

The term 'repertory' is a much used and abused one and, at the risk of stating the obvious, we should perhaps make clear at the outset the sense in which we are using it. Strictly, a repertory theatre is one that stages its plays in rotation, building over a period of a year or more a store of productions that are offered to the public on a regularly changing basis, each play being performed no more than a week at a time but brought back at frequent intervals according to public demand. This, essentially, is the pattern adopted at the National Theatre in London and the norm at most of the large state and civic theatres in the rest of Europe. But the term in Britain has come to be used far more loosely, and it is the looser and more common usage that we employ here. What characterises the average British repertory theatre now – and indeed what has done for most of the movement's history – is that its season of plays, while conceived as a whole, is yet presented in a single linear sequence: each production runs for three or four weeks at a time (much less before the advent of subsidy), with no rotation, no return of plays once done, no 'repertoire' as such. Exceptions to the rule, as might be expected, abound. And there are, and have been, repertory theatres organised on strictly repertory lines. Indeed, symptomatic of the general practice has been the coining of the term 'true repertory' to indicate a theatre system based on the Continental model. It is a term, too, that, for the sake of clarity, we shall employ here when appropriate.

Repertory in this looser, broader sense does, however, contain a whole cluster of other important meanings and associations that need to be pinpointed and recognised before the historical account can begin. Broadly, repertory theatres in Britain have seen themselves as determinedly non-commercial in approach, based in and serving a specific community or region and providing a wide range of plays, new and classic, challenging and popular. Emphases and practice have undergone considerable shifts over the decades. But behind the shifts, the twists, turns and contradictions in the development of repertory has been the sense of a cause to be fought. Repertory, in fact, from the very beginning has been an *idea* in the minds of its advocates as much as it has been a practical method of presenting plays. Already at the turn of the century, the idea of repertory – as a form of theatre opposed in every way to the dominant commercial theatre of the time – had become an integral part of the developing concern with the future of the theatre in Britain. It had become inseparably linked to such other central issues as the need to establish a state-subsidised national theatre organised on repertory principles, the need to encourage new British playwrights, and the need to raise the general standards of production. At the same time, awareness was growing of the theatre's potency as an educative as well as artistic or entertainment medium, and therefore of its importance in the cultural life of the country as a whole – in the regions at least as much as in London. In all such areas the 'repertory idea' was seen to be crucial, and hence came to embrace before long the general concern for renewing the vitality of the theatre and for re-establishing theatre's links with its community. From this general concern it was only a short step to the assertion of the theatre's necessary role as a cultural service, to be supported by public funds just as were libraries, museums and art galleries. Without doubt the inspirational value of the repertory idea together with the movement to translate it into reality – involving failure as much as success – have been at the centre of the subsequent development of theatre in Britain.

Theory and practice have often diverged, of course, and still do – often because of unbending economic realities or the personal whims of artistic directors; but most of all because the theory has never been hard and fast. The repertory movement was not imposed from without, was not part of any national plan, but evolved from a whole gamut of complex factors, not least being the personal visions and driving energies of particular personalities. Similarly the repertory idea itself was never seen as one static goal to be reached but has been subject to constant expansion and redefinition as decades have passed. There are, none the less, larger, underlying patterns in the history of the movement that do present themselves and which this study will attempt to describe. One such pattern demands attention now, for it will help to place the detailed chronological account to follow in clearer perspective and explain, for example, the space given to the nineteenth-century background and likewise our emphasis upon the regional dimension.

The repertory movement was propelled by a double revolt against the Edwardian theatrical establishment: a revolt against the dramatic fare offered by London managers and actors, and against the exploitation of the provincial theatre as the market for metropolitan products. Often the two rebellions coincided, as in the fostering of Irish nationalist drama at the Abbey Theatre, Dublin, or the Lancashire school of playwrights based on the Gaiety, Manchester. Both took sustenance from local pride and local disillusion with London hallmarks. But they were also only the more dramatic signs of the gradual but total transformation of the provincial scene which the repertory movement was to bring about.

Most of the early champions of that movement selected the touring company as their chief target. 'A smudged carbon-copy of last year's West End success' was the standard accusation hurled at the latest attraction in their local Theatre Royal. While one cannot defend *in toto* the touring system established in the last quarter of the Victorian era, it may be salutary to recall that the system was itself hailed as a renaissance of dramatic standards during the 1870s and 1880s. Before that provincial playgoers might see London stars, but they would be supported by an uneven and under-rehearsed stock company and mostly stock (or improvised) sets and costumes. Of course the touring system invited abuse; an organisation as widely spread as the Victorian and Edwardian theatre encouraged managements to undertake mass production, and it was against the second-, third- and fourth-rate companies that the pioneers of repertory mainly made their stand. In the cyclic fashion of human endeavour they looked back longingly to the days of the resident manager, local favourites and even local plays. When one of these pioneers, Alfred Wareing, tried to persuade Miss Horniman, that patroness of early repertory, to finance his Glasgow project, he proposed 'the re-establishment of a stock company with a repertory of modern plays', while some years earlier Granville Barker had planned his venture at the Royal Court in terms of 'a stock season of the uncommercial Drama'.

Although the first wave of repertory subsided as a result of the First World War, there was a steady renaissance of the movement in the 1920s and 30s, much encouraged by the shrinking during this period of the provincial touring circuit at the challenge of first the 'movies' and then the 'talkies'. Again local pride, sometimes sustained by amateur effort in the best sense of labouring for love, contributed greatly. In the 1930s too a species of 'commercial' repertory grew up to challenge the local strain: circuits of 'chain store' companies financed by London impresarios which to some extent took the place of the old touring companies, now decimated by the all-conquering cinema. The ground gained by the repertory movement in this period is graphically summarised in Cecil Chisholm's informative mid thirties survey *Repertory: an outline of the modern theatre movement*. In 1934 the coexistence of thirty-seven repertory and thirty-seven touring companies was noted, whereas twenty years earlier, at the outbreak of the War, there had been 'twelve stock companies and 170 touring companies'. The cinema had taken its toll but not at the expense of the local rep.

This diarchy in the provincial theatre survived and even flourished in the austere siege conditions of the Second World War, expanding in the decade 1945–55, only to fall victim to the television set and home entertainment provided first by the BBC and, from 1955, by commercial television. 'Commercial' repertory sustained a mortal blow but the local brand was saved by increasing blood-transfusions from Arts Council and local government sources. At the same time the label 'rep', now devalued by its identification with the commercial product of the late thirties and forties, was largely discarded in favour of 'regional', a term accurate as far as the appeal and support of the companies in question were concerned but less precise when applied to their personnel and repertoire.

The distinction between 'local' and 'commercial' rep might have disappeared, but another quickly replaced it. In 1971 John Elsom, writing in his *Theatre Outside London* and drawing on his experience with the Arts Council, awarded merit marks for the ambitious programme, which he termed *haute couture* and identified in such salons as Nottingham, Birmingham, Bristol and Oxford, as opposed to 'something for everybody' (termed *prête-à-porter* – 'ready to wear'). Of course this distinction could hardly have arisen without the steady flow of funds into existing companies from the Arts Council and local authorities which characterised the 1950s and 1960s, and more particularly the building of regional theatres by a number of enlightened councils. The welcome assistance from public funds which many reps now received opened up the possibility not merely of new purpose-built homes but also of higher production standards in general.

Today too the repertory company performs a very different function from that envisaged by Miss Horniman in 1907, or by the Arts Council when it established the Bristol Old Vic in 1946. It is even faced with a different task from that for which John Elsom awarded merit and de-merit marks in 1971. It has had to assume the responsibilities of both the commercial repertories and the touring circuit, except for highly specialised offerings such as opera and ballet. Thus Elsom's *prête-à-porter* has become not so much 'off the peg' as 'your only repertory wear'. There is no other shop for the bulk of the provincial playgoing public to buy from.

There remains the sphere of *haute couture*, but it is surely a totally transformed branch of tailoring. In particular the establishment of the National Theatre and the diversification of the Royal Shakespeare Company have taken over some of the tasks once assumed by leading reps as a challenge to the commercial managements. If the repertory company entrusted with a substantial sum of public money has to cater for the playgoing public on the same lines as the librarian caters for the reader, there arises a need for an 'alternative' theatre: avant-garde, experimental, committed, élitist, educational – each adjective and school has its merits and de-merits. But the cyclic movement noted in connection with the Victorian stock company is no less apparent in the history of the repertory company, seen as an alternative to some theatrical 'establishment'. It *is* now the establishment.

The scope of our study, then, is first and foremost the history of the movement in Britain from its origins in the nineteenth century up to the present day, concentrating upon the general underlying patterns and achievements. Inevitably our approach has had to be selective and theatres have been chosen for discussion because they illustrate those patterns and achievements particularly well, not because they are the only theatres worth discussing. We have not dealt in any great detail with repertory developments in London (such as those at the Old Vic, the Royal Court, the National Theatre or the Royal Shakespeare Company's various London homes) except insofar as they represent a pivotal stage in the development of repertory or illuminate especially effectively an important aspect of it. We see repertory as primarily a regional phenomenon. Similarly – for the sake of maintaining the sharpest possible focus – we do not discuss in detail those parallel and influential developments that took place across the seas, in Dublin and in the great theatrical centres of Paris, Berlin and elsewhere in Europe. Those developments were important in their own right and often exerted considerable influence upon British practice and ideas. But repertory in Britain was not an offspring of nor modelled slavishly upon theatre systems elsewhere. Its development was unique (not necessarily better or worse), and it is the study of its growth within and the contribution it has made to British theatre in general that we have felt to be our primary task here.

The chapters we have written separately, though not in isolation. While responsibility for the judgements made in each are the author's own, we have each benefitted from the critical scrutiny and constructive comment of the other. Our emphases and interpretations may be different from chapter to chapter, but a shared belief in the importance of the subject and in the significance of its many achievements underpins our collaboration.

2   The Nineteenth-Century Background

GEORGE ROWELL

N THE COURSE of the nineteenth century the British theatre evolved from a minority interest to a national industry. The impact of the Industrial Revolution was no less extensive on the country's recreation than on its growth and distribution of population. In the Georgian period the scope of the theatre had been severely restricted, as much by legal as by physical limits. London was permitted its two 'patent' theatres – Drury Lane and Covent Garden; its opera house, the King's Theatre; and a 'summer' playhouse, the Haymarket, providing entertainment when the patents were shut. Any competition was liable to infringe the Licensing Act of 1737, a statute designed by Walpole to silence the playwright with political intent, but exploited to muzzle the drama in general. Outside London all stage performances were suspect and subject to the authority of the local magistrates and the greed or spite of the common informer. Some sort of theatrical activity continued, but it was inevitably fugitive and often clandestine. The strolling player was despised as a rogue and vagabond, and his audience forced to play the conspirator and accomplice.

Nevertheless in the latter part of the Georgian era official recognition of the provincial theatre slowly progressed. Patents granted to companies in the more important centres protected their endeavours and earned their playhouses the title of Theatres Royal. Bath, Norwich, York and Hull were so recognised in the 1760s; Liverpool, Manchester and Bristol in the 1770s; Newcastle in the 1780s. This relaxation of the embargo on provincial playmaking also encouraged those companies who moved from town to town, setting up their stage in hall or inn, planning their visits to coincide with a fair, a race meeting or the assizes, and building up a 'circuit' which grew in reputation and respectability. A substantial step forward in this growth was the passing in 1788 of a statute allowing magistrates to license performances for sixty days at any one time, since a two-month season was as much as most communities could sustain.

The way was thus cleared at the turn of the century for a large-scale expansion of theatrical activity for which the country evinced a rapidly increasing appetite. By 1827 Leman T. Rede in his *Road to the Stage* records details of forty-nine companies, several of them based on well-established Theatres Royal, such as Manchester (from which the players travelled as far afield as Shrewsbury and Lichfield), York and Newcastle, but others covering less populated areas. By 1833 the proliferation of playhouses was such that John Miller ('Agent to the Dramatic Authors' Society') could compile *An Alphabetical List of Theatres in the United Kingdom* running to over 200 entries.[1] By no means all of these dared call themselves Theatres Royal or claim to be purpose-built, and many functioned for only a few weeks of the year. Nevertheless their identity and location were well-enough established to figure on the Dramatic Authors' list, and in the majority of cases the inclusion of a manager's name indicated professional continuity and commercial stability. Equally notable is the provision in the bigger industrial centres of a number of halls offering a diversity of entertainment, including music, song, dance and circus, as well as the drama. Liverpool, for example, is listed as providing six, and by the 1840s Glasgow could cap this with seven.

THE STOCK COMPANY

The basis of all this activity was the stock company, a semi-permanent group managed by a leading actor and fulfilling the function of players and family circle simultaneously. Dickens' affectionate portrait in *Nicholas Nickleby* of the Crummles Company (apparently inspired by a Hampshire manager, T.D. Davenport, with a daughter able or at least required to play Shylock, Richard III and Sir Peter Teazle)[2] should not be credited as a just account of the entire theatrical profession outside London in his youth. Not only were many of the Theatres Royal capably managed but some at least of the circuits achieved consistently high standards: Sarah Baker made the Canterbury circuit a recognised training-ground at the start of the century.

Certainly membership of a stock company equipped a young actor for all emergencies, and the demands made on him were daunting. The evening's bill might include four or five items and extend from seven to midnight to appease the 'half price' public, precluded by their working hours from the early portion. The majority of the company would be expected to take part in most of these items, some of which were changed nightly and many of which were changed weekly. A succession of farces, melodramas, pantomimes, interspersed with dancing, singing and acrobatics, stretched them mentally and physically beyond modern comprehension. During his first three years as an actor Irving, for example, undertook 428 characters before making a (dismally unsuccessful) London debut.[3] His contemporary, Squire Bancroft, claimed to have played 346 parts in numerous provincial companies between 1860 and 1865, and was positive that 'the repetition of many of those in standard plays, and some of them often, not only in different theatres but with different actors, was alone of the greatest service'.[4]

As an apprenticeship to acting the stock company was rich in experience if poor in pecuniary reward, but such an output was made possible only by a species of conveyor-belt manufacture on the part of both actor and author. The plays themselves, when original (a flattering term since the majority were adapted from some other source), were products of ready-made theatrical tailoring. The characters proclaimed their cut, being labelled 'Comedy Lead'; 'Character Comedy'; '1st Old Man' (usually fat); '2nd Old Man' (usually thin); '1st Old Woman' (proportions unspecified); 'Singing Chambermaid' (brilliance more important than bed-making); down to the humble 'Utility' and 'Walking Gentleman' (so called because he seldom talked). Actors knew their 'line' if not their lines, and borrowed dialogue from one play for another without the audience's knowing or their colleagues suffering, provided they 'came to cues'.

Indeed these colleagues rarely noticed the loan, since they were supplied only with 'sides' (long sheets of manuscript) which revealed their own lines and the preceding cue. The importance of a part was measured in 'sides', and the actor could only guess at the development of the drama until the first reading or rehearsal. Margaret Webster, descendant of two theatrical houses, the Websters and the Whittys, reprints in her family history a splendidly perplexing extract from such a 'side':

HERO: I love you, my darling, and shall love you till I die.
HEROINE: [*cue*] . . . very much.
HERO: Ah! (*Shoots himself*)[5]

Sometimes the unfortunate actor was not even supplied with a 'side' but required to write out his lines from the manuscript prompt-copy.

Inevitably rehearsals were cut to the bone. As a very young man in the late 1840s John Coleman, an actor who was to preserve the traditions of the stock company into the next century, joined the Lincoln circuit when its troupe were playing at Leicester. The company was then run by Mr and Mrs Robertson, a fertile couple who produced at least seventeen children, including a famous playwright, Tom, and a famous actress, Madge, later Dame Madge Kendal. The matriarchal Mrs Robertson was too pre-occupied to attend rehearsal:

'Mrs Robertson!' called the Prompter.

'Mrs Robertson is looking out the checks. Read for her', grimly remarked Mr Robertson.

'Gabble-gabble,' commenced the Prompter – 'gabble! Now, sir, that's your cue. On you come from behind the centre arch.'

'Where will the arch be?'

'Where will the arch be, Casson?' inquired the Prompter.

'Second grooves', replied the master-carpenter.

'It will be a drawing-room. Here is a chair; there a table', continued the Prompter.

'But I don't see either the one or the other', I replied.

'No, but you will at night . . . Gabble-gabble – squeak. Cross to right, then to left and up centre. Mind you give Mrs Robertson the stage: she wants plenty of elbow-room.'[6]

Other stock companies managed matters better. Madge Robertson herself joined the company at the Theatre Royal, Bristol, for fifty years ruled by the Macready family and at this period (the 1860s) under W.C. Macready's step-brother-in-law, James Henry Chute:

Our governor is a fine-looking man, deep in the chest, broad in the shoulders – well set up, twinkling eyes – that can be severe – broad massive forehead and a large moustache. His hands are Frenchy in their action, and he is never seen without a pair of gloves – which I am told by old hands he has never been known to put on . . .

wrote another aspirant, William Rignold,[7] when joining the Bristol band, where at various times the two eldest Terry sisters, Kate and Ellen, and Marie Wilton (later Mrs Bancroft) also learnt their craft. In this decade another manager, Charles Calvert, raised the prestige of his Manchester stock company, first at the Theatre Royal, later at the newly built Prince's, to gain national recognition. His productions of Shakespeare in particular continued and refined on the traditions of Samuel Phelps (under whom he had served) and inspired those of Irving, who played his first Hamlet at Manchester.

SPECIAL ENGAGEMENTS

What undermined the authority and standards of the stock company was the increasing popularity of visiting performers with a London reputation. Theatrical expansion in the capital matched that in the provinces. By 1850 there were some thirty-five theatres or halls offering theatrical entertainment, and in 1843 the privileges of the 'patent' theatres were recognised as outdated, the distinction between them and the newer 'minors' abolished by the Theatre Regulation Act, and the restrictions on the latter's bill of fare lifted. Until their emancipation the 'minors' had been limited to the 'burletta', an ill-defined term interpreted as any dramatic work with a musical content, often referred to as 'illegitimate drama' as opposed to the 'legitimate' sphere reluctantly upheld by the 'patents'.

One consequence of this greatly increased theatrical activity and the attention paid to it in the expanding popular press was the creation of 'star' actors who could command leading parts and lavish payment by touring. A handful of Georgian favourites had tided over the summer recess in London by accepting engagements in a few provincial theatres, but the early-nineteenth-century stars – Edmund Kean, W.C. Macready, Charles Kemble and his daughter, Fanny, Charles Kean and his wife, Ellen – could arrange to tour for months, if not years, and with North America and Australia offering increasing opportunities, it often paid them better to travel than to remain in London and take the risks.

Until the 1860s they travelled alone, or at most with a supporting player, undertaking a round of parts in a round of plays. The quality and character of the resulting performance may be imagined. There was little time (and with some stars little inclination) for rehearsal. Samuel Phelps, later to make Sadler's Wells the home of Shakespeare for twenty years, was a minor member of the York company in the late 1820s when Edmund Kean joined them to exhibit the remains of his once staggering powers, and found himself cast as Tubal to the star's Shylock:

He didn't come to rehearsal, and although Lee, his secretary, rehearsed carefully enough, I did not know where to find Kean at night, for he crossed here, there, and everywhere, and prowled about like a caged tiger. I never took my eyes off him. I dodged him up and down, crossed when he crossed, took up my cues, and got on pretty fairly, till he thoroughly flabbergasted me by hissing, 'Get out of my focus! Blast you! – get out of my focus!'

Phelps loyally adds: 'With the exception of this trifling hitch the scene went like a whirlwind.'[8]

Yet even with stars prepared to rehearse, the effect of their annexing the leading roles and the public's adulation of the visitor were demoralising to the resident company. In his *Diaries* Macready, a star of a very different stamp from Kean, catalogued a dismal series of supporting actors, incompetent, intemperate or perhaps just terrified of the Great Man. In the performance of *Virginius* at Bath in 1836

The Icilius (a Mr Savile) was either half-stupidly drunk, or is, as is very probable, a born ass. Virginia would have made an excellent representation of Appius' cook, as far as appearance went, added to which she seemed to think that she was playing Virginius, not Virginia, and fortified herself for some extraordinary efforts by a stimulant which was too easily detected on a near approach to her.[9]

Nevertheless Bath was one of the leading provincial theatres and its stock company a nursery for London favourites.

INTRODUCTION OF THE TOURING COMPANY

Even more damaging to the smaller stock companies was the transformation of the repertoire. Until the turn of the century a handful of tragedies (Shakespeare interspersed with the occasional Otway or Addison's *Cato*) and a modest selection of comedies, including afterpieces, had served the strollers season after season. But the nineteenth-century taste was for spectacular scenes and melodramatic plots, depending heavily on the new stage technology of the Industrial Age: gas-light, 'flown' scenery, 'cut-cloths', gauzes, trap-work of various kinds, a full complement of supernumeraries and a squad of technicians to stage-manage miracles. Only the better-equipped houses in the bigger centres could accomplish all this, and even those found themselves hard pressed to do so within the constantly changing bill by which the stock company survived. Visiting stars were an effective if expensive attraction, but provincial audiences became increasingly critical of a Macready supported by born asses and actresses breathing brandy. They looked for a carefully rehearsed ensemble and staging up to London standards. The reform and refinement of theatrical presentation following the Theatre Regulation Act had established those standards, and the rapid growth of the railways made them available to the provinces.

The era of expansion in the London theatre came to a temporary halt after 1843. Those prophets who foretold doom for the drama as a result of the Theatre Regulation Act and *laissez-faire* in the theatre were proved wrong. Instead of a ruinous outbreak of competitive theatre-building the London managers turned to putting their own houses in order. Leadership passed from the former 'patents'; Drury Lane and Covent Garden were too large for the spoken drama and directed their efforts towards opera, pantomime and spectacular entertainment. In their place more manageable theatres became the homes of 'antiquarian' Shakespeare (the Princess's under Charles Kean), 'gentlemanly' melodrama (the Olympic under the Wigan family), and visiting French companies (the St James's), with the Haymarket preserving its traditions of comedy and farce. The initiative of the Royal Family in introducing from 1848 an annual series of Command Performances at Windsor conferred distinction on a profession which had lost much of its patronage as it greatly increased its public.

By the 1860s the former burlesque actress, Marie Wilton, was able to turn a miniature and run-down playhouse off the Tottenham Court Road into a fashionable theatre, the Prince of Wales's, offering drawing-room comedy to drawing-room audiences. Within a few months of opening in 1865 she had found not only a leading man (Squire Bancroft, whom she married) but a resident dramatist, Tom Robertson, whose 'cup-and-saucer' comedies from *Society* to *Caste* and *School* were the mainstay of her programme. Moreover she had earned a reputation for over-all standards of acting, staging, dressing and interpretation which were the envy of her competitors, both in London and the provinces. It was appropriate, therefore, that in 1867 a Bancroft company should blaze the trail by touring a complete production of Robertson's most popular play, *Caste*. Their initiative was a revelation to provincial playgoers but struck a further blow at the stock company, already demoralised by the popularity of visiting stars. It was in the touring company of *Two Roses*, a comedy in the Robertsonian style, that in the summer of 1871 a Dublin boy, George Bernard Shaw, first saw Henry Irving and 'instinctively felt that a new drama inhered in this man, though I had then no conscious notion that I was destined to write it; and I perceive now that I never forgave him for baffling the plans I made for him'.[10] Shaw was then rising fifteen, and Irving within months of his sensational success at the Lyceum in *The Bells*.

The twenty-five years between Irving's arrival at the Lyceum and his journey to Windsor to be dubbed the first actor-knight by Queen Victoria saw a remarkable advance in the standing of the London theatre. The Bancrofts' success in tempting polite society to their pocket-playhouse was achieved by other actor-managers on a bigger scale. Irving became director as well as star of the Lyceum in 1878; Charles Wyndham began a quarter of a century's reign at the Criterion in 1875; John Hare presided over first the Court, then the St James's. In a different but no less influential style Richard D'Oyly Carte brought together Gilbert and Sullivan, established their work at the Opera Comique, and built the Savoy to provide it with a permanent home and an immortal name. Other theatres sprang up in competition, and by the end of the century the West End alone boasted over fifty such, augmented by music halls, suburban theatres and homes of entertainment not easily classified.

All this expansion found a counterpart in the provinces. With rail travel increasingly swift and comprehensive, the example of the *Caste* tour could be readily and profitably followed. In the week of November 1871 when Irving inaugurated a new chapter in theatre history by his performance in *The Bells*, there were still only twelve touring companies 'on the road', and stock companies occupied the majority of provincial theatres. Thirty years later, in November 1901, the columns of the theatrical paper, the *Era*, list 143 touring companies on circuit, and do not name a single stock company. Several of the touring groups offered the same attraction, particularly the newly popular musical comedy; for instance, three versions were available of both *Floradora* and *The Belle of New York*, while the single company playing *Les Cloches de Corneville* claimed to be in its 'Twentieth Year'. Straight plays were less widely represented, but there were three rival productions of *The Sign of the Cross* and two of *The Silver King*, both melodramas made famous by Wilson Barrett, while Mrs Bandmann-Palmer, an actress brave or rash enough to tackle Hamlet, was in her 'Thirteenth Year of Tour with Company'.

STANDARDS OF TOURING COMPANIES

Of course it would be unjust to condemn the touring system on the strength or weakness of its cracked chimes of Corneville or too too solid female Hamlets. The tours of the Lyceum, St James's or Her Majesty's companies brought to provincial audiences standards of performance and presentation they had never previously experienced, even when an Edmund Kean or W.C. Macready played for them. Conversely the success and profits of touring, in North America as well as the provinces, made possible those standards of presentation. Irving and his fellow-managers looked to touring to balance their books and finance new enterprises. But there were only a handful of leading London actor-managers and nearly 150 touring companies operating simultaneously.

It followed that the lion's share of touring fell to 'second line' companies. Some of these, like Frank Benson's or Ben Greet's, struggled manfully under conditions which would have broken less stout hearts. Basil Dean, soon to be a mainstay of the Manchester Gaiety Company, and then director of the Liverpool Repertory Theatre, gives a chilling picture of the touring actor's lot:

Life on tour was not exactly the romantic struggle I had imagined; away from the theatre it appeared sordid and uninspiring. I was left with a lasting impression of tedious railway journeys and uncomfortable lodgings. Few of the cross-country trains had corridors. Occasionally a lavatory was discovered attached to a single compartment; this was allotted to the women; the men had their own way of dealing with the calls of nature. Late journeys were completed in semi-darkness which the gas-jets, encased in glass bowls in the roof, seemed only to accentuate; sometimes the gas escaped; often there was no gas at all. The railway companies did their best to provide heating by means of small metal canisters of hot water, guaranteed to cause chilblains rather than provide warmth. Dining-cars were non-existent, but luncheon-baskets made of brown wicker with the name of the railway and the station of issue stamped on a zinc plate on the lid, were available for those who could afford them.[11]

A few actor-managers, such as Fred Terry and Martin-Harvey, made touring their chief concern, but the great majority of touring companies were operated by commercial managers to whom financial return was paramount and who were prepared to exploit both actor and audience in the process. When the Actors' Association (later absorbed into Equity) was set up in 1891, its provisions were chiefly designed to bind the hands of the touring manager, Article 7 specifically declaring that 'the Association is determined to crush the infamies of bogus managements; it is also most anxious to enforce honest conduct on the part of its members – i.e. to compel the honourable fulfilment of their responsibility to managers, land-ladies of lodging houses etc.'.[12] Interestingly, a specific Provincial Actors' Union was formed at Manchester in 1907, some six months before the first provincial repertory season opened there, although the organisation quickly amalgamated with the short-lived Actors' Union.

AN ALTERNATIVE THEATRE

At the same time touring managements were subject to criticism from the playgoing public for offering 'carbon copies' of London successes. The titles already listed from the *Era* for November 1901 point to the preponderance of melodrama and musical comedy 'On the Road'. This emphasis accurately measured the limitations of theatrical progress over the previous thirty years. The standards of presentation had risen steadily but the quality and character of what was presented, particularly the 'serious drama', still showed a heavy dependence on outdated Continental sources, the French school of Sardou, Meilhac and Halévy, not the Scandinavian school of Ibsen and Strindberg. Certainly a self-respecting Society drama emerged during the 1890s, and it would seem no unworthy aim to 'copy' the St James's production of the latest Wilde or Pinero, but doubtless the 'copy' which had been toured for months or even years became increasingly smudged. Many touring managers did not aspire that high but found a vehicle they could tour year in, year out, as W.W. Kelly offered *A Royal Divorce* with its well-remembered line: 'Not tonight, Josephine'.

By the turn of the twentieth century the ubiquitous touring company had provoked a nostalgic recollection of the stock company which, with all its faults, the provincial playgoer remembered as predictable and seemingly permanent, cherishing its memory with a sense of possession they could never feel for a succession of weekly visitors. The first two declared objectives of the Scottish Playgoers' Company founded in April 1909 were:

> 1. To establish in Glasgow a Repertory Theatre which will afford playgoers and those interested in the drama an opportunity of witnessing such plays as are rarely presented under the present Touring Company system.
> 2. To organise a Stock Company of first-class actors and actresses for the adequate representation of such plays.[13]

Thus from its earliest days the repertory movement combined a search for unfamiliar drama with a return to familiar forms of achieving it.

The various strands which were woven into the fabric of the growing alternative theatre movement in London at the turn of the century will be unravelled in Chapter 3. Here it may suffice to point out that fifteen years before the first repertory theatre opened in Manchester, that same city had responded to the capital's initiative. London's Independent Theatre, founded in 1891 'to give special performances of plays which have a literary and artistic rather than a commercial value',[14] and chiefly recalled for its sponsorship of Ibsen and Shaw, inspired a Manchester Independent Theatre between 1893 and 1897. Like its prototype it offered occasional productions by a company performing for the cause rather than the cash, but several of its keenest supporters encouraged Miss Horniman in her enterprise later.

But before this development could follow, a clearer lead was needed than the Independent Theatre or its successor, the Stage Society – both essentially play-producing societies rather than ensembles – was able to offer. In Dublin the resistance to (mostly English) touring companies was sharpened by nationalist pride and prejudice. Starting as a group of artistic amateurs, the Irish National Theatre Society was able through the reputation of W.B. Yeats and the subvention of Miss Horniman to establish itself at the Abbey Theatre in 1904. In the same year the success of the Stage Society encouraged the young Granville Barker, who had acted in and directed several of the Society's productions, to look for a more permanent home. With Shaw's support he found it in the little Royal Court Theatre in Sloane Square.

3 First Steps: The Beginnings of a Movement

ANTHONY JACKSON

THE Royal Court venture, under Barker's direction but with the indispensable aid of his business manager, J.E. Vedrenne, lasted for only three seasons, from 1904 to 1907, but its achievements were many. In presenting no less than eleven plays by Bernard Shaw the management triumphantly established Shaw's reputation as the major British dramatist of the day; a remarkable range of new or 'uncommercial' drama was introduced to the English theatre; through Barker's work as a director new standards of acting and production were set on the London stage; and, not least, a powerful impetus was given to the repertory theatre movement.[1]

In July 1907, shortly after the management at the Court had come to an end, Barker, summing up what he believed to have been the most significant aspects of their artistic policy, remarked:

At the Court we have by no means started a repertory theatre or anything like it, but we have introduced a system which may prove the artistic necessity of such institutions. We have opposed to the long run system the short run system. It has many disadvantages, perhaps, but it keeps the plays fresh . . . I think we may claim that the plays are more alive now, both from a business and an artistic point of view, than they would have been had they simply been run callously to the fullest limit of their popularity.[2]

Only months later Britain's first permanent repertory theatre company began work in Manchester, organised on the 'short-run system' and drawing much of its inspiration, several of its actors and a good deal of its repertoire from that pioneering Court venture. Not only was the Court's impact an immediate one, but it remained a constant point of reference for the repertory movement for a decade and more.

But the Court venture was itself only the culmination of a whole series of challenges to the actor-manager's hold on the London theatre that had been made during the final two decades of the previous century. Before looking at the Vedrenne–Barker achievements in more detail we must first set them in that larger context.

ORGANISING THE THEATRE

British theatre has rarely if ever been static, but while the newly predominant touring system in the regions and the various commercial

16

managements of the West End were, as the previous chapter has shown, evolving in their own ways and at their own pace, the calls for a theatrical reform of a much more urgent and radical kind grew increasingly persistent. In part they arose from a frustration with the limited theatrical fare available in London, dictated as it was by the market forces of supply and demand as interpreted by the commercial managers, in part from an awareness of the new, challenging and often disturbing dramas of modern life appearing from the pens of Ibsen, Strindberg and other Continental writers, and in part, too, from the stimulus of a number of visits to London by theatre companies from abroad. Of these companies the three that made perhaps the most striking impression and had the most influence upon the germination of the repertory idea were the Comédie-Française in 1879, the Meiningen Company in 1881 and the Théâtre Libre in 1889: a long-established and state-aided (though not state-run) national theatre company, a more recently formed though heavily subsidised Court theatre company and the small, amateur, subscription-funded, independent company devoted almost wholly to new and recent drama. Both the Comédie-Française and the Meiningen companies showed what could be achieved with a classical repertoire and a permanent, ensemble company of actors (although the Meiningen's lead actors were rarely members of the permanent corps, it was the superlative crowd scenes that above all so impressed and influenced both Irving and Frank Benson). Antoine's Théâtre Libre, on the other hand, offered a model of the kind of theatre devoted to the encouragement and presentation of new writing that J.T. Grein endeavoured to inaugurate with his Independent Theatre just two years later.

It was, too, the Comédie-Française visit that inspired Matthew Arnold's oft-quoted and influential polemic, 'The French Play in London', published in *The Nineteenth Century* in August 1879. Not only was he impressed by the quality of their performances and by their repertoire of the great classics of French culture, but the Company represented for him a shining example of what could be gained by *organising* the theatre. State grants allowed for permanence and for a wholehearted commitment to 'the famous and classic plays of the French nation' without at the same time undermining the Company's self-governing status. No matter how good the English theatre might occasionally be, the constrictions imposed by the constant need to make a profit would, he argued, always deny the nation the opportunity of having any remotely similar kind of theatre: a theatre that could genuinely fulfil its potential as a civilising influence in society. His stress was upon the need for a national theatre enterprise rather than upon a regional network but he did not, on the other hand, see such a theatre as confined to the West End of London; and it was his forceful call for state subsidy that rang in the ears for decades to come as the advocates of national and regional repertory theatres endeavoured to find ways of pursuing an organised and worthwhile theatre in practice. Archer and Barker themselves chose to use a lengthy quotation from the essay as the opening shot in their own plea for a National Theatre, a quotation that ended with Arnold's now famous declaration:

The people *will* have a theatre; then make it a good one . . . The theatre is irresistible; organise the theatre![3]

Examples from abroad of how the theatre should or at least could be organised in England were sought and proffered with increasing frequency during the last two decades of the century. Foremost in this respect was William Archer, drama critic and one of the leading champions of Ibsen in Britain. He came to realise with growing clarity during the eighties the essential connectedness of the various and sporadic calls being made at the time for the establishment of a National Theatre, for permanent and subsidised theatre companies, for the introduction of a Continental-type repertory system and for the encouragement of new English playwriting. Inspired not only by the visits of foreign companies to London but further by what he learned at first hand from his visits to numerous theatres in France and Germany, he mounted an increasingly vigorous campaign in the press, emanating in such influential articles as 'A Plea for an Endowed Theatre' (in *The Fortnightly Review*, May 1889) and 'On the Need for an Endowed Theatre' (in *The Theatrical World of 1896*, published in 1897). Though he rejected state subsidy (as beyond the bounds of possibility in the England of his day) in preference to some form of private endowment, Archer argued strongly and uncompromisingly for the institution of a full-fledged repertory system on Continental lines. His definition of a true repertory theatre, made in 1889, with the Berlin Schauspielhaus very much in mind, was quoted at length by P.P. Howe more than twenty years later as a helpful measure by which to assess the first London experiment along such lines at the Duke of York's Theatre in 1910, and is worth quoting again here to indicate just how 'foreign' repertory of this kind was to the dominant long-run practice of the contemporary West End stage:

When we speak of a repertory, we mean a number of plays always ready for performance, with nothing more than a 'run through' rehearsal, which, therefore, can be, and are, acted in such alternation that three, four or five different plays may be given in the course of a week. New plays are from time to time added to the repertory, and those of them which succeed may be performed fifty, seventy, a hundred times, or even more, in the course of one season; but no play is ever performed more than two or three times in uninterrupted succession.[4]

THE INDEPENDENT THEATRES

The natural evolution of the English theatre was clearly seen to be insufficient when viewed in the light of the achievements both of the Continental companies and of playwrights such as Ibsen. William Archer, J.T. Grein and Shaw were all in the forefront of the movement to bring the plays of Ibsen to London, not only because the plays deserved to be seen but, equally, because they might act as a catalyst for new British playwrights. There was a production of *A Doll's House* given at the Novelty Theatre in 1889 but it was not until the formation of Grein's Independent Theatre in 1891, followed by Archer's New Century Theatre in 1897 and the Stage Society in 1899, that the so-called 'New Drama' was given any sort of positive boost.

The work of these pioneering societies was, during the final decade of the century, limited in scope, irregular and somewhat haphazard, and, in the case of Grein's and Archer's ventures, confined to very small memberships (total membership of the Independent Theatre in any one year never exceeded 175).[5] But their modesty of scale belied the significance of what they set out to do and indeed managed to achieve. Whilst little advance was made, or attempted, in terms of acting style or stage design (single performances given at West End theatres on dates and at times when those theatres happened to be free allowed very little opportunity for rehearsal, let alone imaginative settings), enormous gains were made in the cause of the playwright. The play, its intellectual challenge and literary quality, unfettered by considerations of likely popular appeal, was what now took precedence. As well as giving the first London performances of such plays of Ibsen's as *Ghosts* (which in 1891 met with the now legendary howls of protest from the London critics) and *The Wild Duck* (in 1894) and of Zola's *Thérèse Raquin* (1891), Grein's society made considerable efforts to encourage new plays from English writers. George Moore's *The Strike at Arlingford* (1893) and Shaw's first play, *Widowers' Houses* (1892), were two notable contributions but little more of any worth materialised: there was certainly no generation here of the renaissance in English drama for which Grein had hoped. The effects were instead indirect, delayed and cumulative. When Archer's short-lived society was formed in the year that Grein's came to an end, the promotion of new plays was now being linked explicitly in its statement of aims with the formation of a national Repertory Theatre. And the remarkable growth in membership experienced by the Stage Society within its first few years of operation (the maximum limit of 300 had to be raised to 500 in 1900), together with the wide scope of its objectives, provide some measure of the growth of interest that had occurred in the New Drama and in the idea of repertory. The founders declared confidently and ambitiously that their aims were no less than the restoration of vitality to the English theatre, the encouragement of the writing and performance of new, serious and experimental drama, and the permanent establishment of a Repertory Theatre in London.[6]

As the calls intensified during the final years of the century for an 'organised theatre', two distinct strands of thinking on the subject began to emerge, strands that are drawn together particularly well in some reflective articles written by Shaw in 1896 and which in some respects anticipate one of the major debates on arts funding that was to run through the nineteen-sixties and seventies. While Archer campaigned unceasingly for the establishment of a national, centralised repertory theatre in London, Shaw was beginning to see a greater challenge and possibly more pressing need, which was to extend the national repertory theatre idea to encompass towns and cities throughout the country. Reflecting upon Beerbohm Tree's massive rebuilding operation at Her Majesty's Theatre and noting the vast investment of capital in theatres generally in central London, he argued that the real task faced by the theatre if it was to take itself seriously was less to do with raising standards at the centre for the benefit of the few and more to do with widening the theatre's reach. We must, he proposed, 'discard our fixed idea that it is the business of the people to come to the theatre, and substitute for it the idea that it is the business of the theatre to come to the people'.[7] And the job had to be done, he argued, by the elected representatives of the people, not left to private enterprise which was, in the theatre at least, 'immoral, irresponsible, full of the gambling spirit, always ready to sacrifice the public welfare to the magnitude of its dividends'. Public enterprise had to be 'responsible to public opinion' and really had no more excuse for failing to provide a theatre for its locality than to provide 'public libraries and baths . . . museums or picture galleries'. The theatre, 'a great social force for good or evil', should not be abandoned to 'exploitation by commercial speculators'. He therefore was happy to leave Archer to work out the plan of his repertory theatre as 'a model central house' while declaring his own interest in 'the establishment of local theatres, without which we can never become a nation of playgoers'.[8]

The idea of a National Theatre and even of municipal theatres did not, it must be said, belong exclusively to Archer, Shaw and the reformists. Proposals for a National Theatre were already in the air early in the 1870s. Indeed in 1878, the year in which he took control of the Lyceum, Henry Irving – soon to be cast in the role of enemy of theatrical progress – had himself addressed the question of a National Theatre (in a speech given to the Social Science Congress) and offered some tentative thoughts on the kind of role it might fulfill and how it might be run.[9] He also allowed the possibility at some future date of theatres funded and run by municipalities but expressed unease at the possible hampering effect of public subsidy upon the 'free' system of British theatre. (Later he was to give more positive support to the idea of municipal theatres to complement the work of the London-based touring companies.) The model he suggested in 1878 for a National Theatre – a central theatre setting the highest artistic standards and then touring to the major theatres in the regions – proved to be not unlike the pattern he forged with such commercial success at the Lyceum. It came as no surprise therefore that in 1904 he agreed to be one of the signatories to Archer and Barker's scheme and estimates for a National Theatre: opponent of the Independent Theatre and of the whole New Drama movement he may have been, but the National Theatre was for him (as it was not for others) a quite distinct issue.

Less resistant to new writing but no less a symbol of all that was seen to be wrong with commercial West End theatre was Herbert Beerbohm Tree. An energetic exponent of the actor-manager system and the long run, he did none the less demonstrate a degree of openness to and curiosity about the new plays and new ideas that were emanating through the work of the small theatre societies and in the press. In 1893 he became the first actor-manager in the West End to stage a play by Ibsen with a matinée production of *An Enemy of the People* at the Haymarket. And while his tenure of that theatre was dominated by popular long-running productions, Tree's unashamed catholicity of taste did lead him to stage a series of special Monday night and Wednesday matinée performances of new or 'uncommercial' plays, plays that according to his biographer, Hesketh Pearson, Tree considered 'above the average playgoer's intelligence'.[10] In 1905 he ventured further and inaugurated an annual Shakespeare Festival at His Majesty's Theatre, which quickly developed from an initial six days' duration to three months in length by 1911, and in its later stages came to include, as well as his own presentations, visiting productions by Frank Benson and William Poel. It has even been argued that in this respect Tree was 'the founder of the repertory movement in England',[11] and that 'at His Majesty's the Edwardian West End did have a sumptuous "repertory" stage, never officially recognised in that chilling term'.[12] But claims such as these surely fall very wide of the mark. The fare offered at Tree's theatres hardly constituted a genuinely balanced and varied repertoire, and his 'Monday Nights' proved little more than a costly and somewhat patronising if well-intentioned indulgence on the part of an impresario whose major commitment to the successful long run was never in doubt. The larger objectives that were part and parcel of the argument for repertory – involving long-term financial security, artistic freedom, the development of a wide-ranging programme of plays each season chosen on merit rather than commercial profit-making potential and representing the best of the old drama and the new, and the avoidance of long runs – were totally absent from the policy at His Majesty's. That strongholds in the West End, however, were showing at least some responsiveness to new ideas – even if only minimally – was itself reflective of the depth of the impact those ideas were beginning to have upon the theatre at large.

Other developments during this period gave further signs of the change that was brewing. Parallel to the activity of the independent societies in London was the growth of an Irish independent theatre movement leading to the formation in 1898 of the Irish Literary Theatre in Dublin under the aegis of W.B. Yeats, Lady Gregory and Edward Martyn. This in turn led

directly to the founding of the Abbey Theatre in 1904 – of which important development more will be said later in this chapter. Frank Benson's
company, formed in 1883 and committed almost entirely to a Shakespearean repertoire, toured the British Isles for several decades, dedicated
to the cause of popularising Shakespeare and from 1886 until the outbreak
of the First World War was responsible for the annual summer season of
Shakespeare at the Memorial Theatre in Stratford-upon-Avon. Though
constantly beset by financial difficulties Benson did manage to maintain a
relatively permanent, if all too small, company of actors whose ensemble
performances were frequently admired, and his dedication to a classical
repertoire within the constraints of a commercial operation was a rare and
admirable endeavour.

Another dedicated Shakespearean, one whose dedication took the form
of an almost fanatical opposition to the commercial stage practices and
values of the time, was William Poel. The cause that he championed above
all was the performance of Shakespeare's plays in the manner of their own
time – in Elizabethan costume and on an Elizabethan 'open' stage thrust-
ing into the auditorium – so freeing Shakespeare from the paraphernalia of
lavish stage production. His Elizabethan Stage Society (formed in 1894)
gave infrequent but momentous presentations of Shakespeare's plays in a
staging that came as close to Elizabethan practice as current knowledge
and Poel's own predispositions allowed. Though for the most part
amateur and sometimes self-consciously educational in conception and
execution, these productions proved to be a major influence upon the
staging of Shakespeare in the new century, and, indirectly, upon the much
later movement in theatre design away from the tyranny of the proscenium
arch.

Granville Barker had himself been one of Poel's actors, having taken the
title role of Richard II in Poel's 1899 production. As a young professional
actor he had already spent a number of years on tour, playing in the traditional touring companies (notably in those of Ben Greet and Mrs Patrick
Campbell) and occasionally appearing in the West End. But the work
lacked intellectual and creative challenge and inspired in him only a long-
lasting distrust of the actor-manager system and all that went with it: the
long run, the type-casting and the 'star' performers. It was in the work of
Poel and of the independent theatre societies that he began to get a sense
of the new direction that the English theatre so badly needed. In 1900 he
joined the Stage Society, where he was able to act in a wide variety of challenging roles and to try his hand at directing. The conditions under which
the productions were mounted were far from ideal: financial resources
were almost non-existent and performances took place only on Sunday
evenings and at occasional matinées, generally on a bare, curtained stage.
But these limitations did reveal to Barker new possibilities in the art of the
theatre. Perhaps for the first time he realised the value of 'ensemble' acting.

While the stock companies had thrived on the exploitation of one or two 'stars', the actors engaged by the Society – for merely nominal fees – were drawn together primarily by a common interest in the play. Through an emphasis on teamwork in the acting and simplicity in the staging, the Stage Society performances, while they may have lacked the polish of a commercial production, at least allowed the author's intention to emerge clearly and without distortion.

THE ROYAL COURT VENTURE

The serious and enthusiastic interest in the New Drama which the Stage Society was so effectively fostering in the early years of the century was still, however, a specialist cult and had not yet affected the English stage as a whole; the conditions of the commercial theatre, especially the need to produce plays that promised a long run, presented a formidable barrier. Barker's purpose in embarking upon the Court venture was therefore to extend the work of the Stage Society into the public London theatre. But there was a wider purpose too. During these early years Barker was also collaborating with William Archer in preparing plans for a proposed National Repertory Theatre, and an important letter written to Archer in 1903 reflects his impatience to begin preparing the way for such a theatre on a practical basis. The work of the Stage Society, valuable as it was, was not enough for Barker:

I think there is a class of intellectual would-be playgoers who are profoundly bored by the theatre as it is. Matinée productions don't touch these people (who are all workers) and Sunday evening is expensive and incapable of expansion. Our actors – and worse still our actresses – are becoming demoralised by lack of intellectual work – the continual demand for nothing but smartness and prettiness.

I think the Independent Theatre – the New Century Theatre – the Stage Society – have prepared the ground, and the time is ripe for starting a theatre upon these lines, upon a regular – however, unpretending – basis.[13]

He explained that he wanted to take the Court Theatre (which was an ideally small theatre, seating roughly 600) and run there 'a stock season of the uncommercial Drama', adding that he would 'stake everything upon plays and acting – not attempt "productions" '. There were then three aims: to prepare the way for public acceptance of 'the repertory idea' and particularly of a National Theatre; to encourage a wider interest in the new avant-garde drama of Europe; and to present such plays simply and unpretentiously, allowing them to make their full impact, unhampered by elaborate sets or star performers. When, with Archer's help, his plans eventually materialised (the first Vedrenne–Barker season began on 18 October 1904), these aims were clearly reflected in the policy he pursued as artistic director.

His responsibilities as artistic director involved him in a vast amount of work, including the selection of plays, casting, designing sets and rehearsing (in addition to which he acted in a number of plays during the first two seasons). Of the thirty-two works presented by the management, all but the eleven plays of Shaw were personally directed by Barker, and the variety of his Court 'repertoire' was considerable. Among the playwrights whose work was represented were Euripides, Ibsen, Maeterlinck, Hauptmann and Yeats, and new English playwrights such as Galsworthy, St John Hankin and Granville Barker himself. Shaw, whom Barker had met in the Stage Society and who became closely involved in the work of the venture, directed all his own plays at the Court, and offered constant support, criticism and advice throughout the season.

Fundamental both to his policy as artistic director and to his method of production was Barker's commitment in principle to the 'repertory idea'. Archer and Barker had argued in their book – *A National Theatre: Scheme and Estimates*, published in 1907 but privately circulated in 1904 – that the advantage of repertory was that it would provide for a wide range of plays to be kept constantly before the public for as long as interest was shown in them; at the same time it would avoid the evils of the 'long-run' system by ensuring a frequent change of bill, never allowing one production to play for more than three or four performances in succession.[14] Such variety would of course be of particular value to the actors, enabling them to progress through a large number of widely different roles and preventing performances from becoming stale.

Financial restrictions prevented Barker from operating the Court as a full-scale repertory theatre as he would have wished, but he did insist on the next best thing: the 'short-run' system. Thus new plays were given a run of six matinées spread over two weeks (or, later, eight or nine matinées spread over three weeks), then taken off and replaced by the next play. Shaw's most popular plays, such as *Man and Superman* and *You Never Can Tell*, would sometimes run for as much as six weeks at a time in the evening bill, in addition to the matinées of other plays running during the same period, but at no time did Barker allow a truly long run of a popular play. Such a concession he believed would be detrimental to the vitality of the performances. His aim was to keep plays and actors fresh and alive in performance, and he was aware that variety in the repertoire would benefit actor and audience alike.

A second major feature of the proposed National Theatre was to have been the existence of an acting company that would work together as an ensemble. 'A permanent company, formed, so to speak, by natural selection and survival of the fittest, used to each other's methods, and working in harmony, may be trusted to give a far sounder performance of any play than the most brilliant "scratch" company that can be got together.'[15] Although Barker, working within severe financial limits, was never able to build up a really permanent company of players at the Court, the opportunities that his productions provided did draw serious artists of the highest calibre. Among the nucleus of the actors who appeared regularly at the Court were Lewis Casson, Edmund Gwenn, Amy Lamborn, Lillah McCarthy, Dorothy Minto, Norman Page and Harcourt Williams. Others who appeared, though less frequently, included Henry Ainley, Louis Calvert, Robert Loraine and even, on occasion, Ellen Terry and Mrs Patrick Campbell. But despite the wealth of acting talent at his disposal, Barker consistently refused to exploit them for their potential 'star' appeal. In 1907, looking back over the seasons, he declared that he would rather think of his actors 'as a company, brilliant individually as they may be', for he strongly felt that 'it is the playing together of a good company which makes good performances'.[16] His constant striving for 'unity of effect' in performance, the subordination of the individual to the total pattern, inevitably made great demands on the performers, but it was an ideal that seems to have been wholeheartedly shared by those who played regularly at the Court. Lillah McCarthy, for instance, stressed that this policy was maintained consistently throughout the seasons, and with remarkable results. She later wrote: 'No one of us was allowed to act away from the rest of the company, nor away from the play as a complete pattern', and also confirmed a point made by innumerable contemporary critics – that the same actors, when they went to other theatres and acted under other directors, experienced 'a loss of power' in their performances; this she attributed to the inspiration, originality and discipline of the Court pro-ductions: 'When we went elsewhere the part was everything: but at the Court the whole was greater than the part.'[17]

Careful attention was paid in rehearsal to the acting of every role, no matter how small, and everyone was encouraged to see that his contri-bution was vital to the whole effect. As Lillah McCarthy explained: 'Any of us would cheerfully take a small role, for we knew that even so we should not have to be subservient, negative or obsequious to the stars – for . . . there were no stars.' 'Rightly in my judgement', commented Archer at the end of the first season in 1905, 'they thought completeness of presen-tation as essential to their enterprise as to that of any long-run manager, and did not regard the fact that a play was announced for only six or nine performances as an excuse for slovenly mounting or inferior casting . . . This would have been a very interesting and creditable record even for a thoroughly equipped and endowed Repertory Theatre'; and, he con-cluded, perceptively, that 'this unassuming enterprise, in which intelli-gence and hard work supply the place of large and material resources, is full of promise for the future, both of English authorship and of English acting'.[18]

There is little doubt that Barker's approach to play production as it evolved during these three seasons – an approach that firmly placed the director in the auditorium rather than on the stage, that proved ideally suited to the naturalism of so much of the new drama and that above all stressed the play rather than the star – was to have a major influence upon the English theatre. That influence made itself felt in large measure through the actors with whom he worked and who then brought their experience to bear in companies elsewhere. When the Court seasons ended many of Barker's actors went on to work with him during the subsequent season at the Savoy Theatre. But between 1907 and the outbreak of the First World War a considerable number also moved on to work in each of the new repertory ventures in Manchester, Glasgow and Liverpool. At Manchester, for example, the actresses Clare Greet, Irene Rooke and Penelope Wheeler, all of whom were Vedrenne–Barker actors, took major roles, while Lewis Casson, one of the Court stalwarts, joined the Gaiety company in 1908 as an actor and later the same year directed *Hippolytus*, a play in which he had himself played the part of the Messenger at the Court in 1906; he was to become artistic director at the Gaiety in 1911.

At Glasgow some thirteen of the eighty actors who worked with Wareing at his Repertory Theatre between 1909 and 1913 had previously worked with Barker at the Court, and Barker himself actively lent his personal support to the venture, delivering a lecture on the ideals of a civic theatre at the beginning of the first season and directing a play (*The Witch*) for them in 1910.[19] At Liverpool, Madge Mackintosh, another Court actress, went on to play a key part in the development of the Repertory Theatre there, becoming its artistic director in 1914.

Not only in acting and direction but in the repertoire too the influence of the Court was pervasive. A number of the most artistically successful and interesting of the plays first performed at the Court became regular features of the programmes at the new reps, often helping to provide a kernel of modern work around which the ventures were able to develop their own increasingly distinctive repertoires. During the first full season at the Gaiety, for example, Manchester playgoers saw four plays from the Court repertoire – *Hippolytus* (in Murray's new translation), *The Silver Box*, *The Charity that Began at Home* and *The Return of the Prodigal* – while at Glasgow most of the Shaw plays produced during the first two seasons were first seen publicly at the Court. *The Voysey Inheritance*, *The Return of the Prodigal* and *The Silver Box* proved particularly ubiquitous: the first was seen as Glasgow, Liverpool and Birmingham many times before 1914; the second was seen early on at Liverpool and Birmingham as well as at Manchester; *The Silver Box* was played during the opening seasons at both Manchester and Birmingham.[20]

THE SAVOY SEASON, 1907–8

If the Court Theatre experiment appeared to demonstrate the commercial viability of an artistic theatre, in that at the end of its third year it had just about paid its way without private or public subvention, the following season was to throw any such easy optimism back into serious doubt. Certainly the Court had benefitted from a happy marriage of 'artistic endeavour and sound business sense'.[21] While the long run and the safe choice of play were consistently opposed, the management were sensible enough to revive those productions that proved to have most box office appeal (such as *Man and Superman* and *You Never Can Tell*, *The Silver Box*, *Voysey Inheritance*, *Return of the Prodigal* and even *Hippolytus*), and to keep performances of plays that lacked popularity to a minimum (Harcourt's *A Question of Age* and Penn's *Convict on the Hearth* were given only two performances each). In the circumstances this showed a degree of flexibility in programming that could justifiably be seen as true to the repertory idea (although Howe points out that so heavy was its dependence upon the popularity of Shaw's plays, the Court might be more aptly described as a 'Shaw Repertory Theatre').[22] It was this flexible use of the short-run system that the later repertory pioneers in the regions picked up and adapted to their own purposes.

Both financial and artistic success proved elusive at the Savoy during the 1907–8 season. Boosted by the success at the Court, the management planned to extend the enterprise into the heart of London's West End. The Savoy Theatre was almost twice the size of the cramped Royal Court and could therefore hold larger audiences and lend itself better to the more demanding stage requirements of larger productions such as the Euripides plays; it was also in Central London and offered the chance for the management to prove the worth and enhance the prestige of their enterprise. Five productions were given – three plays by Shaw, Galsworthy's new play *Joy* and the *Medea* of Euripides – again on the basis of short runs in the evening together with special matinées of the less popular fare. The Court spark, however, was missing: the productions lacked lustre in the larger space of the Savoy; audiences were smaller (even the loyal core of the 'Court audience' – largely the middle-class intelligentsia – proved wary of the new scheme); and disagreements arose between Vedrenne and Barker over matters of policy, with Vedrenne increasingly distrustful of Barker's long-term commitment to repertory. The Savoy season ended in deficit – as did other limited forays into the West End within a short space of years (for single productions of plays by Shaw and Masefield, among others). As Shaw, one of the backers of the partnership, put it, 'the receipts barely kept us going and left no reserves with which to nurse new authors into new reputations', and, as debts began to accumulate, 'so the firm went down with its colors flying, leaving us with a proved certainty that no National Theatre in London devoted to the art of the theatre at its best can bear the burden of London rents and London rates'.[23]

Barker himself expressed his frustration with 'the whole vicious circle of the system' in an interview given at the end of the Savoy season: 'The important thing for the public to consider is this, that if they want anything in the shape of a theatre like this they cannot have it under the present conditions that obtain in London of enormous rents. If the public want even so much of a repertoire theatre as we have been running, the building must be kept rent free.'[24] As it was, he argued, managers were driven constantly to look for plays that could run for 200 or 300 nights, irrespective of the worth of the play or the effect upon the quality of acting that this would have: 'If you are going to have various sorts of plays which will appeal to various sections of the public, you must alter your present system.' Here in a nutshell was the repertory idea: an idea that linked variety of play programme, breadth (rather than volume) of theatre-going public, vitality of performance and a change in the economic structure of the theatre.

Everything that had happened at the Savoy seemed only to confirm for Barker what he had already perceived in his new preface, written in 1907 for the general publication of his and Archer's book, *A National Theatre*: that the first of the new repertory theatres might be started in a provincial centre more easily than in London, for there the policy of the management would be freer of the 'vitiating influence of fashion'; and, prophetically, that 'I think it will not be until shamed into action by other cities' good fortune that we shall have our central repertory theatre.'[25]

REPERTORY AT THE DUKE OF YORK'S, 1910

But there was to be one last major attempt to put the ideal of repertory to the test in Central London before the outbreak of war, and it was to be repertory in the true sense. Financed by the American manager, Charles Frohman (after a good deal of persuasion from James Barrie), a full-scale repertory programme was launched for a trial season in 1910 at the Duke of York's Theatre. The opening production (on 21 February) was Barker's powerful and acclaimed staging of the new Galsworthy play, *Justice*, followed two nights later by Shaw's *Misalliance*; in the next week a Triple Bill entered the repertoire (consisting of two short plays by Barrie, *Old Friends* and *The Twelve Pound Look*, and Meredith's *The Sentimentalists*), joined in the third week by Barker's own new play, *The Madras House*. The schedule for this third week[26] illustrates clearly the full-fledged nature of the repertory scheme adopted:

7 March	Thur.	Triple Bill
8 March	Tue.	*Misalliance*
9 March	Wed.	*The Madras House* (première)
10 March	Thur.	(mat.) *Misalliance*
	Thur.	(eve.) *Justice*
11 March	Fri.	*Justice*
12 March	Sat.	(mat.) *The Madras House*
	Sat.	(eve.) Triple Bill

Fully conforming to Archer's earlier definition (see p. 18) of the essential components of a true repertory system – involving no one production's running for more than two or at most three consecutive performances – the scheme also proved, as may be imagined, both costly and exhausting to operate given the severely limited back-stage facilities of the Duke of York's. The season lasted just seventeen weeks, the latter half being dominated by a highly successful revival of *Trelawny of the Wells* and a more moderately successful revival of *Prunella* by Barker and Housman. Ten plays had been presented (including the plays on the Triple Bill), of which all but *Trelawny* and *Prunella* were new or hitherto unperformed works. Although Miss Horniman's Manchester company had visited London the previous year with a three-week performance of plays presented in true repertory (at the Coronet Theatre in Notting Hill), the enterprise at the Duke of York's represents the first occasion in London on which a whole new season of plays was launched on a true repertory basis – at least since the days of the old stock repertory companies of a century earlier.

It was an ambitious undertaking and artistically not without its achievements. Without doubt the outstanding critical and popular success of the season was *Justice*. A plea for greater humanity in the treatment of convicted criminals, Galsworthy's play not only stirred its audiences but, unusually, played a significant part in the campaign to reform the penal system of the time. Almost immediately, too, it became taken up by the reps at Manchester, Glasgow and Liverpool. Financially however, if not

1. *Justice*, by John Galsworthy. Duke of York's Repertory Season, 1910, directed by Harley Granville Barker. Photo: Victoria and Albert Museum.

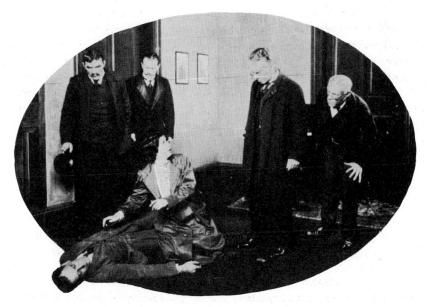

artistically, the repertory experiment was a failure. Audiences were unfamiliar with the rotating schedule of performances and did not adjust to it. They were also (if critical reviews are anything to go by) disconcerted by the enormous differences in the types of play presented. Clearly, as Archer and Barker had foreseen in 1904, the creation of a new repertory theatre in London needed 'time to establish itself and take hold upon the public'.[27]

If the success of the Court seasons had proved the need for a proper repertory theatre in London (let alone a full-scale National Theatre), the financial failure of the Duke of York's season proved – even more emphatically than the earlier failure at the Savoy, because of the artistic standards achieved – the need for long-term subsidy and for the permanence and security of operation that only subsidy could bring. Audiences for repertory could not be built in a mere seventeen weeks.

P.P. Howe, in his detailed and searching 'record and criticism' of the venture, *The Repertory Theatre*, published the following year, saw in both its success and its failure evidence of the deep 'disturbance' that theatre as a whole was undergoing and signs of hope that the 'repertory idea' would soon take root in London. The lessons that Barker himself learnt from the season were augmented further by visits he made shortly afterwards to repertory theatres in Germany (notably Reinhardt's theatres in Berlin and the Schauspielhaus in Dusseldorf) and later to Stanislavsky's Moscow Art Theatre (in 1914). Likewise, a more recent convert to repertory, Basil Dean, reported on his own visits to German theatres to the inaugural meeting of the Liverpool Repertory Theatre company in 1911 – a report considered important enough to be published in pamphlet form under that recurring title, *The Repertory Theatre*. Again the example of repertory practice abroad was to provide inspiration and confirmation for the proponents of the repertory movement in England as it began to gather momentum. Certainly Barker's own growing familiarity with Continental practice strengthened his personal dedication both to the repertory idea and to the establishment of a National Theatre, and he was to continue his campaign through speeches, pamphlets, articles and books and through such organisations as the British Drama League for another three decades, long after giving up active work in the theatre. What he helped to articulate, perhaps more forcefully and consistently than any other theatre practitioner of his day, was the ideal of a theatre that could be seen as necessary to its society and accepted as a normal part of social life. 'The struggle', he argued later in 1910, was 'to capture the Theatre in the interests of . . . the average man and woman'.[28] What was needed – in addition to a National theatre – was a 'Normal Theatre' available to people throughout the country, producing 'normal plays about and for normal people, capable of normal success under normal conditions'. Municipal subsidy and/or private endowment, freedom from censorship, permanent companies of highly trained actors, open-minded critics and above all repertory would all be essential components of such a theatre.

If his argument is sometimes expressed in terms that, for our taste, smack too much of Victorian notions of self-improvement and moral good health (it was vital that the theatre should be 'of good report, clean, wholesome, making for righteousness . . . ') then that should not deter us from acknowledging the very real battle that Barker and his fellow pioneers were waging to persuade their countrymen that theatre was an art form and, potentially, a service to society that merited serious attention and support from public funds. Barker protested – as the early leaders of the repertory movement in the provinces did too – that the 'organised theatre' did not open up 'an arid, educational prospect', that its plays were not always serious, intellectual and gloomy. But his analogy of a repertory theatre with a public library (keeping a play 'on the shelf of a theatre, so that, as from time to time a reasonable number of people is likely to want to see it, it can be taken down without overwhelming trouble and expense'[29]) not only served to illustrate the method of true repertory and the variety of fare that could be available within a given period of time, but also, perhaps unintentionally, suggested an aura of public utility and institutionalised education that was reflected to some degree in the earnestness of atmosphere that pervaded the first repertory ventures and in the severity of Barry Jackson's design for his own repertory theatre in 1913.

THE ABBEY THEATRE, DUBLIN

One further development of significance demands attention: one that had its origin partly in the avent-garde theatre societies in London at the turn of the century but more so in the entirely separate and indigenous circumstances beyond London's orbit. The story of the Abbey Theatre, Dublin, has been well documented elsewhere and its history falls outside the scope of this survey, but because of the important threads that connect the opening of the Abbey with the repertory movement in Britain generally a brief résumé here may be useful. Indeed the Abbey has a legitimate claim to be the first permanently established repertory theatre in the British Isles, antedating Miss Horniman's Gaiety venture by nearly four years.

The two main impulses towards the formation of Ireland's national theatre were, first, as was the case with the independent theatre societies in London, dissatisfaction with the theatrical fare available on the commercial stage (fare that in Dublin relied heavily upon touring companies from England and was rarely Dublin-created); and, secondly, the growing cause of Irish nationalism. For W.B. Yeats, who stands indisputably at the centre of these movements, dramatic art offered a unique means of linking his own crusade for a 'Celtic revival' in the arts with the wider nationalist cause. Prominent in literary circles in both Dublin and London during the last decade of the old century, and having formed Irish literary societies in both capitals, he had his dramatic ambitions boosted by the offer from the wealthy and admiring Miss Horniman to finance a production of his play *Land of Heart's Desire* for a series of special matinées at the Avenue Theatre, London. The performances took place in 1894. Four years later, Yeats, along with Lady Gregory and Edward Martyn, formed the Irish Literary Theatre in Dublin. Opposed to everything that the commercial London theatre represented, as was Grein's theatre of seven years earlier, it was designed to be distinct from the Ibsen-oriented societies in London in its uncompromising dedication to the Irish literary revival. Their plans were, in Yeats' own words, 'for the most part remote, spiritual and ideal'.[30]

In these early years the performances were organised on an infrequent, *ad hoc* and wholly amateur basis and given in various halls in Dublin. A more professional, theatrical and overtly nationalistic complexion was brought to the enterprise by the brothers W.G. and Frank Fay. It particularly disturbed the Fays that so much was made of English rather than Irish actors, a feeling that was exacerbated for many by the visit of the Benson Company to Dublin in 1901 who performed, among other pieces, Yeats' and George Moore's *Diarmuid and Gráinne* in what must have seemed a desperately incongruous style. The next important step was, then, in 1903, the merging of the Irish Literary Theatre with W.G. Fay's own amateur company of Irish actors, the Irish National Dramatic Society, to form the new Irish National Theatre Society, with Yeats as its president. The declared objects of the society were 'to create an Irish National Theatre, to act and produce plays in Irish or English, written by Irish writers, or on Irish subjects; and such dramatic works by foreign authors as would tend to educate and interest the public of this country in the higher aspects of dramatic art'.[31]

The Society performed as before in various halls in Dublin and on an occasional basis because of its continuing amateur status. But the presentations increased in frequency, and that their standards of performance went beyond 'amateurishness' is evidenced by the enthusiasm with which London critics greeted their brief visit to London in May 1903. Their productions of, amongst others, *The Hour Glass*, *Cathleen ni Houlihan* and *A Pot of Broth*, were given with simplicity and freshness and were marked especially by the almost musical quality of their speaking.

Miss Horniman's continuing admiration for Yeats and her involvement in the work of the Society (designing and making, for example, the costumes for *The King's Threshold* in 1903) were such that in 1904, with her own fortunes in the tea business rising in the stock market, she offered to buy for the Society its own theatre building. Despite some argument among Society members about being beholden to an Englishwoman – who, moreover, was known to have little sympathy with the nationalist cause – the offer was accepted, and the small music-hall attached to the

Mechanics Institute on Abbey Street, after some basic alterations had been carried out, opened as the Abbey Theatre on 27 December 1904 – some three months after the opening of the Vedrenne–Barker seasons in London but none the less on a permanent rent-free basis rather than on a temporary lease as at the Court. Under Willie Fay's direction three Irish plays fittingly opened the theatre, Yeats' *On Baile's Strand* and *Cathleen ni Houlihan*, and Lady Gregory's *Spreading the News*.

Despite the continuing amateur basis of the work – which meant among other things that performances could be given only one week in every month – it was a significant date, marking the birth of a repertory theatre that was to play a major part in the development of twentieth-century drama in Europe. In the early years, however, progress must have seemed erratic and uncertain. By October 1906 the need for professional status and for greater continuity in the work had become paramount. It was again Miss Horniman who stepped in to provide the subsidy required for the payment of actors' salaries – though again to the discontent of many in the Abbey company who resented the constant dependence of the theatre upon Miss Horniman's money. But that money did allow the theatre the opportunity to grow, and already the ground was being prepared for the move to fuller independence: in 1906 the Society became formally registered as the Irish National Theatre Society Ltd, its board of directors being Yeats, Lady Gregory and the Abbey's new and exciting playwright, J.M. Synge. By 1907 the logic of the theatre's development towards complete autonomy had become inescapable, and Miss Horniman withdrew entirely if grudgingly from the Abbey, leaving it thenceforth wholly in the hands of its Board of Directors, and finally severing all her legal ties with it in 1910. Instead she turned her eyes towards the prospect of a completely new and perhaps more easily manageable repertory venture on the English mainland.

Already then, within the early years of the century, another example had been provided of the necessity of subsidy if a repertory theatre committed to new plays and high artistic standards were to flourish. Clear too were some of the dangers implicit in such a theatre's dependence upon endowment from a single, private source.

In 1907, in his preface to *A National Theatre*, and even before the failure of his Savoy season, Barker had suggested that a preliminary step towards the realisation of such a theatre in London ought to be the devising of a 'second set of figures suitable to the foundation of an adequate repertory theatre in Manchester, Birmingham, or some such provincial centre. For it is to one of these cities, easier to stir to the expression of civic opinion, rather than to the monstrous and inarticulate London, centre of all English thought and action though it may claim to be, that I look for the first practical step in theatrical organisation.'[32]

Miss Horniman's arrival in Manchester at once confirmed Barker's diagnosis and guaranteed the significant role to be played by 'provincial centres' in the development of British theatres during the forthcoming century.

4   1907–1918: Manchester to Birmingham

GEORGE ROWELL

THE diversity and importance of the links between Granville Barker's work at the Court and the growth of the repertory movement outside London have already been indicated. The early provincial repertories drew on the resources of the Sloane Square enterprise in every department: plays, players, producers, ideas, above all inspiration. Even before the first of these repertories had opened its doors Barker accurately forecast this development. His speech at the testimonial dinner given in his and Vedrenne's honour on 7 July 1907 mentioned Manchester or Birmingham as the likely home of 'the first repertory theatre of the new order', a sentiment reiterated in the passage from *Schemes and Estimates for a National Theatre* already quoted. Moreover he was always ready to practise what he preached. He frequently spoke on the repertory idea in centres planning such a company, and in 1910 he and Lillah McCarthy joined the Glasgow repertory to recreate their original roles in *Man and Superman*, after which Barker stayed on to direct the first production of John Masefield's adaptation of *The Witch* before he introduced it to the London public.

The contribution of his 'graduates' to the various provincial companies has already been touched on. Their names and achievements could be treated at length, but perhaps the record of Lewis Casson calls for particular examination and may stand as representative of the whole group. Casson, who had appeared regularly at the Court throughout the three Barker–Vedrenne seasons, joined Miss Horniman's company on tour in December 1907 and remained with them playing leading roles for the next two years. In December 1908 he married a fellow-member of the company, Sybil Thorndike, and in 1911 he succeeded Ben Iden Payne as artistic director. This appointment was terminated in December 1913, but the following month he became director of the Glasgow repertory, until that company was wound up on the outbreak of war. Effectively he devoted the first ten years of his career to the repertory cause.

The movement's debt to the Court was also evident in their programmes, particularly during the early years when the various companies were still grooming their own authors. Shaw's work was a rallying-point for them all, its popularity limited only by his reluctance to cede the performing rights of his more recent plays. Thus Manchester fell back on the little-known *Widowers' Houses* (which figured repeatedly in their first few seasons); Glasgow opened with *You Never Can Tell*, dubbed by Shaw 'the *Charley's Aunt* of the repertory movement', and an early Liverpool offering was *Arms and the Man*. A Court author perhaps even more to provincial taste was Galsworthy, with his social conscience and his direct, dispassionate approach. *The Silver Box* won Manchester's immediate respect, and in due course *Strife* and *Justice* joined it in the repertory lists. *Strife* was picked as the opening play of Liverpool's try-out season in 1911, and *Justice* was given its Glasgow première on the same night as London saw it initiate the Frohman season at the Duke of York's. Another playwright associated with the Court who figured prominently in the repertories' programmes was St John Hankin, although the detached, cynical tone of *The Return of the Prodigal* and *The Cassilis Engagement* pleased the press more widely than the public. A more sombre choice was *The Tragedy of Nan* by John Masefield, who had also begun his theatrical career when Barker staged *The Campden Wonder* at the Court.

MANCHESTER

As an inspiration to the repertory cause in Britain the Abbey, Dublin, rated next to the Court under Barker and Vedrenne. Clearly the nationalist aims of the Irish enterprise precluded the exchange of plays and players, but Dublin's lead was acknowledged in several important respects, not least in provoking Miss Horniman to seek another sphere of influence. 'I want to teach these impossible people in Dublin that I have other fish to fry', she told Iden Payne, who had been serving as the Abbey's stage director when she approached him to start the Manchester experiment.[1] In fact the extended tour of the provinces undertaken by the Irish National Players in 1906 stimulated interest wherever they performed, and their booking manager for this tour was Alfred Wareing, who tried unsuccessfully to persuade Miss Horniman to finance his plan of establishing a repertory company in Glasgow.

Manchester, however, proved her choice. It had already supported an Independent Theatre Society between 1893 and 1898, an offshoot of the London group, and a number of the earlier Society's committee gave Miss Horniman's initiative their blessing. The prestige of the Hallé orchestra attested Manchester's interest in the arts, an interest often attributed to the city's influential German community. The Manchester press too was receptive to the idea and exceptionally well equipped to assess it; the *Guardian* already boasted a dramatic critic of national standing in C.E. Montague and had recently added James Agate and Allan Monkhouse to its staff. Moreover Payne was a product of Manchester Grammar School, which was to prove a forcing-ground of writing talent for the new company.

Before committing herself fully, however, Miss Horniman decided on a preliminary season to be staged in the 'Midland Theatre' (in fact the ballroom of the new and exclusive Midland Hotel), which ran for five weeks from 23 September 1907. This was successful enough to encourage her search for a permanent home, resulting in the purchase of the Gaiety Theatre, a brave choice since its capacity was 1350. Meanwhile the company undertook an extended tour until the Gaiety was available. Touring in fact was an important aspect of their work from the start; there were sometimes two companies performing simultaneously, and the resident company fitted matinées at nearby towns into its Manchester schedule. (Payne reports the comment of the stage-carpenter at Oldham, which proved resistant to all such opportunities: 'It's only to be expected at Oudam. You wouldn't get folk to come to a theayter if you was to give 'em the Crucifixion with the original cast.'[2]) Later there were to be regular and greatly influential seasons in London and North America.

Although structural changes and redecoration were scheduled for the Gaiety, a start was made there with the production on 11 April 1908 of *Measure for Measure* with William Poel in command and playing Angelo. Poel's insistence on the fundamentals of Elizabethan staging ran wholly contrary to the illusionary aims of most leading actor-managers of the day, and the Gaiety was thus early committed in its Shakespearean work to bold new beliefs. The introductory season at the Gaiety was suspended after a month to allow the refitting to be completed, and finally on 7 September 1908 the 'new' Gaiety opened its doors and the Manchester company settled into their permanent home.

From their first meeting a complete and fruitful understanding developed between Miss Horniman and her artistic director, Iden Payne, nourished no doubt by their experience as aliens in the Abbey Theatre administration. She showed her confidence in him by abstaining from any interference in artistic matters, and in his words: 'Never made so much as a suggestion regarding life beyond the curtain'.[3] Although Payne's contract stipulated that she retain a veto on all plays and he submit scripts before announcing his programme, Miss Horniman returned the scripts without comment. Whitford Kane, a member of the company for the 1910–11 season, attested that after the first performance of *Justice*,

a tall, maidenly lady dressed in a mediaeval green dress and wearing a gold chain with an opal dragon, took a bow from a box. It was Miss Horniman, and it was the only time we saw her during the year.[4]

The extent of her trust in Payne may also be measured by the stormy and sudden end to the term of office of his successor, Lewis Casson.

Although indebted in the early days to several veterans of the Court seasons, Payne knew that the particular demands of the enterprise called for particular and preferably local talents, and set about assembling a resident team. He showed especial insight in engaging a Lancashire actor, Charles Bibby, who was a mainstay of the company from its inception until he enlisted and unhappily was killed in the War. Payne judged him quite simply 'the finest character actor I have ever known',[5] and Rex Pogson, historian of the Gaiety, affirmed: 'None, save Payne himself, had a greater share in establishing the Gaiety acting tradition.'[6] By the time the company played its first London season in 1909 that tradition was recognisable enough to be hailed by the critics. E.A. Baughan of the *Daily News* contrasted the performance of Henry Austin, another local recruit, in Sudermann's *Vale of Content* with West End ways:

An actor-manager taking the part of Weidemann would have upset the balance immediately. He would have gasped and groaned in the centre of the stage and, if possible, he would have made the author insert a few long set speeches. The truth is that our particular type of star actor has been the ruin of our drama.[7]

This suggests a less than fair comparison between the best of repertory acting and the worst of actor-managerial egotism, but Payne had a remarkable flair for finding and nursing talent. Another of his early discoveries was Basil Dean, then a 'juvenile' but soon to mature swiftly and prodigiously as a director. A local actor whom Payne engaged to walk on was Herbert Lomas; by 1912 he had progressed to the point of creating the crucial role of Nathaniel Jeffcote in *Hindle Wakes*, although he was still only twenty-six. A less happy choice was Mona Limerick, who became Payne's wife. Though striking in appearance and overpowering in the right part (for example Blanche Sartorius in *Widowers' Houses*), she lacked range and, perhaps more seriously, was disrespectful to Miss Horniman.

The cohesion which Payne quickly secured endowed his company with great flexibility in a theatrical era characterised by long runs and stereotyped casting. Although true repertory was possible only on special occasions such as their London seasons, regular and rapid revivals were well within their grasp and a feature of their programme. Their various tours sometimes involved dividing forces, but this too the company took in their stride; on joining them in 1910 Whitford Kane found himself playing Burgess in *Candida* to 'three different daughters during the week'.[8] Nevertheless 'everyone seemed to be alive, down to the stage doorkeeper. There were many jealousies, of course, but they were healthy and stimulating ones.'[9] His tribute is all the more eloquent since he came direct from the Frohman repertory season at the Duke of York's, where he found some far from healthy jealousies between the 'Barkerskites' and the 'Boucicaultites' (protégés of the younger Dion Boucicault, who shared artistic command with Barker).

The Gaiety's commitment to touring grew rapidly. Their first London excursion, to the Coronet Theatre in Notting Hill Gate in 1909, became an annual visit either there or to the Court, with seasons sometimes as long as

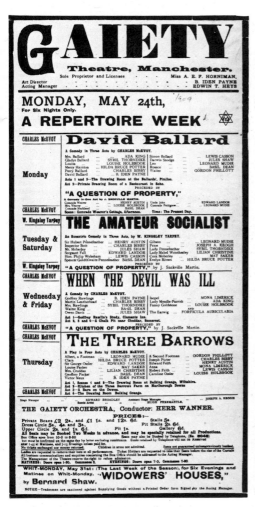

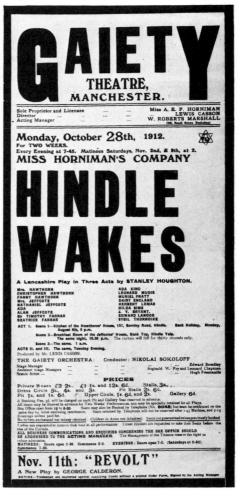

2A. Poster for the short 'Repertoire' season at the Manchester Gaiety Theatre in 1909.
2B. Poster for *Hindle Wakes* at the Manchester Gaiety Theatre, 1912. Photos and copyright for 2A and 2B: Theatre Collection, Manchester City Public Libraries.

eight weeks (in 1913) or nine in the following year. In addition, tours of Canada and the United States were undertaken in 1912 and 1913. In one sense these expeditions seem a contradiction of the company's resident status and regional character, but undoubtedly they built up the Gaiety's reputation and allowed it greater scope and influence, above all in making their local playwrights nationally and internationally known.

39

ımediately she had chosen Manchester as the base of her operations,
Iiss Horniman announced in the local press:

want to find English dramatists who will write better than the Irish. We ought to be
ashamed of ourselves. If Lancashire playwrights will send their plays to me I shall pledge
myself to read them through. Let them write not as one dramatist does, about countesses
and duchesses and society existing in imagination, but about their friends and enemies
– about real life.[10]

Predictably her aim of cultivating a Lancashire drama drawn predominantly from Manchester playwrights took time, and was in fact helped by
some of her competitors, notably Liverpool and more surprisingly
Glasgow. Any assessment of their efforts therefore relates to the repertory
movement as a whole and will be attempted in its place. While the
Manchester school was learning its craft, the Gaiety, as has been seen, had
to rely largely on those forerunners of intellectual drama whom the Court
seasons had identified. But it would be misleading to equate the Gaiety
repertoire solely with social drama and social issues. Both Iden Payne and
Lewis Casson found room in their programmes for lyric drama, old and
new. Not only did Shakespeare inaugurate the Horniman régime at the
Gaiety; his plays featured regularly thereafter, particularly as a Christmas
offering. There were also excursions into Ibsen's history plays (*The
Vikings at Helgeland*) and period plays by contemporary authors (*The
Cloister* by a Belgian, Emile Verhaeren, and *The Feud* by David Garnett),
as well as a brave essay at Greek tragedy, with *Hippolytus* and *The Trojan
Women*.

A notably successful feature was the revival of costume plays, particularly at Christmas. Starting with the virtually unacted *Knight of the Burning Pestle*, the Gaiety proceeded to offer revivals of old favourites such as
The Critic, *The School for Scandal* and *She Stoops to Conquer*, as well as
some more recent and less familiar (*The Fantasticks*; *Prunella*). Less
happily it was a Shakespeare revival which led to major conflict between
Miss Horniman and Lewis Casson, resulting in Casson's resignation. His
decision in the autumn of 1913 to stage *Julius Caesar* in the swift,
simplified style then being practised by his master, Granville Barker, at the
Savoy, carried the critics but not The Lady herself, to whom the permanent
set smacked of Gordon Craig. *Measure for Measure*, as directed by
William Poel, had at least been reconstructive and so tolerable, but this
was just 'freakish', and a second dose (with *The Tempest* at Christmas)
unthinkable. She stepped in where she had hitherto foreborne to tread, and
cancelled the Christmas production; Casson resigned, to be succeeded by
a more amenable if less distinguished figure, Douglas Gordon.[11]

LIVERPOOL

Meanwhile Manchester's example had begun to be copied. Alfred
Wareing, although denied Miss Horniman's help, persevered in his deter-

mination to establish a Glasgow repertory company and, backed by a group of leading citizens, opened his first season at the Royalty Theatre in April 1909. A much closer neighbour, Liverpool, also took up Manchester's challenge and, following their lead, opted for a short experimental season to test public support. This took place at Kelly's Theatre (managed by the sponsor of *A Royal Divorce*, W.W. Kelly) for six weeks from 20 February 1911, and drew on Manchester both for inspiration and personnel. A Gaiety actress, Miss Darragh, was the leading lady, with the backing mostly provided by an admirer of hers, Charles Kenyon, and Basil Dean, abandoning his acting career, took charge of production. He decided to open with *Strife*, a brave choice at a time of serious unrest in the Liverpool docks. Against all the odds it proved a critical and popular success, though Whitford Kane, moving from Manchester to play the strike-leader, Roberts, noted that only those in the company cast as steel-masters were invited to the first-night party given by the Earl of Derby.[12]

Nevertheless the remainder of the season, with plays taken from the Court repertoire (*The Cassilis Engagement*) or approved by Manchester audiences (*The Vale of Content*; *The Tragedy of Nan*), as well as some familiar and less familiar one-acters (*The Twelve Pound Look*; *The Dear Departed*), resulted in a profit of £1600, an uncharacteristic outcome for a repertory season.[13] Spurred on by this success, enough support was found amongst Liverpool's men of substance to buy and rename the Star Music Hall in Williamson Square as the Liverpool Repertory Theatre. Basil Dean was appointed director and a young Liverpool artist called George Harris, then unknown but shortly and justly to be celebrated, became resident designer. After a week's try-out at the Gaiety, the company opened their new home on 11 November 1911 with *The Admirable Crichton*.

By choosing Barrie's tested comedy to open, the Liverpool Board, twelve representatives of the city's commercial and professional interests, gave a clear indication of their future policy. The theatre was financed by 900 shareholders, not a single patron as in Manchester and later Birmingham. The shareholders' taste had to be considered, and that taste was inevitably cautious. This did not mean reneging on the brave start made six months earlier; authors represented in the first few years included, as expected, Shaw, Galsworthy, Barker, Hankin and Masefield. But there were more performances of plays by 'commercial' names, notably Pinero and Wilde, than figured on Manchester's or Glasgow's bills, and Continental drama was very sparingly represented. Ibsen, for example, received only four productions in the first sixteen years. There was also a strong emphasis on comedy, mostly contemporary but with a steady showing of Sheridan and Goldsmith and a less regular foray into Shakespeare. Amongst the numerous loyal and much-loved members of early companies were Estelle Winwood, J.H. Roberts and Wilfred Shine, but perhaps

Ronald Squire won most hearts, even if his memory sometimes failed the author and his fellow-players. The quality of civilised good humour he radiated nicely summed up the Liverpool style.

Safety, however, was not wholly to Basil Dean's taste. He aimed to introduce new plays and also some experiments, a less happy move in the Directors' eyes. Crisis point was reached in March 1913 with his choice of Hauptmann's elaborate expressionist play, *Hannele*. Artistically the production was a proud moment; Grace Wyndham Goldie, historian of the company, judged it 'the most expensive, the most ambitious and the most difficult yet attempted in the Repertory Theatre',[14] and Dean himself called it 'a personal triumph'.[15] Historically it is probably remembered for introducing to Liverpool audiences Noel Coward (aged thirteen) and reintroducing Gertrude Lawrence (aged fourteen) as Angels of Light. But for the Board it was marked by alarming expense and damned by heavy loss: £800. They objected and Dean resigned.[16]

The Liverpool venture owed its survival over the next five years as much to the faith of its players as to the support of its public. Dean was succeeded as producer by a senior member of the company, Laurence Hanray, who guided it out of the stormy seas left by the Hauptmann hurricane, and restored stability sufficiently to allow a short spell of true repertory in the spring of 1914. But the outbreak of War rekindled the Directors' alarm, and the Board recommended closure. Only a firm stand by two leading ladies, Estelle Winwood and Madge McIntosh, who persuaded their colleagues to form a 'Commonwealth' in traditional theatrical fashion, induced the Directors to change their minds and confirm Madge McIntosh in her new appointment as artistic director.

By 1917, when this 'Commonwealth' came to an end, the fortunes of the theatre had been restored; its name had been changed (in 1916) to the Liverpool Playhouse; and the company had paid two visits to London. The second, to the Coliseum with a home-made revue, *Hullo Repertory*, withered in alien ground, but the first, to the Kingsway in May 1915 with a wide-ranging programme including the premiere of Galsworthy's *A Bit o' Love*, won critical approval, if not much financial reward. It put the Liverpool company on the metropolitan map and in particular confirmed the reputation of a leading actor, William Armstrong, who played the central role in the Galsworthy and was presently to play a central role at the Playhouse over a long and illustrious period of time.

LANCASHIRE DRAMA

The lasting legacy of the pre-War repertory movement was the modest but significant body of original drama it fostered. It is customary to describe this as 'Lancashire drama', and its authors as 'the Manchester school', a custom manifestly apt in the case of its two most famous titles,

Hindle Wakes and *Hobson's Choice*, since these plays are quickened to life by Lancashire folk and the Lancashire idiom, and were written by two Mancunians born and bred: Stanley Houghton and Harold Brighouse respectively. What is perhaps less apparent is that this original drama and its school of playwrights were powerfully assisted by other early repertories, and that many of the plays in question received sympathetic hearing not only at the Gaiety but as Glasgow and Liverpool as well. Thus Brighouse was given the first production of his *Dealing in Futures* by Alfred Wareing at Glasgow, where two of his short plays, *The Price of Coal* (with the scene moved from Lancashire to Lanarkshire) and the much-admired *Lonesome Like*, also received their premières. Liverpool was similarly receptive, staging his full-length piece, *The Game* (with a footballer as its hero), and accepting another offering from the Manchester journalist, Allan Monkhouse, which had perhaps seemed too lightweight for the Gaiety management, *The Education of Mr Surrage*.

In fact the repertories' net was cast more widely than identification with the Lancashire drama seems to permit. Glasgow, as will be seen, bravely pioneered the work of an obscure and, to British audiences, unperformed Russian, by name Anton Chekhov. Manchester accepted from St John Ervine, an author then familiar only to Belfast playgoers, a piece entitled *Jane Clegg*, which provided Sybil Thorndike with one of her earliest and most enduring triumphs. In the same month, October 1913, Manchester and Liverpool both tackled new plays by a novelist closely associated with Devon and its farming community. Manchester chose *The Shadow* and Liverpool staged *The Mother*, two of Eden Philpotts' earliest essays in playwriting, both exploring the Devonshire scene which ten years later he was to make the subject of string of successful comedies.

Nevertheless, the peak of Manchester's achievement, from which the repertory movement as a whole earned respect and reputation, was the emergence of a school of local playwrights gifted enough to win national and lasting fame. Not surprisingly trial and error were needed before this aim could be realised. Iden Payne's first choice of a 'house' dramatist was Charles McEvoy, a Londoner of Irish descent who had chosen to live in wildest Wiltshire. His study of social pretension in Pimlico, *David Ballard*, opened the 'experimental' season at the Midland Theatre, and was hailed by James Agate as 'not easily distinguished from a masterpiece',[17] but the judgement proved premature. *When the Devil was Ill*, chosen for the opening of the 'new' Gaiety, must have commended itself to Miss Horniman by poking fun at 'the Guild of Woodland Worshippers' and 'the Keen Order of Tinker-Lovers' who claim to practise the simple life and speak in 'the sing-song of the Irish Players'. For the Manchester audience, however, its qualities seemed inbred and slight, and a later McEvoy play, *The Three Barrows*, lacked the modest entertainment value of its predecessors.

The true pupils of the Manchester School were to be found nearer home and mostly amongst the Old Boys of its illustrious Grammar School. Harold Brighouse was encouraged by both Glasgow and Liverpool, but it was understandable that his affection and loyalty should principally be given to his birthplace. His work and success increased steadily in substance and stature. *The Price of Coal* and *Lonesome Like* were brief but evocative studies in, respectively, Lancashire stoicism and Lancashire sentiment. An early full-length play, *Dealing in Futures*, challenged Galsworthy on his own ground by its strong similarity to *Strife*, though Brighouse's friend and colleague, Stanley Houghton, comforted him by pointing out: 'You concentrate on the people and Galsworthy on the social problem', a penetrating comment.[18]

A later full-length play, premiered by the Gaiety, was *Garside's Career*, which tells of a working-class MP seduced by fashionable Society until his wife opens his eyes to his stupidity, and does not stand up as successfully to comparison with Barrie and *What Every Woman Knows*. But *Hobson's Choice* not only survives the comparison; it transcends it. Maggie Hobson is a flesh-and-blood Maggie Wylie, Willie Mossop a John Shand without education and without whimsy. Not strictly a 'repertory' play, since it received its first production in the United States and later in London, *Hobson's Choice* is none the less a tribute to the flair and faith of the pioneers of that movement, as the play's continuing popularity testifies.

The historian of the Gaiety, Rex Pogson, has placed on record the view that whereas Brighouse and Houghton would have emerged without their Manchester platform, this is not true of Allan Monkhouse, adding: 'but for the Gaiety, he would not have been a playwright at all',[19] and citing the writer himself as his source. On first hearing this statement sounds unlikely, for none of Monkhouse's major plays tackles the Lancashire scene at all. *Mary Broome*, easily his most successful and substantial contribution to the Gaiety programme, is a sensitive reworking of a familiar Edwardian theme: the mutual attraction of the son of a well-to-do household and a parlourmaid, leading to an arbitrary and ill-fated marriage when the girl becomes pregnant. Set in London, it is characterised by the strength and power of survival which the girl in question displays. *The Education of Mr Surrage*, on the other hand, takes a fashionable country-house gathering as its starting-point, and satirises with skill and good humour the younger generation's worship of 'artistic' people, who, not surprisingly, exploit that worship to their own advantage. A much shorter piece, *The Grand Cham's Diamond*, which the Birmingham Repertory introduced, is a broadly comic (and Cockney) extravaganza on sensational thrillers. Nothing, in fact, of Monkhouse's pre-1920 output conformed to the closely observed picture of Lancashire working-class people which the 'Manchester school' epitomises.

What lay behind Pogson's statement was rather the realisation that a writer with the skill and versatility Monkhouse possessed would not have been drawn to the drama without the Gaiety and its company to encourage him. His turning playwright was in fact a tribute to the standards and achievement of the Manchester pioneers. Stanley Houghton on the other hand needed no such stimulus, since he found in Lancashire and its people a ready-made subject and inspiration. All his successful plays were written for the Gaiety, and by the sad accident of his death in 1913 at the age of thirty-two his career fell entirely within the heyday of the Manchester 'school', whereas both Brighouse and Monkhouse wrote acceptably for the post-1918 theatre, and even McEvoy had a late flowering with *The Likes of Her* in 1923.

Moreover Houghton's career demonstrated fully the harvest which cultivation by directors as understanding as Payne and Casson and a patron as considerate as Miss Horniman could produce. *The Dear Departed*, a one-act piece perfectly devised for its modest comic aim, led to *Independent Means* and *The Younger Generation*, both full-length, both set in recognisibly Mancunian middle-class households, both neatly plotted, but the latter more assured in tone than its predecessor, and both lacking the full force of inspiration harnessed to experience.

That full force exploded in *Hindle Wakes*, which by an odd theatrical twist was first given not at the Gaiety but for the Stage Society in London, though with a solidly Manchester cast. Here was the complete 'Lancashire drama': serious in theme certainly, but often drily comic in tone and full of human understanding throughout. Fanny Hawthorn, the mill-girl found out after her weekend in Llandudno with the millowner's son, yet retains the audience's respect and even admiration. Her shrewd analysis of his reluctant offer of marriage is worthy of Shaw, and the courage with which she dismisses him and faces the consequences on a par with Nora's rejecting her doll's house.

It is difficult after seventy years to conceive the reactions, both approving and hostile, which *Hindle Wakes* provoked, feelings reminiscent of those aroused by *Ghosts* twenty years earlier and as influential as the reception of *Look Back in Anger* forty years later. For Lancashire drama and the repertory movement the play proved a climax, at once planned and unplanned, since Houghton's death within a year and the outbreak of the War within two years called for a conclusion the movement and its makers never sought. Without doubt *Hobson's Choice* has proved a more popular play, as its greater range and more varied tone deserve, but comparisons are hardly necessary, since between them Houghton and Brighouse justified the hopes and labours of the repertory pioneers. Brighouse himself declared modestly: 'In the long run, if the one-act plays can be ignored, Houghton and I are one-play men',[20] to which both critic and public would reply: 'Yes, but your one play is worth twice the other men's entire output.'

GLASGOW

While Manchester was finding its feet and before Liverpool had attempted to follow, Alfred Wareing, although denied Miss Horniman's support, found sufficient interest amongst Glasgow industrialists to provide the £1000 he needed for a lease of the Royalty Theatre, and the Scottish Playgoers' Company opened on 5 April 1909 with *You Never Can Tell*, a hopeful if cautionary choice of title. In some important respects the Glasgow repertory lacked advantages enjoyed by Manchester and Liverpool, and still more by Birmingham. There was no experimental season; the company never owned their home, and indeed had regularly to move out while the proprietors, Howard and Wyndham, brought in some favoured touring attraction. Nor was there a wealthy patron to write off the debts, although there were debts in plenty: the accounts reveal losses of £3019 in 1909–10, £1539 in 1910–11,[21] and James Bridie, then an aspiring medical student in Glasgow, writes drily of the early days:

The theatre was there, the plays were there, the actors were there, but the audiences stayed away in their homes or elsewhere, congratulating themselves on the vision and pioneering genius of their city.[22]

Moreover Wareing's health was too frail to allow his vision full expression; he relied on several assistant directors, often good – Norman Page, Madge McIntosh – on one occasion great – for Granville Barker not only recreated John Tanner in *Man and Superman*, but stayed to direct Masefield's adaptation of *The Witch* before its London showing. Given the difficulties that confronted them, Wareing's persistence and his backers' patience in guaranteeing his losses were nothing less than heroic.

Even had he not sought the comparison, Wareing's initiative would probably have stimulated his public to demand what he lacked the means to supply: a Scottish National Drama comparable to that with which Yeats and Synge were endowing the Abbey, Dublin. He had some success with Scottish plays, particularly as Christmas attractions. John Joy Bell was one author who met this need in *Oh! Christine* and *Wee Macgregor*; Neil Munro was another with *Macpherson*, and George Hamlen a third with *Colin in Fairyland*. But the precarious finances of the venture precluded the nurturing of a truly native drama, since the financiers had no great enthusiasm for it and the enthusiasts no great financial means.

Wareing then was compelled to build his programme around the established names of the day, placing Shaw and Galsworthy beside Pinero and Henry Arthur Jones. Nevertheless his choice of play could be bold to the point of recklessness. Introducing *The Lower Depths* (shown previously only by the Stage Society) was probably a calculable risk and paid off. The Glasgow public had the necessary insight, and the *Glasgow Record* commented approvingly: 'Gorki shakes hands with Burns and broadcasts the meaning of our great human phrase: "A man's a man for a' that".'[23]

Undertaking the first performance in Britain of a Chekhov play was a bolder decision, and Glasgow audiences found themselves predictably puzzled by *The Seagull*. 'If on occasion the audience last night was disposed to laugh at the wrong places', reported the *Glasgow Herald*, 'this was in no way the fault of the playing nor of the piece',[24] and it is tempting to wonder whether it was this production which drew the audience of three schoolteachers reported by James Bridie.[25] An equally brave gesture, two 'private' performances of *Mrs Warren's Profession* (refused a licence for twenty years by the Lord Chamberlain), was better supported, its audience including the Lord Provost and leading members of the community.

Whether brave or foolhardy on occasion, Wareing's work earned respect in the theatrical profession itself. Granville Barker's participation both as actor and director has already been noted; Galsworthy thought highly enough of the company to permit a Scottish première of *Justice* on the same night as its first London production, which inaugurated the Frohman repertory season at the Duke of York's. The leading part of Falder was played at Glasgow by Milton Rosmer, who had created Konstantin in *The Seagull* with Mary Jerrold as Arkadina. It is a tribute to Wareing's talent-spotting, though it cannot have consoled him at the time, that the Glasgow players were soon wooed elsewhere. Rosmer and his partner, Irene Rooke, were claimed by Manchester, while Mary Jerrold was recruited by Granville Barker for his Duke of York's company. The Glasgow programmes also listed in much smaller print the name of an assistant stage-manager, William Armstrong, whose contribution to the repertory cause was to prove far from small.

Wareing's dedication began to make an impression at the box office, and the company's losses for the seasons 1911–12 and 1912–13 were reduced to £322 and £125 respectively.[26] But his health deteriorated; he was forced to take sick leave in the autumn of 1912, and in the following year he resigned. The directors, learning that Lewis Casson had just parted company with Miss Horniman, offered the post to him, and Casson took over in January 1914. His six months in charge were outstandingly successful; not only did the company record a profit of £790,[27] but Casson found in *Campbell of Kilmohr* by J.A. Ferguson a Scottish play which press and public alike agreed met the test of a 'Scottish National Drama'. Its grim tale of a staunch Jacobite betrayed by the sweetheart who puts her trust in an unscrupulous Government man captured something of Yeats' tragic dimension and was told in the cadenced prose adopted by Synge. Of the original plays staged by the Glasgow company it alone found a lasting place on the bills and in play anthologies.

Ironically this success came too late for survival. The season ended in July 1914. A month later the War broke out and Lewis Casson, like many in his profession, volunteered for military service. Howard and Wyndham, proprietors of the Royalty Theatre, deemed escapist entertainment a sounder wartime offering than repertory and realism. The company's lease was not renewed; its personnel were dispersed, its assets frozen. The Glasgow venture, second only to Manchester in the chronology of repertory, was the first to fall.

A VISIT TO BRISTOL

In December 1913 the Gaiety company paid a visit to Bristol's historic though long-neglected Theatre Royal, with a programme including *Candida* (played by Sybil Thorndike) and *Hindle Wakes*. The effect of such advanced fare on an audience accustomed to sensational melodrama and traditional pantomime was to say the least equivocal. At one performance the sentiments of Marchbanks, as voiced by Lewis Casson, provoked an appeal from the gallery for 'someone to wring his neck'.[28] To more discerning Bristolians, however, the plays and their playing opened up vistas of a repertory company of their own. Encouraged by the influential Bristol Playgoers' Society, one of the Manchester cast, Muriel Pratt, who had played Fanny Hawthorn in the December production of *Hindle Wakes*, undertook to bring repertory to the 150-year-old Theatre Royal, starting with an experimental season in May 1914, with the first full season scheduled for the following August.

High hopes and players of promise were sadly insufficient to establish a new venture at such a time and in such a home. Although the director of productions (and at that time Muriel Pratt's husband) was W. Bridges-Adams, later to command at Stratford-upon-Avon, and his programme included the première of Masefield's *Philip the King*, the response was muted, and grew predictably weaker as the War fastened its grip on the public mind. By May 1915 this shortest-lived of repertories had expired, leaving the Theatre Royal to its ghosts and its tawdry touring companies, until thirty years on the magic wand of the Council for the Encouragement of Music and the Arts achieved a transformation scene, and the Bristol Old Vic Company entered with repertory banner flying.

BIRMINGHAM

Manchester, Liverpool and Bristol had all been prepared for repertory by short introductory seasons which proved successful enough to warrant the launching of a full-scale operation. The pre-history of the Birmingham Repertory Theatre was of a different nature and extended over six years. In 1907, when Miss Horniman was making her plans for Manchester, a number of Birmingham enthusiasts responded to the call of the young Barry Jackson, son of the founder of the Maypole Dairies empire, to form the Pilgrim Players, a group chiefly devoted to the rediscovery and presentation of English poetic drama. Thus their first significant production was the sixteenth-century *Interlude of Youth*, and amongst their number was John Drinkwater, at that time an insurance clerk but presently to emerge as a major poet and playwright. The Pilgrims were also associated with a working-class Birmingham parish, St Jude's, under its farsighted vicar, Arnold Pinchard, and the spirit of Christian fellowship which inspired their endeavours prevailed when they moved their base to the more secular Edgbaston Assembly Rooms.

Barry Jackson, who had been apprenticed to an architect, was blessed with talent as well as fortune; a designer of distinction, an author and actor of sensitivity, he shepherded the Pilgrims through the trials and triumphs of performing a wide-ranging programme in a diversity of locales, often open air but sometimes professional and prestigious. By 1910 they had achieved sufficient status to commend them to W.B. Yeats, who encouraged them to give *The King's Threshold* as part of a London season of Irish plays at the Court Theatre. Opportunities like this and an invitation to

3. Auditorium of the old Birmingham Repertory Theatre, designed by S.N. Cooke for Barry Jackson and built in 1913. Photo: *Birmingham Post and Mail*.

play *Deirdre* and *The Interlude of Youth* at the Liverpool Repertory in 1912 inspired Jackson with an ambition to build his own theatre and form a full-time professional company. The Pilgrim Players took the name of the Birmingham Repertory Company in 1911, and by September 1912 he had chosen a site in Station Street and commissioned an architect, S.N. Cooke, to design this, the first purpose-built repertory theatre in the country. He also appointed John Drinkwater manager, and the insurance world's loss was the theatre world's gain. On 15 February 1913 the curtain rose on Barry Jackson's production of *Twelfth Night* with a company including Felix Aylmer as Orsino and Drinkwater as Malvolio, preceded by the director's reading the manager's 'Lines for the Opening of the Birmingham Repertory Theatre'. The Birmingham adventure was under way.

In several important respects Jackson's enterprise was unique. Whereas the Manchester, Glasgow and Liverpool companies had all taken over large commercial houses, seating upwards of 1000 people, Birmingham's architect was restricted by the site chosen to an audience of 464, a difference in scale which was to influence materially the style and scope of the programme offered. The décor, too, restrained to the point of severity, contrasted strongly with the Victorian plush and gilt of the established repertory theatres. Again, the nucleus of Pilgrim Players who formed the basis of the company ensured a degree of ensemble without the trial period undertaken by Manchester and others. Above all, Birmingham possessed in Jackson a combination of patron and artistic director unique in British theatrical history and comparable only to such Continental figures as Duke George of Saxe-Meiningen.

This asset endowed the Birmingham programme with a quality at once eclectic and highly personal, since Jackson, freed from the restrictions imposed by the board of directors at Glasgow and Liverpool, could satisfy his own taste unchecked. That taste lay principally in imaginative and poetic drama; although the early seasons contained their measure of standard repertory fare (Shaw, Galsworthy, Hankin), Shakespeare was far better represented on the Birmingham bills than at Glasgow or Liverpool, and unfamiliar ground was regularly explored. *Everyman*, *The Interlude of Youth*, the Chester Mystery plays, were brought out from the existing Pilgrim Players' store, and Maeterlinck, Yeats, Rostand and even Euripides provided additions to that store. No less significant was the steady encouragement of Drinkwater as a dramatist. All his early successes were achieved under Jackson's wing: at first limited to the one-act form (including such favourites as *The Storm*, *The Faithful* and $X = 0$), these culminated in 1918 with the triumph of his full-length play *Abraham Lincoln*. This marked a turning-point for both author and theatre. Confining his use of verse to the two chroniclers who comment on the story, Drinkwater essayed a major study of his central character, seen in successive moments of decision during his Presidential career. The resulting portrait of a man of peace accepting the burden of making war inspired an immediate and intense response from the Wartime playgoer. The piece transferred to the Lyric, Hammersmith, achieving a run of well over a year. It bore Drinkwater away from Birmingham on its tide of success; it laid the foundations of Nigel Playfair's distinguished reign at Hammersmith; and it established Jackson as a London impresario of flair and far-reaching importance.

THE END OF THE BEGINNING

The building of Britain's first repertory theatre marked a high point for the movement, unhappily followed by the outbreak of the War the following year. Wartime conditions transformed the London theatre, sweeping away many of its actor-managers in the process, and in the provinces severely curtailed support for the kind of drama with which the repertory companies were associated. Glasgow was an immediate casualty; Bristol, as has been noted, fixed on August 1914 for the opening of

4. The Liverpool Repertory Theatre production of *The Mother*, by Eden Philpotts, 1913, designed by George W. Harris. Cast: F. Pennington-Gush, Gertrude Sterroll, Laurence Hanray. Photo: Liverpool Playhouse.

their venture at the Theatre Royal and foundered in the difficult days which followed. Manchester struggled on, but a city whose artistic life drew substantial support from its German community could not provide the same response in wartime. By 1917 Miss Horniman was compelled to close down her resident company and allow the Gaiety to revert to its original role of a touring 'date'. In 1921 she was reduced to appealing to the commercial interests in the city to take over the financial burden, but her appeals came to nothing and a cinema-circuit bought the building. Invited to attend the last live performance there, her reply was: 'Of course I shall be there. Every corpse must attend its own funeral.'[29] In fact she proved a veryresilient corpse, but although she was created Companion of Honour in 1933 and lived until 1937, she played no further part in the repertory or any other theatrical movement. Alone amongst the pre-War companies, Liverpool and Birmingham survived to carry on the name and traditions of repertory into the 1920s.

A last look at the repertory companies active before 1914 provides some useful conclusions. Manchester, Glasgow, Liverpool, Birmingham, Bristol all constituted big commercial and industrial centres greatly expanded by the effects of the Industrial Revolution and conscious that their commercial importance was not matched by artistic enterprise on a comparable scale. Out of this realisation grew support for the theatrical pioneers who put dramatic art on the same aesthetic level as music and painting. At Glasgow and Liverpool financial responsibility for their resident company was assumed by leading members of the community, and the short-lived Bristol enterprise was guaranteed by the local Playgoers' Society. Manchester and Birmingham were in a different category, since the funding was found by two wealthy individuals dedicated to the drama and blessed by an inheritance from tea and dairy products respectively. Nevertheless public support for the Gaiety and the Birmingham Repertory also derived from civic pride and recognition that these companies constituted a theatrical equivalent to the public library, the concert hall, the museum and the art gallery.

By contrast, the country's main professional and intellectual centres – for instance Oxford, Cambridge, York, Edinburgh – as yet showed little or no interest in the repertory movement, though several of these were to provide valuable initiative and example in the 1920s and 30s. There may be some reflection here of the anti-theatrical prejudice then strongly held in British educated circles. Literature and the stage were still viewed as wholly incompatible in most scholarly minds, and theatre-going widely regarded as frivolous if not actually sinful. On the other hand commercial centres like Manchester and Birmingham, with their lines of communication to Continental cities firmly established, had plenty of evidence available of the benefits which patronage of the arts, whether from public or private resources, conferred on their European colleagues. At any rate during these years the provincial public in this modest handful of cities showed a seriousness of taste and a sustained loyalty to its resident team that London audiences of the time could not, or at least did not, emulate. Though the notion of theatre on the rates had to wait another thirty-five years for legal authorisation, and even longer for widespread implementation, the germ of such provision can be traced back to the pioneering playgoers at Manchester and their fellow-enthusiasts elsewhere in those stirring days before 1914.

5   The Inter-War Years

THE earliest repertory companies were established to provide an alternative to the dramatic fare and standards of the commercial managers operating the provincial circuit. The repertory movement in the 1920s and 30s, however, was confronted by a much more seductive counter-attraction: the cinema, scattering its images all over the country, internationally financed and so cut-priced, commanding lavish and spectacular means which not even the largest theatre, still less a modest 'rep', could rival. Particularly after the introduction of 'talkies' in the late 1920s, the theatre in both its forms, commercial and non-profit-making, faced a struggle to survive. On the other hand the very ubiquitousness of the film created, if unwittingly, the genre of 'live' entertainment. Before the first films all entertainment was live; now the theatre, though steadily shrinking, possessed a charm of its own, and since it was the commercial managements whose stock-in-trade more closely paralleled the cinema's, the repertory movement claimed a larger share of the credit for offering 'something different' as well as 'something local'.

This is particularly true of the 1930s when the triumph of the 'talkies' brought about the building of hundreds of new, often palatial, cinemas, to which the modest repertory theatre afforded a definite if austere alternative. It is notable that whereas the majority of the pre-1914 'reps' were housed in former theatres, those established in the 1920s had mostly to look elsewhere for a home (Bristol's chamber concert hall, Sheffield's YMCA, Hull's lecture-room, Oxford's 'Big Game' Museum), whereas several of the second wave (York and Windsor, for example) reoccupied theatres which had been converted to cinemas. The actual building of a repertory theatre, however, remained a rich man's privilege, as Barry Jackson had demonstrated and Eric Dance was to prove at the 'second' Oxford Playhouse.

BIRMINGHAM AND BARRY JACKSON

Among the pre-War companies Glasgow was an immediate and Manchester an ultimate casualty. The two survivors, Birmingham and Liverpool, rightly assumed a special status in the repertory ranks during

54

the 1920s. Although Liverpool achieved great artistic and commercial success in these years, what gave Birmingham precedence in the public eye and theatrical records was Barry Jackson's central and commanding position in the 'intellectual' theatre throughout the country. From the transfer of *Abraham Lincoln* to the Lyric, Hammersmith, in February 1919, to the production of *1066 and All That* at the Strand in April 1935, not a year passed without at least one presentation by Jackson in London. For long periods the playbills of the Court and Kingsway were monopolised by his name, and their stages graced by the taste and standards he maintained.

Nor were his activities restricted to London and Birmingham. In a letter he wrote to J.C. Trewin in 1957,[1] he selected a single year – 1932 – and listed five companies operating under his banner at some point in that year (marked both inside and outside the theatre by contracting markets, growing unemployment and political problems). The list includes seven presentations in London (amongst them the premières of *Too True to be Good* and *For Services Rendered*); a Birmingham programme which featured Shaw, Maugham, Philpotts, Robert Sherwood, Elmer Rice and Molière, beside many others; the Malvern season (one of the 'historical surveys' with plays by Jonson, Southerne, Fielding and Boucicault included); a national tour of *Too True to be Good*, and a Canadian tour with *She Stoops to Conquer*, *Heartbreak House* and *Dear Brutus* as its chief attractions. It is difficult to conceive how even an organisation as well endowed today as the National Theatre or Royal Shakespeare Company could achieve such miracles within twelve months. As the output of a single impresario it is no less than astonishing.

While compelling astonishment and admiration, however, it complicates any assessment of Birmingham's particular contribution to the repertory movement in the 1920s and 30s. What, for example, qualifies as a 'Birmingham production'? The road from Station Street to Sloane Square was emphatically two-way. The brave and breath-taking enterprise of staging *Back to Methuselah* in full occupied the Birmingham stage in October 1923 and that of the Royal Court in February 1924. On the other hand the controversial (but admired) modern-dress *Hamlet* and controversial (and disparaged) modern-dress *Macbeth* opened at the Kingsway in 1925 and 1928 respectively, and then transferred to Birmingham as part of the relevant season. It would be unjust to hail *Back to Methuselah* as a Birmingham achievement and then label *Hamlet* and *Macbeth* as 'direct from the Kingsway Theatre, with full West End cast'.

What can be safely argued is that without the experience he gained at Birmingham, Jackson would never have ventured into London management; and without the knowledge that Birmingham audiences would receive his London experiments with interest, if not always enthusiasm, he would never have risked a modern-dress *Hamlet*. Even after the 'crisis' of 1924, when he insisted on 4000 season ticketholders being found to share financial responsibility,[2] and the setting up in 1935 of a Theatre Trust (on which the Corporation, the University and a number of important civic societies were represented), Jackson saw Birmingham as the nerve-centre of his theatrical enterprise. West End productions might open and close, national and international tours ebb and flow, but season followed season in Station Street, and both the theatrical public and the theatrical profession looked to it for a lead.

Training tomorrow's stars became an accepted function of the Birmingham company. It may at first glance seem strange that the schooling of actors was seen as a prime responsibility of the repertory movement when well-endowed institutions such as the Royal Academy of Dramatic Art and the Central School were now established to carry out that task. But though such centres existed to train actors, they could not by their very nature supply the experience of progressing from 'super' to 'small part' to 'supporting role' to 'principal' which the actor-managers and the touring companies had provided before 1914. A London theatre world, controlled by commercial managements setting up productions singly (and often quitting the scene if unsuccessful), had no means of 'nursing' the prentice player, and the touring circuit was not merely subject to the same commercial hazards but gradually contracting under the fierce competition of the cinema.

The repertory companies could and did undertake such 'nursing', to the parental pride of their public who saw their favourites growing in stature and reputation on their home ground, and later in the wider and more cutthroat arenas of London and New York, Ealing Studios and Hollywood. At the same time some distinction should be maintained between a promising pupil who earned a good end-of-term report and went off to seek honours elsewhere, and the new boy who progressed steadily from Lower Fourth to Upper Sixth, and then moved gracefully to higher institutions of theatrical art, wearing his old school tie with pride and honour. In theatrical annals, for example, the Liverpool Playhouse shines with the reflected glory of launching Rex Harrison on his stage career and giving Michael Redgrave his first leading roles. But Liverpool playgoers with long memories might be tempted to point out that in his two seasons Harrison was confined to minor roles and that Redgrave moved on to the Old Vic after a couple of years, whereas such long-term members of the company as Cyril Luckham and Ena Burrill graduated from cameo parts to Shakespearean leads: in the latter's own words 'from Bessie Legros to Lady Macbeth'.[3]

Birmingham's roll of honour is even longer, not least because of the constant interchange of productions between Station Street and London, but in this list too some discrimination may be allowed. Peggy Ashcroft made her professional debut at Birmingham in 1926 as Margaret in *Dear Brutus*, and appeared there the following year in Drinkwater's *Bird-in-Hand*.

Recognition then rapidly directed her to Town. Her 'stage-father' in Barrie's play was Ralph Richardson, whose Birmingham career was also restricted to a single season, though he went on to great distinction elsewhere under Barry Jackson's banner. His stay overlapped that of a younger actor, Laurence Olivier, who remained for two years, 'playing leading and other parts',[4] besides appearing for Jackson on tour and in London. On the other hand Cedric Hardwicke was a Birmingham actor from 1922 to 1925, starting in a one-acter with 'undoubtedly the worst performance in memory' (according to Jackson),[5] and rising by way of the He-Ancient in *Back to Methuselah* and Shotover in *Heartbreak House* to Churdles Ash in *The Farmer's Wife*, which took him to the Court for a year's run. Even after London and New York had recognised his quality he returned annually to the Malvern Festival, where King Magnus and Edward Moulton-Barrett were amongst the many parts he created.

5. *Back to Methuselah*, Part V, by Shaw. The Birmingham Repertory Theatre production, 1923, designed by Paul Shelving. Photo: Birmingham Repertory Theatre.

THE MALVERN FESTIVAL

Barry Jackson's responsibility for the Malvern Festival during the first nine years of its life (1929–37) aligns the Birmingham enterprise with the Oxford and Cambridge ventures of the 1920s, to be examined in detail later. In all three cases the theatres offered strictly limited seasons to a highly sophisticated, homogeneous audience, although the affluent patrons of Malvern covered a wider age-range than the undergraduates who made the pilgrimage to Woodstock Road, Oxford, or Barnwell, Cambridge. There was a strongly intellectual flavour about audiences and programmes at all three places, particularly Malvern during the 'theatre-through-the-ages' seasons (1931, 1932, 1933) when Jackson chose to spare Shaw from over-exposure and instead revived some rare items from the English repertory. Amongst the rarest were *Hick Scorner*, *The Play of the Wether*, *The Fair Maid of the West* and *The Dancing Girl*.

The concept of Malvern as an Academe of Dramatic Art was strengthened by the introduction of morning lectures and teatime talks, a nice distinction being observed between the specific gravity of the two. Lest all this suggest some dry-as-dust unearthing of dramatic cadavers, it may be apt to quote T.C. Kemp's comment on the 1932 production of *Tom Thumb the Great*, which endeared itself so much that it was revived in 1937:

... the sort of thing that may be enjoyed by anyone who has seen half a dozen plays and is blessed with a sense of humour. Even the six plays may be foregone, for this parody of dramatic pomp and passion has an extravagance of its own.[6]

But of course the *raison d'être* of the Festival remained Shaw, who presided over the occasion, whether his plays were performed or not. Overall his work was as essential to Malvern as it had been to the Royal Court seasons nearly thirty years earlier. It may be noted that *The Apple Cart*, *Too True to be Good*, *The Simpleton of the Unexpected Isles*, *Geneva*, *In Good King Charles's Golden Days*, and (much later, in 1949) *Buoyant Billions*, all had their British premières at Malvern; that only twice was Shaw's name totally absent from the Festival playbills; and that in 1930 no less than seven Shaw plays were presented in a two-week season. Even after Jackson relinquished direction of the Festival to the Theatre's lessee, Roy Limbert, Shaw remained its centrepiece, as witness the 1938 revival of *St Joan* with Elisabeth Bergner.

THE LIVERPOOL PLAYHOUSE

If Liverpool did not catch the public eye or the press's attention as often or as widely as Birmingham, this was simply because it did not possess – and did not need – a Barry Jackson, and thus did not impinge so largely on the London scene. What it did possess was a continuity of artistic direction and administration unrivalled elsewhere. William Armstrong, who had earlier acted at the Playhouse, became its director in 1922, and Maud Carpenter, who had worked there from the very first season, was made business manager in 1923. Their partnership was both successful and enduring: Armstrong remained director until his retirement in 1944, at the age of sixty-two, and Maud Carpenter continued to manage the Playhouse until the 1950s.

Their collaboration set the pattern of Liverpool playmaking. The theatre, after its early vicissitudes, settled into a steady rhythm of highly professional standards and highly responsive audiences. Runs, normally three weeks, were sometimes extended up to six, in itself an extraordinary achievement in an era of 'weekly rep'. Armstrong and Miss Carpenter did not take risks – the emphasis was on the established modern British and American playwright – but equally they did not pander to the public. The Playhouse historian, Grace Wyndham Goldie, defines their course as 'steering firmly between the merely popular and the rashly adventurous'.[7] The theatre's capacity, 900, compared with Birmingham's 300 or the 200 of Bristol's Little Theatre, was at once a reason for not gambling and a source of substantial box office support, without the patronage of a Barry Jackson or Terence Gray. The Liverpool roll of honour was as long and, if a little less glamorous, just as solid as Birmingham's. To the names already mentioned might be added Diana Wynyard, Robert Donat, Robert Flemyng and Wyndham Goldie: with the proviso (applicable to all such lists) that as many must be left out as included, and that one ground for inclusion must inevitably be the artist's subsequent success, not always proportional to the value of his repertory training.

Birmingham and Liverpool were the twin pillars of the repertory movement between the wars –at once survivors and leaders. The newcomers in the 1920s can usefully be divided into 'avant-garde' and 'self-help', inadequate as most labels prove to be. The 'avant-garde' was dominated by Oxford and Cambridge, not coincidentally, as may emerge. 'Self-help' was the motive behind the founding of a number of companies during this decade. If emphasis is placed on three – Bristol, Sheffield and Northampton – it is not intended as a slight to others' achievement. All the 'self-help' companies were brought into existence by the communities they served, were supported and financed by those communities, and at least in the case of Sheffield drew largely on the community for their early personnel. On the other hand the two 'avant-garde' companies who wrote their names large in the records of repertory at this time were in no sense indigenous, either in their leadership or their following.

It has been suggested that the creation of repertory companies at Oxford (in 1923) and Cambridge (in 1926) was no coincidence. The older universities had made no contribution to pre-War repertory. Perhaps the Victorian prejudice against the theatre lingered longer by the Isis and Cam than by the Mersey or Clyde. Perhaps too Oxford and Cambridge men and women found it easier (and free from disciplinary action by the University authorities) to do their playgoing in London, a recourse denied the students at Liverpool and Glasgow. Certainly the seasons at both the Oxford Playhouse and the Cambridge Festival Theatre were geared strictly to University terms. Eight one-week runs were the basis of both, with a strong emphasis on autumn and spring. Indeed after 1925 the original Oxford company did not attempt a summer season at all. It has been argued that neither could have tackled a year-round programme; their artistic objectives (and, in the case of the Oxford Playhouse, physical shortcomings) were limiting factors which precluded longer seasons. It should also be noted that their respective homes were significantly sited on the 'fringe' of the University area. The first Oxford Playhouse was a former 'Big Game' Museum in the Woodstock Road. The Festival Theatre, Cambridge, originally a Georgian playhouse, the Theatre Royal, Barnwell, was some way along the Newmarket Road, itself a cause for alarm to the University authorities.

Both projects were initiated from without, but here the resemblance ends. James Bernard Fagan, who founded the Oxford Playhouse, was a vastly experienced man of the theatre, an actor (with Benson and Tree), author (for Alexander and Mrs Patrick Campbell) and director (of the British première of *Heartbreak House*, as well as of pioneering Shakespearean productions at the Court). A Balliol man, he had returned to direct for the University Dramatic Society, whose productions since their inauguration in the 1880s had launched a large number of careers. Terence Gray, who both founded and financed the Cambridge Festival Theatre, was educated at Eton and Magdalene. That he possessed flair and originality is undeniable; that he also lacked staying power is also undeniable. He was, in the most creditable sense of the terms, an amateur and a dilettante.

THE FIRST OXFORD PLAYHOUSE

The Oxford Playhouse opened in October 1923 with a production of *Heartbreak House*, in which the acting honours seem to have been stolen by a recent graduate of the OUDS, Richard Goolden, as Mazzini Dunn. The young Flora Robson was oddly cast as old Nurse Guinness, and the equally young Tyrone Guthrie, having lost the part of Captain Shotover at the readthrough, was eventually moved to that of

Hector Hushabye. Although the programme contained an appeal from J.M. Barrie, Arnold Bennett, Lord Curzon, Edward Elgar, Thomas Hardy, John Galsworthy, Gilbert Murray, A.W. Pinero and Shaw, amongst others,

to the Members of the University and the Citizens of Oxford . . . to support a movement which promises to supply Oxford with a distinguished source of entertainment,[8]

the opening had been postponed for six months because the management failed to obtain the Vice-Chancellor's permission to play. Indeed throughout the theatre's early history there was a distinct lack of support from both Town and senior Gown, leaving the company at the mercy (sometimes literally) of the undergraduates.

So long as Fagan remained in command (until 1929) the bill of fare remained resolutely highbrow in tone. Shaw, who graced the last performance of *Heartbreak House*, was reported as asking: 'If Oxford is not "highbrow", what on earth is Oxford?',[9] and Fagan evidently concurred. His advocacy of 'unpopular' Shaw entitled him to the same respect as Barry Jackson gained with *Back to Methuselah* at Birmingham, and of course he lacked Jackson's financial resources. The enterprise started with a capital of some £500, and though in 1925 the Carnegie Foundation made a grant towards an 'Oxford Arts Theatre Guild',[10] this does not seem to have been repeated, and Fagan's hopes of enjoying two weeks' rehearsal were never realised. At the end of his régime he told the *Oxford Magazine* the company had lost an average of £330 a year on a season of about eighteen weeks;[11] after 1925 they did not attempt to play in the summer term, and in 1928 and 1929 opened only in the autumn.

Not only did they lack funds, they were desperately short of facilities. The 'Big Game' Museum was as far artistically from the ideal venue as it was from the centre of Oxford. The auditorium was small, noisy and comfortless; the stage and backstage were more so. Indeed the stage facilities were so lamentable that Fagan contrived to make a virtue of necessity by insisting on his 'Presentational' method of production, setting every play in white drapes, with only an inner stage suggesting a specific location. The white drapes were a particular source of strain on the stage-staff, notably on Tyrone Guthrie, who, when not impersonating Hector Hushabye or Sir Lucius O'Trigger, had to look after them, and concluded:

Much as I admired Mr Fagan, it was soon apparent that the Presentational Method was not a very good idea. For one thing, the audience became very tired of the white curtains; for another, the white curtains became very tired of themselves. I know this for a fact, because one of my daily duties was to remove the fingermarks and damned spots by rubbing the beastly things with an evil-smelling concoction called Gudasnu.[12]

Against all the odds — human, technical, financial — the company achieved several miracles (though inevitably also experienced several disasters). If one such triumph is selected, it need not detract from the overall achievement of a repertoire which also included Ibsen and Strindberg, Sophocles, Shakespeare, Synge and Shaw. But the production on 26

January 1925 of *The Cherry Orchard* does exemplify Fagan's courage and artistry. It was the Stage Society's showing of this piece in 1911 which had tied a tin-can to Chekhov's tail as an unplayable author. Yet at Oxford a first-night witness, Norman Marshall, records its triumph:

I went to the Playhouse rather doubtfully that Monday evening, expecting to be bored and bewildered. It was one of the most exciting evenings of my life . . . I only knew that I had seen a play full of the beauty and strangeness of life, its humour and its sadness and its absurdity, a play full of understanding and tenderness unblurred by sentimentality, by a man without illusions but without bitterness. For the first time I realised that the theatre can achieve a reality deeper and more poignant than is possible in any other art.[13]

The Cherry Orchard, with a cast including John Gielgud as Trofimov, was revived in May and immediately transferred to the Lyric, Hammersmith. Its success there led to the season at Barnes directed by Komisarjevsky from which Chekhov's acceptance in the British theatre is often dated.

THE FESTIVAL THEATRE, CAMBRIDGE

The physical limitations of the Woodstock Road building dictated 'Presentationalism'. The Theatre Royal, Barnwell, Terence Gray's chosen base at Cambridge, suffered from fewer drawbacks, although it had long been disused as a theatre. But the very idea of restoring it, either to its original Georgian form or to an orthodox 'picture' stage, was anathema to this cosmopolitan man, imbued with Continental staging and lighting ideals, many of them paradoxically originating with an Englishman, Gordon Craig, though hitherto only widely practised in European subsidised theatres. Gray and his skilled lighting designer, Harold Ridge, applied the lessons they had learnt on their European travels to the shell of the old Theatre Royal. The acting area was stripped of its surviving fittings and proscenium, and an open stage backed by a cyclorama replaced them. Gray's justification of this change struck a strongly prophetic note, pointing to modern developments at Stratford (Ontario), Minneapolis and Chichester (all masterminded by Tyrone Guthrie, who directed a season at the Festival Theatre):

The spectator's eye is not the single eye of the camera: it is an argus-eye that in its widest range can see from every part of a semi-circle at one and the same time. In brief every actor is seen in the round and must therefore learn to act in the round.[14]

The open stage was provided with a permanent, curved cyclorama, 'built from two layers of hollow tiles curved with sirapite and surfaced with cement',[15] a complete break from the flimsy cloths of many contemporary stages. Ridge introduced a lighting system costing over £2000 and featuring the Schwabe lamps newly designed for the Dresden Opera House, which provided an unprecedented range and subtlety of colour. Accordingly Gray favoured what he termed 'isometric scenic design' — bold arrangements of screens, steps, rostra and architectural forms, painted pale grey and coloured by the lighting designer, not the scenic artist (Ridge also described this method as 'Presentationalism', distinguishing it from 'Representationalism').[16] A revolve and sliding sectional stages were installed, and, as a further move against the picture-stage, entrances from the auditorium were regularly employed.

The programme was also purpose-built. Greek drama suited it well; the opening play was the *Oresteia*, and over the years not only were Aeschylus, Sophocles and Euripides well represented but Aristophanes and even Roman comedy. Modern European authors were regularly heard, often for the first time across the Channel. Expressionism found a congenial platform at Cambridge; the Germans Kaiser, Klabund and particularly Toller, and the Czech Capek brothers. American Expressionism followed; Elmer Rice, predictably, and a pair of O'Neill's early plays (*The Emperor Jones* and *The Hairy Ape*). Less predictable were several productions of Pirandello, not an author obviously amenable to 'Presentational' methods.

English drama did not fare so well. Gray caused considerable stir by his Shakespearean productions, in which he showed his strong German allegiance, notably to Leopold Jessner in his handling of *Richard III*. Less readily explained were the treatment of *Romeo and Juliet* in 'flamenco' style, an inspiration attributed to the films of Rudolph Valentino, or the presentation of all the characters in *Henry VIII* as playing-cards and several in *Twelfth Night* on roller-skates. But the Elizabethans yielded more in Gray's hands than did the 'picture-stage' playwrights, for whose aims he expressed total contempt:

What in the name of Dionysus has Illusion got to do with Art anyhow? All the hotchpotch of proscenium and flies, grids and strips and wings and tormentors and all the rest of the mumbo-jumbo – clean gone, surviving only in its rightful place – a child's playbox.[17]

This rejection extended even to Ibsen, whose *Wild Duck* was given an absurdist interpretation, culminating in a curtain-call chorus of 'Daisy, Daisy, give me your answer, do'. Gray seems to have despised not only illusion but the dramatist who aspired to be a man of letters, claiming 'The theatre is being rescued from the degradation of being a place for the exhibition of the work of men of letters, a printer's rival . . . Aeschylus was a dancer, Shakespeare and Molière were comedians; none of them was a man of letters',[18] and certainly dance figured high in his priorities. He early employed the young Ninette de Valois (his cousin) to choreograph his productions, and later made the theatre available to her for complete ballet programmes. She was particularly successful in working on Wilde's *Salome* and a production of *On Baile's Strand* which encouraged Yeats to write *The King of the Great Clock Tower* expressly for her.

Despite the success of *On Baile's Strand* Gray attempted nothing else by Yeats, perhaps because living authors of such distinction could prove inhibiting to his aims. After leaving Cambridge he prophesied: 'The verbal framework will be created by a poet perhaps, but by a poet who is also a worker inside the theatre, and even his text will be no more sacred than Shakespeare's was to Burbidge . . . but will be moulded according to the director's theatrical conception as a whole.'[19] His failure (or refusal) to attract a 'Cambridge School' of playwrights as Miss Horniman had created the 'Manchester School' was judged by Norman Marshall, his assistant for much of the Festival's life, as a matter for regret:

It was a weakness of Terence Gray's policy that he very seldom gave a first performance of a play. More important to him than the play was the manner in which it would be presented, so his energies were devoted less to finding new plays than to finding new methods of presenting old ones . . . Had he from the beginning been ready to encourage authors and to collaborate with them a whole new school of playwrights might have grown up around the Festival.[20]

Restlessness and dissipation of effort were two strains in Gray's make-up. During the seven years he held the theatre's lease he twice handed over responsibility. In 1929–30 Anmer Hall, a wealthy patron of the drama, took over and engaged Guthrie to direct the season, marked by productions as diverse as *Six Characters in Search of an Author* and *Lady Audley's Secret*, both triumphs for Flora Robson, while in 1932 Norman Marshall took charge. In 1928 and again in 1929 there were exchanges of productions between Oxford and Cambridge, and one of the last presentations at Oxford under Fagan was *Iphegenia in Tauris* by a Cambridge company led by Robert Donat and Flora Robson. While Cambridge seems to have taken Oxford's offerings in its stride, the Oxford public viewed Gray's experiments with some suspicion. His plan to link the Festival Theatre and the Playhouse with a London base to be established at 43 King Street, Covent Garden (formerly the home of the National Sporting Club), broke down when the Oxford authorities refused him permission to extend the Playhouse frontage.[21] In 1931–2 he also attempted to link the Festival Theatre with the London Gate Theatre under Peter Godfrey, though the needs and organisation of the two proved too disparate for close cooperation.

In 'Festival', Gray chose a suitably 'not everyday' name for his theatre. If it is now chiefly remembered for the programmes printed on black transparencies, to be read during the performance, that is not wholly inappropriate. His resources permitted him a measure of whimsicality and luxury denied the Oxford venture: the theatre boasted the best restaurant in Cambridge (an innovation from which the Arts Theatre was to profit in the next decade) and suited its menu to the play, e.g. for Shakespeare, 'porterhouse steak, Surrey capon, fish pingle and roast swan'. His appeal to the undergraduate population was even more exclusive than Fagan's; although 8:30 was the usual curtain-time, Tuesday's performance was given an hour earlier to meet the women students' strict 'gate' or curfew.[22] He regularly challenged the Lord Chamberlain's powers of censorship (Miss Julie, Salome and Lysistrata were all heroines whose embraces he

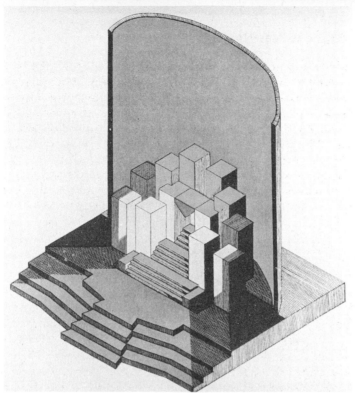

6. Terence Gray's design for *Oedipus Rex* (Sophocles, trans. by J.T. Sheppard). A Cambridge Festival Theatre Production, 1927, directed by Gray. Design reproduced in the *Festival Theatre Review*, vol. 4 no. 77 (30 May 1931). Photo: Bristol University Theatre Collection.
7. The set for Gray's *Oedipus* production. Photograph by Scott and Wilkinson, reproduced in *Festival Theatre Review*, vol. 2 no. 41 (2 June 1928). Photo: Bristol University Theatre Collection.

invited and St James's Palace forbad or frowned upon). The bar stocked only choice wines and eschewed beer and spirits. Gray even flirted with such uncommercial notions as suggesting that 'Any member of the audience wishing to see the play a second time could do so free of charge', and 'Once every week there will be a free bar night' (but kept the secret to himself).[23]

In June 1933 he gave up the Festival Theatre, claiming in his valediction published by the *Festival Review*: 'Whatever we believed to contain truth and to be worth saying or doing we have said or done without hesitation', and adding an intriguing note of speculation: 'Perhaps the Festival will become what is termed a provincial repertory theatre',[24] which suggests a sharp distinction between his vision and the practical policies of Liverpool, for example. Consistent with his dedication to the theatre as an art and his contempt for the 'trade theatre' as he termed the established order, Gray's break with the stage was final. On quitting Cambridge he took up viniculture in France and later bred horses in Ireland. Enough financial backing was found to continue running the Festival under Joseph Macleod, one of Gray's disciples, for a couple of years more, but it could not survive competition from the Arts Theatre (opened in October 1935), the creation of John Maynard Keynes, which owed a good deal, including its name and restaurant, to Gray's inspiration. The Festival Theatre dwindled into the home of short 'repertory' seasons by visiting companies on the 'trade' basis he had foreseen and rejected. It has not been used as a theatre since 1939.

A PENNINE MALVERN

During the years that Gray pioneered Continental ways and plays in Cambridge, a pioneer from the earliest days of repertory, Alfred Wareing, attempted on a modest scale something similar in the less congenial setting of the Theatre Royal, Huddersfield, of which he had become manager in 1918. The theatre was part of a commercial circuit with touring companies for the greater part of the year, but Wareing introduced an annual summer 'repertory season' between 1921 and 1931. Frequently this was provided by an established Shakespearean company (Benson, Baynton, Doran and on one occasion the Old Vic), but Wareing favoured a more contemporary and Continental programme, billed as 'International Masterpieces', including several of Pirandello's plays, notably the world première of *Lazzaro* in 1929. Wareing's 'incredible gallantry' in trying to make Huddersfield 'a Pennine Malvern' (Ivor Brown's verdict)[25] was at least ten years premature. Pirandello and International Masterpieces were still caviare to the general playgoer at Huddersfield or elsewhere, and the owners of the Theatre Royal decided to turn it into a 'twice-nightly' house, provoking Wareing's resignation.

THE 'SELF-HELP COMPANIES'

Fagan and Gray, Guthrie and Marshall were the trend-setters of the repertory movement during these years. But there were other labourers in the cause who followed more closely the lead of the pioneers before 1914. Even the War years were not wholly destructive. In December 1915 a repertory company was established at Plymouth. Its location, at the junction of Princess Square and Westwell Street, was more impressive than its accommodation, in the Mechanics' Institute. J.C. Trewin, who began his apprenticeship to the critic's craft there, remembers 'an absurdly constructed stage, a tilted tea-tray on the top of a spiral staircase, cubby-holes for dressing-rooms and an auditorium that held over 400'.[26] The moving spirit was a local professional, George King, described by the leading lady in 1922, Colette O'Niel, as 'a little man with a comical egg-shaped face and a wisp of dark hair brushed down into his eyes', and also 'an ironic sad, sardonic smile'.[27] Given the tea-tray of a stage, the repertoire had to be restricted and cautious. The opening play was *A Bunch of Violets*; by 1929, '*A Pair of Silk Stockings* has proved so popular that it has been staged eight times.'[28] Nevertheless there was more solid fare, and Trewin recalls Bernard Coppin, once a member of the Manchester Gaiety company, who took over in the late 1920s as an impressive Captain Shotover, before the company closed down in 1935.

THE LITTLE THEATRE, BRISTOL

As has been seen, Bristol came late and fleetingly to an appreciation of resident companies, and Muriel Pratt's seasons at the Theatre Royal ended ingloriously in the spring of 1915. But Plymouth's response to the challenge of the Mechanics' Institute may have encouraged Bristol to explore the facilities of the municipally owned Colston Hall. This included both a main and a 'lesser' hall, and it occurred to several enthusiastic members of the Rotary Club that the latter might house a theatre company. When the scheme was put to the Club in June 1923 the President's comments sounded more warning notes than rallying cries, castigating alike 'that kind of popular sentimental play . . . associated with the glamour that radiated around the matinée idol' and 'that most acute form of disappointment which was known as an intellectual treat'. Indeed his only positive call was for 'plenty of nonsense but of course intelligent nonsense'.[29] Nevertheless his caution struck the right note for his hearers; financial support was found, an artistic director, Rupert Harvey (then a leading actor at the London Old Vic), appointed, and the first night fixed for 17 December.

Sir Arthur Pinero was persuaded to give an opening address in which he welcomed the announcement that the theatre was to be run on 'commonsense lines', because 'the word commonsense conveyed to his mind the assurance that the repertory theatre was not to be exclusively highbrow'.[30] Could he have had second thoughts about signing the appeal to support the Oxford Playhouse only three months earlier? At any rate the choice of opening play – a light comedy, *Other People's Worries*, by a lightweight playwright, R.C. Carton – can have given him no concern, especially as Carton was of his own generation. In a comment on the venture *The Times* noted:

This new scheme is of unusual interest because of the fact that the Little Theatre in Bristol is the first Repertory Theatre in the country which has started with direct civic encouragement.[31]

– no doubt a reference to the City's making the lesser Colston Hall available at a non-commercial rent. There was no other 'direct encouragement', although the artistic policy was subject to an Executive Council of alarming size, which embraced representatives of more than half a dozen local dramatic societies (including the Commercial Travellers' and the British Empire Shakespeare Society), all with members on the parallel 'Ladies' Committee', though both bodies seem to have exercised their powers sparingly.

Like Oxford and Cambridge the Bristol company offered a new play each week, although unlike them the season extended to some forty-eight weeks. The strain, particularly on Rupert Harvey himself, must have been overwhelming – not surprisingly a local critic commented a year later: 'He has disappointed us but once, and that was when he had an almost perfect innocence of his words in *Young Imeson*. It became infectious.'[32] Nevertheless the Bristol company prospered, and when Harvey returned to London in 1926, other hands, notably those of Ralph Hutton, an experienced comic actor, took over, while the 'safe' policy adumbrated by the opening choice was sufficiently varied by productions of Shaw, Shakespeare, Galsworthy, St John Ervine and like names hallowed by earlier repertory example.

SHEFFIELD AND NORTHAMPTON: THE EARLY YEARS

Parallel with the history of Bristol's Little Theatre ran the course of Sheffield's repertory company. This had antecedents in amateur drama: a group called the St Philip's Dramatic Society had been formed there in 1919 under the guidance of a railway clerk who was to prove a key figure in the repertory movement between the Wars, Herbert Prentice. The following year they changed the name to the Sheffield Repertory Company, which for the next ten years played in a succession of halls, gradually acquiring more professional status, thanks to their success and a grant from the Carnegie Foundation. Prentice left them in 1926 to work at the Festival, Cambridge, whence he moved on to direct the Northampton

Repertory and to play an important part in the history of the Birmingham company.

Sheffield continued steadily with a succession of directors, and from 1928 operated in a specially constructed auditorium in the Comrades' Hall, Townhead Street. The name nicely epitomises the community spirit of the company, and was changed to the Playhouse only ten years later. Though comradely, the hall had its limitations. Alfred Wareing described it in the *Stage Year Book* for 1928 at 'not an alluring place. It is squarish and like a chapel with the pews removed.'[33] The chapel image seems also to have discouraged the local inhabitants, who were reluctant to attend because 'It's only for 'igh class people, such as school-teachers.'[34]

Sheffield and Bristol were companies created by self-help on the part of their citizens in halls not designed for theatrical purposes. Northampton, which opened in January 1927, offered a variation on this theme, since it was housed in an existing theatre which local playgoers felt could be more beneficially employed. It was also an early example of the 'twice-nightly' principle operating in repertory, a way of life which might strike terror into today's actors. As such the Northampton company was viewed askance by some commentators. The *Stage Year Book* article already cited observes:

Northampton's claim to inclusion in the list of towns ennobled by the possession of a Little Theatre is admitted – but only just admitted – by the production of *A Midsummer Night's Dream* which ran for 22 performances and showed a profit. By that production the Northampton Repertory Players took a bold step forward from a popular twice-nightly policy, and came into line with those Little Theatres which are doing fine and more ambitious work.[35]

In fact Northampton had to return to a twice-nightly system, and the artistic consequences, particularly in the early part of the week's run, must have been damaging; significantly they abandoned twice-nightly performances on Mondays in 1935. But it is only fair to contrast their perseverance with the loss of the repertory seasons and resignation of the director (who wrote the *Stage Year Book* article in question) when the Theatre Royal, Huddersfield, turned to a twice-nightly programme.

The account of Northampton should not be broken off without a reference to the arrival there in 1928 of a young scenic designer by name Osborne Robinson. He rapidly established himself as a principal asset of the company, and his designs, conceived and carried out within the strictest limitations of time and money, if not of space, put Northampton playgoers into a favoured class of audience. If the reputation of the Birmingham company in the area of décor was largely attributable between the Wars to one man, Paul Shelving, the standards at Northampton were even more dependent on Osborne Robinson, who was still designing their productions thirty years later.

8. Design by Osborne Robinson for *Northampton Harlequinade* at the Northampton Repertory Theatre, 1951. Photo: Bristol University Theatre Collection.

THE LITTLE THEATRE MOVEMENT

Alfred Wareing called his article in the *Stage Year Book* 'The Little Theatre Movement, its Genesis and its Goal', thus opening up a related but confusing aspect of the subject. Alongside the repertory companies established from the 1920s there appeared a number of producing groups dedicated to offering their audiences an alternative to the merchandise of the commercial managements, but operating spasmodically and combining professional leadership with unpaid support. Undoubtedly the 'Little Theatre' movement, which had a proportionally bigger impact on North America, contributed much to the range of drama experienced by the post-1918 generation, and in so doing assumed some of the early repertories' function. There is little in the records of their successors to challenge the achievement of the Manchester School or the Irish national drama. The majority could not afford to put experimental or untried work before their audiences, and were even chary of 'advanced' work by leading dramatists. Ronald Russell at Bristol had to battle for the inclusion of Coward's *Private Lives* and Maugham's *Sheppey* in his 1935 list because 'one or two of the older generation stirred uncomfortably in their seats when the

70

language became a little more staccato'.[36] Adventurous companies like Oxford and Cambridge were chiefly concerned to introduce Continental masters to English playgoers. The contemporary writers whom the enlightened Barry Jackson is now remembered as championing are Shaw, Drinkwater and Philpotts, all of whom were prominent before 1920. Responsibility for experiment passed to London's proliferating club theatres, and to the Little Theatre movement.

Its guiding hand was widely recognised as that of Nugent Monck, an inspiring director who even before 1914 had established in Norwich a group which in 1921 transferred to the converted church known then and since as 'the Maddermarket Theatre', reproducing the essentials of Elizabethan staging. Though not exclusively Elizabethan in its pro-ramme, the Maddermarket found in poetic drama its strongest and most characteristic voice.

The North country proved an especially bracing climate for the growth of the Little Theatre. Sheffield's evolution from amateur group to fully professional repertory has been noted. At Hull a similar though shorter story unfolded when a professional actor, A.R. Whatmore, founded a repertory company in 1923, and by concentrating on limited seasons was able to strengthen his company with professional actors. Colette O'Niel, joining in 1925, found Roland Culver and Colin Clive amongst her col-leaigues and *John Gabriel Borkman* and the Brtish première of Björnson's *Leonarda* amongst the plays. The Hull company was also blessed with a versatile designer, Eric Hillier, who transformed its miniature stage, in fact the platform of a lecture-hall, from week to week. A venture of this kind depended on the magnetism of its director, and after Whatmore moved back to London in 1930 the Hull company lost impetus and did not survive the pressures of that period. At Leeds the movement took more diverse form, including an Industrial Theatre drawing on employees from local factories, an Arts Theatre undertaking new verse drama, and a Civic Playhouse operating in the Albert Hall (with a capacity of 1000) and funded by a silver collection. Across the Pennines three long-lived organis-ations emerged in the Manchester Unnamed Society, founded as early as 1916 and turning a carpet-warehouse into its own Little Theatre, and two Garrick Societies, at Stockport and Altrincham. The list could readily be extended.

Nevertheless the singularity of the Sheffield story and the disappearance of the Hull group suggest that the Little Theatre movement contributed more to the evolution of community drama than to the growth of the repertory theatre. Conditions in both the country and the theatre fostered a widening and deepening interest in what before 1914 had been largely confined to light-hearted entertainment by leisured entertainers. The foun-dation in 1919 of the British Drama League by Geoffrey Whitworth pro-vided a focal point for this transformation. But the Little Theatre and the repertory theatre overlapped only occasionally, and in the 1930s the repertory movement had to face its own crisis.

Despite the success of the moving picture, the theatre until the late 1920s possessed a trump card: it could talk, and the cinema was silent. But with the introduction of the 'talkie' the cinema gained another stride over its rivals, and the challenge was felt immediately and increasingly by the repertories. In December 1929 J.B. Fagan left Oxford for good and the Oxford Playhouse closed down, albeit only temporarily. In that year also Bristol lost the support of the Rotary Club, although some individual members sustained it until 1934. At the same time Northampton underwent a serious financial emergency. As has been seen, Terence Gray gave up the Cambridge Festival Theatre in 1933, and the following year not only was the Sheffield company in grave difficulty but even Birmingham displayed distress signals, when Barry Jackson announced that he had underwritten the Repertory to the tune of £100000 and must call a halt.[37] In the spring of 1935 the Bristol company came within days of closing down, and that year marked the end of both the Plymouth and Cambridge enterprises.

These last constituted the two poles of the repertory globe, Plymouth improvising a popular programme with minimal resources, Cambridge serving an intellectual élite in an expensively equipped theatre. Significantly those companies following a middle-of-the-road policy proved more resilient. At Birmingham an appeal for help produced only a modest £3000, but in January 1935 a widely representative Theatre Trust was set up with Jackson as governing director. Elsewhere public response confirmed an eagerness to preserve the local repertory. At Sheffield the response was so strong that the company took the plunge and turned wholly professional. Bristol audiences also provided the backing for a new team, the Rapier Players, a new captain, Ronald Russell, and a new captain's lady, Peggy Ann Wood, all of whom were to hold the stage for thirty years. Northampton showed its metal by raising a cricket team under its new Director, the former MP Robert Young, and extended its activities to other fields of play. On one January day in 1934 the Northampton company

- rehearsed *Bull Dog Drummond*,
- played a matinée of *Jack and the Beanstalk* (with a young actor called Erroll Flynn as Prince Denzil),
- gave two evening performances of *Sweet Lavender*,
- broadcast the one-acter, *The Dear Departed*.[38]

Another feature of the movement's answer to the threat of the 'talkies' was the emergence of non-resident repertory companies playing seasons of varying length in what had hitherto been touring theatres and so helping the provincial circuit to survive. In 1934 at a critical point for the movement Cecil Chisholm, a journalist whose career stretched back to Miss Horniman's régime at Manchester, published *Repertory: An Outline of the Modern Theatre Movement.* The appendices list nineteen resident and fifteen non-resident companies, and a competition organised by the *Sunday Dispatch*, which Chisholm adjudicated, awarded the *prix d'honneur* 'for unattached repertory companies' to the Brandon Thomas troupe, whose seasons in Edinburgh, Glasgow and the North of England were highly regarded. In effect they constituted the backbone of professional theatre in Scotland, where the example set by the Glasgow pioneers before 1914 had been slow to take fire.

One rather tenuous link with Wareing's seasons at the Royalty did survive through the foundation in 1921 of the Scottish National Players from funds still standing in the Repertory's bank account. The Players were talented amateurs, their director paid from a Carnegie grant, and their tours covered wide areas of Scotland. For one season, 1926–7, their director was Tyrone Guthrie and their reputation appropriately advanced. But they never achieved continuity or a permanent home, and by 1930 they were forced to suspend activities, although the establishment of repertory theatres at Perth (in 1935) and Dundee (in 1939) was in some measure attributable to the Players' pioneering work in these towns.

Elsewhere there was a growing demand for 'live' drama which neither the beleaguered touring system nor the twenty-odd resident companies could satisfy. Theatrical managers stepped in to supply this demand with twice-nightly repertory companies playing 'popular' programmes at 'popular' prices. The product offered was cheap in every sense – without subsidy or civic support it had to be – especially when compared with the best that Birmingham or Liverpool could offer. But it met a need and sustained a public which otherwise might have been swallowed up by the lavish resources and universal appeal of Hollywood. Cecil Chisholm's book lists fifteen non-resident companies, but reference to the *Era* for 10 May 1933 (a week chosen to avoid both pantomime and summer attractions) provides twenty-three companies in this category. Particularly notable are the presentations of two impresarios. Terence Byron had six companies playing that week, all in the North of England, and Alfred Denville had five (although his entry in *Who's Who in the Theatre* records that he 'has had over twenty repertory companies playing at the same time').[39] It could not be claimed on Byron's or Denville's behalf that their standards were high; it could and should be claimed that they kept actors employed, theatres open, and audiences aware of the alternatives to cinema and radio, as well as giving a lead to other 'multiple storemen' of the repertory scene. As a profession these also contributed to the survival of the provincial circuit. In the week in question Byron's companies were appearing at the Grand, Oldham; the Empire, Dewsbury; the Hippo-drome, Mexborough; the Prince's, Bradford; the Royal, Chester; and the Royal, Barrow-in-Furness – all touring dates and all reminders of how far the provincial theatre had once extended.

RECLAMATION AND REBUILDING

After the first impact of the 'talkies' certain theatres were even reclaimed from use as cinemas, including the Theatre Royal, Windsor, which despite its situation in the shadow of Windsor Castle hardly justified its name. John Counsell, an undergraduate at Oxford during the Fagan era, served his apprenticeship when the Playhouse reopened in 1930, stage-managing, playing juvenile leads and ultimately producing. He had early set his heart on running a repertory company at Windsor, and when the chance was offered in 1933 he took it, perhaps too readily. The reasons he gives for initial failure throw light both on the state of the touring theatre and the repertory movement at that time:

The Theatre Royal had always suffered the inconsistent policy of a second-rate touring date. As such it had never attracted the well-to-do potential audience which live within a radius of ten miles . . . They automatically went to London for their playgoing. Then the theatre had become a cinema and lost even the public that had gone there before. We were thus trying to build up an audience completely from scratch. Another deterrent was that the word 'Repertory' was associated in many people's minds with 'amateur' . . . Even after they had seen as good a company as ours, some people continued to believe that we were a kind of hard-working local amateur dramatic society.[40]

Undercapitalised and lacking experience, Counsell's first venture at Windsor collapsed after a few months, though he had the bitter-sweet experience of welcoming the future King George VI and Queen Elizabeth to one of the final performances. But in 1938, wiser and better backed, he returned to run a carefully devised programme for more than forty years. A similar rescue was effected at the Theatre Royal, York, where in 1935 a former theatre was reclaimed from use as a cinema and began an unbroken career as a repertory.

But perhaps the vicissitudes of the Oxford Playhouse best illustrate the struggle for survival which the repertory cause underwent in this decade. After the departure of Fagan's pioneers the theatre was 'dark' for nine months, and miniature golf was played where Chekhov and Shaw had been heard. But in October 1930 a new Oxford Repertory Company opened – improbably in *Rookery Nook* and even more improbably under the direction of Ben Greet, the touring Shakespearean actor-manager.

The driving force behind this reopening was Stanford Holme, an actor and director who shrewdly trimmed the theatre's sails to the chilly blasts of the 30s. The fare offered was undemanding. Reviewing *The Silver Box* in April 1933, the *Oxford Magazine* observed tartly:

Since the Playhouse programme for the rest of the term does not threaten to impose any great strain upon the intelligence of the audiences, this production is not to be missed.[41]

If playgoers were sometimes scarce, funds were always scarcer. John Counsell recalls that in his scenic artist's capacity 'The state of the budget demanded that I should keep off the more exciting and expensive colours.'[42] But a public was reclaimed, and, by introducing summer seasons in the grounds of Worcester College, a virtually continuous programme was gradually built up. Stanford and Thea Holme remained the leaders of the enterprise, but their endeavours were steadily augmented by a succession of dedicated helpers. Amongst these was a recent Oxford graduate named Eric Dance, who determined that the company should be more fittingly housed, and, having so determined, found the funds to implement his decision.

The last performance in the Woodstock Road was given in March 1938, when the Wilde comedy then played might aptly have been retitled *The Importance of Being Central*, for it was to Beaumont Street, in the heart of academic Oxford, that the company moved, and there on 22 October 1938 the Playhouse known to succeeding generations of Oxford players and playgoers was opened, still under Standord Holmes' direction. The chosen piece was by the fondly remembered (but unhappily dead) J.B. Fagan, *And So To Bed*, a tribute to a founding father.

The 1930s, which had opened with financial crisis in repertory after repertory, saw a steady revival of the movement. Not only did the audiences themselves respond to the emergency with guarantees and regular support; the setting up at Birmingham of a Theatre Trust was perhaps a clearer signpost to future development. If some similar Trust had been formed at Oxford in 1929 or Cambridge a little later, Fagan need not have abandoned the Playhouse for the American film industry or Terence Gray the Festival for viniculture in France. Nevertheless the number of repertory companies grew, even if their identities sometimes changed. In addition to those already touched on, Cecil Chisholm's account in 1934 mentions resident companies at Coventry, Croyden, Harrogate, Manchester (Rusholme) and Rochester. Not all of them survived, but the establishment in the later 1930s of companies still active more than forty years later, such as Colchester, Oldham, York and Windsor, suggests a hardier stock. The purely commercial operations of syndicates like Terence Byron's or Alfred Denville's were themselves evidence of a demand for the product, however answered. The challenge of the cinema had been met; the next threat was to come from Hitler, not Hollywood.

6   The War Years and After

GEORGE ROWELL

THE First World War had marked a watershed in theatrical history and a serious set-back to the repertory movement. The challenge to the actor-managers from purely commercial interests resulted in a transformation of the London scene, and the claims on money and manpower put an end to two pioneer provincial companies, Glasgow and (ultimately) Manchester. The Second World War threatened to wreak a similar havoc: in the first weeks of what proved to be the 'phoney' War, 1939–40, all places of entertainment were closed, and while both the West End and the provincial touring circuit gradually stirred from this enforced slumber, certain repertory companies made major decisions. The Sheffield rep, for example, migrated to Southport for the duration, both Birmingham and Liverpool closed down for some months and then reopened under significantly different circumstances, while the wholesale reorganisation of Britain in wartime, with its blackout, its bombing, its austerity, its enforced control of labour, made decisive changes in playgoing patterns.

In the long run, however, these patterns were by no means destructive to theatrical life in general or repertory in particular. Restrictions on travel, for instance, cut off a substantial portion of the playgoing public from their regular theatre visits and directed them towards their local rep. The strain of living under wartime stress made theatrical diversion welcome to many. Above all a gradual recognition by authority that the arts were an essential tonic for national morale led to financial subvention on a hitherto unimagined scale and variety. The 1914–18 War had done its worst to destroy the existing theatrical fabric; the 1939–45 War ultimately replaced one existing fabric by another, of manifestly superior quality in ever-multiplying quantity.

It is salutary to reflect that while the repertory movement owes its survival and standards, at least from the mid 1950s, to increasingly generous government (via the Arts Council) and local (from the ratepayers' pockets) assistance, that assistance was first conceived as helping to bring music and drama to threatened and deprived areas of the country by way of the touring unit.[1] The precedent was set by purely private initiatives, grants from the Pilgrim Trust (founded by the Harkness family, an American philanthropic venture) and Carnegie Foundation to certain artistic endeavours. Notable amongst these was the work of the Pilgrim Players under Martin Browne, whose tour of the beleaguered South Coast in the summer of 1940 with *Murder in the Cathedral* and *Tobias and the Angel* was a gesture of faith in the country and its artistic values. In their modest way the company displayed the 'Battle of Britain spirit' no less proudly than the magnificent 'small boat' armada organised to rescue the Dunkirk survivors or the heroism of the 'First of the Few' fighter pilots later that summer.

THE CREATION OF CEMA AND CORT

The initiative of such private Trusts prompted the government to earmark limited sums for related purposes, originally through the Ministry of Education and only from 1945 directly by the Treasury. The foundation of the Council for the Encouragement of Music and the Arts, set up on 19 January 1940, was undoubtedly a milestone in British artistic history. It should be emphasised, however, that where the theatre was concerned its purpose was to endow theatreless areas (South Wales, the North East) with dramatic diversion, not to sponsor new or existing repertory companies. In this regard CEMA might be categorised as the civilians' ENSA (though the extension of the slogan 'Every Night Something Awful' would be equally unjust to both endeavours). As they did with music, the authorities saw the newly opened (and secretly sited) ammunition and related factories as important theatreless areas; those towns already provided with theatres, whether commercial or repertory, did not enter into their calculations.

On the other hand certain theatrical developments in these early War years combined to promote the repertory cause on a semi-official basis as importantly as the craving for diversion on the part of the civilian assisted the provincial theatre. The transfer, for example, of the bombed-out Old Vic Company to the Victoria Theatre, Burnley, in January 1941 set a precedent which could not be denied, even though the Company itself returned to the New Theatre, London, in 1942 (leading to the epoch-making seasons under Olivier and Richardson from 1944). An offshoot of this transplant was the reopening of the Liverpool Playhouse by a newly formed Old Vic Company in 1942. Other important repertory companies struggled back into operation with municipal encouragement. Summer seasons in Cannon Hill and other Birmingham parks were features of the Birmingham scene in 1941, 1942, 1943 and 1944. The Repertory Theatre itself, closed for a year from December 1940, played host to several visiting companies until November 1942 when Barry Jackson resumed its direction, offering as his reopening production *The Farmer's Wife*, a reassuring choice.

Nor was the repertory movement itself slow in capitalising on wartime support for its source of diversion and inspiration. On 5 May 1944 a number of repertory theatre leaders met (in a temperance hotel in Birmingham, though the choice of venue seems to have been unintended) to found the Conference of Repertory Theatres, conveniently abridged to CORT and with Council substituted for Conference at Morecambe in 1950.[2] Among the founding groups were Colchester, Dundee, Oldham, Oxford, Windsor and York, with G.E. Geddes from Dundee elected to the Chair. A channel of communication for all repertory companies, however sponsored, was thus established; it summed up a growing confidence in the movement after the setback of the early War years.

CEMA AS A LESSEE

An equally significant development was the assumption by CEMA of the lease (at a rent of £300 p.a.) of the historic Theatre Royal, Bristol, Britain's oldest working theatre. When the last commercial management quitted it in 1941, local enthusiasts saved it from various fates including conversion into a warehouse.[3] CEMA's bid for the lease, which occurred almost by accident and against their constitution, was characteristic and auspicious. The claims of a 175-year-old building found a sympathetic hearer in J.M. Keynes, who had become Chairman of CEMA in April 1942. In a letter to the *Times* later, on 11 May 1943, he wrote of the Council's 'anomalous constitution' which allowed it 'to do by misadventure or indiscretion what obviously no one in his official senses would do no purpose . . . Thus in an undisciplined moment we accidentally slipped into getting mixed up with a theatre building.' Whether accidentally or not, the consequences of the Council's leasing a theatre (as opposed to subvention for its productions) were to be momentous. From 1943 for the remainder of the War a series of CEMA-backed touring productions occupied the stage of the Theatre Royal.

Meanwhile north of the border a movement was afoot to prove that Scotland could emulate the Southrons under wartime theatrical conditions. James Bridie, the only contemporary Scottish playwright with a reputation transcending mere borders, had joined CEMA in 1942 and spoke for Scotland at its meetings. Foremost in his plans was the revival of the Glasgow Repertory Theatre which had flourished thirty years earlier. A modest start was made with the production of his *Holy Isle* at the Athenaeum, Glasgow (the base of the Scottish National Players during the 1920s), on 11 October 1943, the venture's being presented by 'the Glasgow Citizens' Theatre' with a graceful reference back to one of Alfred Wareing's descriptions of his objective.[4] But the history of the Glasgow Citizens' Theatre is more usually dated from its reopening under that name in the old Princess's Theatre in the Gorbals on 11 September 1945. Where Wareing, Casson and Guthrie had laboured and left, Bridie and his supporters worked and won. The Glasgow Citizens' Theatre remains in its Gorbals home (when all about has been demolished), though Bridie himself lived only five years beyond its opening at a permanent address.

The last years of the War proved a period of boom for theatres, metropolitan and provincial. The public, civilian and service, developed an insatiable appetite for some inspiriting alternative to the stress and danger of their occupations, and the military potential in the audience was greatly enlarged by the arrival in Britain of large numbers of troops from overseas, particularly North America. Charles Landstone, since 1942 Deputy Drama Director of CEMA and architect of the involvement of the Council in the fortunes of the Bristol Old Vic and other repertory companies, reports a profit at the Theatre Royal, Bristol, of £16 000 (over a half being bar takings) between 1943 and 1946, and one of £10 000 at the Liverpool Playhouse under its Old Vic Company during 1945–6 alone.[5] That wartime conditions assisted enormously in these rewards is self-evident; Landstone himself also records that after the wartime boom in audiences 'a residue remained – say twenty per cent – and it is this residue which proved in the post-War years to be the backbone of support for the Repertory Theatre Movement'.[6] There may be doubt about the proportion suggested, but no doubt about the provenance of that support.

THE ARTS COUNCIL AND THE BRISTOL OLD VIC

The closure of ENSA and the transformation (on 9 August 1946) of CEMA into a royally chartered Arts Council of Great Britain substantially changed the direction of that body's activities. Touring theatrical enterprises, whether for the Forces or theatreless areas and wartime factories, became irrelevant or subsidiary to such national concerns as the reopening of Covent Garden and the reestablishment (in 1950) of the Old Vic *at* the Old Vic, or the steadily expanding role of the Shakespeare Memorial Theatre, Stratford-upon-Avon. On the other hand the success of the 'provincial' Old Vic Company at Liverpool pointed to another, permanent, foundation at Bristol's Theatre Royal, to replace the touring attractions for which CEMA had been responsible. Consequently the Bristol Old Vic Company was launched under the direction of Hugh Hunt in February 1946. In 1950 the Arts Council withdrew as lessees of the theatre in favour of a Trust on which they, the Old Vic, and local interests were all represented, and the choice of the then Vice Chancellor of Bristol University, Philip Morris, as Chairman proved admirable.

There was a certain historic aptness about this first important development in the post-War repertory scene's occurring at the theatre in which the last enterprise of the pre-1914 movement had breathed so briefly. There was also a much greater artistic aptness in launching a repertory of the highest standards in so historical a home. The subsequent success of the

9. The Bristol Old Vic Company's Theatre Royal: the eighteenth-century auditorium of Britain's oldest working theatre (built 1766). Photo: Derek Balmer.

Bristol Old Vic Company was also due to the astonishing adaptability of the Theatre Royal to plays of any period. Unlike so many Continental theatres of equal venerability, it proved congenial not merely to Sheridan and Goldsmith, its own contemporaries, but to plays of every period and style. Though both stage and auditorium had been and would continue to be the subject of refitting, the theatre maintained its unique receptivity to drama ancient and modern, grave and gay, spoken and sung. If its modest capacity (640 seats under modern conditions, though the 1942 bills of sale had suggested something nearer twice that figure)[7] limited its box office return, it also preserved its intimacy and assured its exclusiveness.

THE GROWTH OF ARTS COUNCIL GRANTS

While the foundation or encouragement of resident companies like Bristol or Glasgow had become the Arts Council's main theatrical interest in the provinces, it did not abandon altogether its wartime prin-

80

ciple of touring. Several mobile or resident-with-touring-duties groups were established in the immediate post-War years, with varying fortunes. The Midland Theatre Company, founded in 1946 and based on a Coventry Technical College, kept alive a theatrical torch destined to illuminate in 1958 the Belgrade, Britain's first purpose-built civic theatre. The company covered at various times Nuneaton, Dudley, Loughborough and Wolverhampton. From 1951 it received substantial civic support (made possible by the 1948 Act authorising rates expenditure on cultural activities) and in 1955 the Arts Council withdrew from the project, leaving the local authority to assume financial control.

Not all such projects proved so fruitful. Two Arts Council creations in strongly contrasted areas failed to find a public. The West of England Theatre Company operated from Exmouth over a terrain so scantily populated as to preclude large audiences, and more seriously the West Riding Theatre, an exchange scheme between Huddersfield (where in the 1920s pioneer Alfred Wareing had tried to bring intellectual drama to a less than intellectual Theatre Royal), Halifax and Wakefield, failed totally and expensively. At Swansea too the public responded none too warmly when the Arts Council tried to upgrade the Grand Theatre and thus fund drama in South Wales.

A more rewarding experiment was that based on Salisbury, whose Arts Theatre (later the Playhouse), a converted chapel-to-cinema-to-theatre, became the base of a circuit including over the years Southampton, Winchester and Basingstoke, a nicely reminiscent return to the old Georgian itinerary followed by strolling players in Wessex. Eventually, as at Bristol, the Council also withdrew from direct management at Salisbury in favour of a Trust set up in 1951. In all these enterprises, when the balance of failure and success was drawn, Treasury funds were required. Such expenditure included structural improvements in the directly managed theatres; safety precautions at Bristol in 1948–9, notably 'an Iron Curtain in the West' as Christopher Hassell's witty reopening prologue deemed it, cost the Council £20000.[8] But it was the production costs of both directly managed and assisted companies which figured largest in their accounts. Expenditure had exceeded £70000 a year by 1949 and was to rise steadily in the 1950s.[9] By 1963 the Arts Council grant to all repertory theatres was seven times that of 1952,[10] and, even allowing for inflation to raise its then small but ugly head, this clearly represents a big increase in both the number of companies and level of Treasury funding.

In the late 1940s and early 1950s the ranks of CORT were steadily swelled by new recruits. Interestingly several of them (Guildford in 1946, Ipswich in 1947, Leatherhead in 1951) were housed in adapted buildings, though they were later to acquire splendid purpose-built homes. Guildford and Ipswich, for example, started as club-theatres in local halls, Kidderminster (1946), Chesterfield (1949), Canterbury (1951) and Leatherhead

as cinemas, Derby (1951) as a public hall. The Manchester Library
Theatre, given house-room in the basement of the Central Library from
1947, was an interesting parallel with Bristol's Little Theatre, which had
been started in a municipal concert hall a quarter of a century earlier. Some
theatres, already established, were able greatly to enhance their standards
of production with Arts Council assistance. Nottingham, a veteran of the
commercial rep circuit, received Arts Council help from 1949, as did
prestigious Birmingham from 1954 (£500, which had risen to £35 000 by
1969).[11] In 1956 when CORT celebrated fifty years of the repertory movement's existence (dating its birth from that of the Manchester company,
which was tidy if disputable), 'about thirty repertory companies' were
receiving Arts Council help.[12]

A NEW DEAL FOR DIRECTORS

A valuable consequence of increased funding for leading
companies like Birmingham, Bristol and Glasgow was the greater freedom
enjoyed by their directors. Before 1939 even enlightened men such as
William Armstrong and Herbert Prentice had to restrict their choice of
play to what they judged their audience would pay for. Grants, particularly from the Arts Council with its broader horizon, allowed the favoured
companies to cast their nets far more widely. If a comparison is made
between Northampton's programme for 1930 and Bristol's for 1950
(Appendix 2), the increase in time and concentration that an Arts Council
company could devote to rehearsal is at once apparent. Prentice and his
designer had to mount forty-five full-length plays in one year, and his
company to give 540 performances of those plays. The Bristol Old Vic
twenty years later prepared twelve productions over the twelve months,
giving 284 performances in all. Money, talent, above all time, were generously provided in the new repertory scheme.

Any comparison of programmes must inevitably be arbitrary but certain distinctions can be made. Northampton relied heavily on successful
authors of the day, particularly authors of comedy: Coward (four plays);
Lonsdale (three); Ben Levy (two). Shakespeare was represented only by an
extract with strong local interest, the murder of Prince Arthur from *King
John*. There were predictably a number of now forgotten titles, including
one first performance on any stage, but nothing that could be called
innovatory, and for very sound reasons. In 1950 the two Bristol directors,
Allan Davis and Denis Carey, between them mounted three Shakespeare
productions and a wide selection of comedy (Molière; Vanbrugh; an
obscure Goldsmith; Pinero; Barrie). The only 'West End success' in their
programme was a recent experiment in verse, *The Lady's Not For Burning*. The new play (*Captain Carvallo*, by a virtually unknown Denis
Cannan) and the nearly new one (*Blind Man's Buff*, by the distinguished

but unregarded Denis Johnston) both achieved later London productions, if with varying fortunes. Even allowing for the random selection of company and year, the greater depth achieved by a company under post-War provisions is apparent.

Not only were leading repertory directors now blessed with time and funds. The recognition of quality companies provided a career structure which their pre-War colleagues had had to carve out for themselves. John Fernald, Director at Liverpool from 1946 to 1949, moved on to a six-year tenure (with Alec Clunes) of London's Arts Theatre during which the tiny club-theatre emerged as a National Theatre in miniature. Hugh Hunt, having established the Bristol Old Vic, came up to the Waterloo Road to direct the senior Company. Douglas Seale moved from Birmingham to the London Old Vic in 1958. Barry Jackson's reign at Stratford from 1946 to 1950 furthered comparable exchanges, particularly for Michael Langham, director at Birmingham from 1948 to 1950. Young directors could gain valuable experience at senior reps and move on nationally and internationally: Peter Brook graduated from Birmingham to Covent Garden and then to widely scattered theatrical centres. Some of the smaller sponsored reps launched directors on paths leading to more responsible posts: Denis Carey was director at Salisbury before going to Bristol, and Frank Hauser moved from the Midland Theatre Company to found the Meadow Players at the Oxford Playhouse.

A similar traffic in plays began to build up. The prestige of the repertory movement was enhanced not only by transfers to London of plays tried out by various companies but more particularly by the presentation of complete productions whose attraction was as much the ensemble of the company as the promise of the play. Thus the Bristol Old Vic were invited to play in the Waterloo Road on several occasions, amongst the most successful being *Two Gentlemen of Verona* in 1952 and *War and Peace* in 1962. Birmingham's admired production of the unconsidered *Henry VI* transferred to the Old Vic in 1953. The following year Bristol provided the West End with the musical *Salad Days*, and could claim not only the company and a production destined for a record long run, but also the author and composer, Dorothy Reynolds and Julian Slade, both members of the Bristol Old Vic team.

REPERTORY GRADUATES

The distinction which almost from its start the repertory movement had brought to the ranks of leading actors gained pace and numbers in the late 1940s and 50s. In the last years of the War Birmingham had launched Paul Schofield, and a little later Ian Richardson and Albert Finney thrilled Station Street before delighting Stratford-upon-Avon and London. John Stride, fresh from RADA, played leads at Liverpool before joining the London Old Vic for a ten-year career, including speaking the last words at the inaugural production there of the National Theatre, in which he played Fortinbras. Richard Briers played Henry Irving's role in *The Bells* in Williamson Square (at the age of twenty-two) before achieving comic pre-eminence on stage and screen. A complete list of 'Bristol Old Vicars' who became London luminaries would be long if flattering, but names like Paul Rogers, Robert Eddison and Yvonne Mitchell from the earliest days, and later Dorothy Tutin, Donald Sinden, John Neville, Eric Porter and Peter O'Toole justify their selection. There was a nice sense of past and present achieved in the choice of companies for the first 'Festival of British Repertory Theatre' staged in London in 1948. The contributors were Liverpool and Birmingham, both giants from the pre-1914 period; Sheffield, representing the 1920s generation; and the Bristol Old Vic. These last were very much the new boys, though the loyalty of Bristol playgoers to repertory had been sustained over the years by the gallant Rapier Players and their predecessors at the Little Theatre. There was also a strong personal link with the origins of repertory in the organiser of the Festival, Basil Dean, a founding father both as actor and director.

THE COMMERCIAL COMPANIES

A divisive if inevitable consequence of increasing Arts Council and local aid to repertory was the disparity in standards between commercial and non-commercial companies. In the immediate post-War period the sheer numbers and diversity of companies concealed this growing division. The *Stage Guide* for 1946 (its first appearance since 1928) ventured the statement that the total of 'repertory theatres and travelling repertory companies . . . has now mounted to 238, and is steadily growing'.[13] That for 1949 reports 'about 250 companies in operation'[14] although of course this does not imply that all 250 were active full-time or in occupation of their own theatres. The report also stretches the category of 'theatres presenting repertory companies' by including such as the Mechanics' Institute, Otley, and the Pavilion, Penmaenmawr. Many of these companies were presented by commercial managers operating in the surviving touring theatres. In particular two impresarios dominated the touring repertory field: Frank Fortescue and Harry Hanson had inherited the mantles and methods of Terence Byron and Alfred Denville.

A spot-check from the *Stage* for 29 May 1947 reveals forty-seven repertory companies performing in that week, and of these no fewer than seventeen were presented by Frank Fortescue. In that week his flag floated over seventeen Northern theatres, many of the companies listed paying return visits. For example, the troupe at the Theatre Royal, Wigan, were 'in their eighth season', those at the Theatre Royal, St Helen's, and the Hulme Hippodrome 'in their sixth year'. Elsewhere Harry Hanson and his Court

Players effectively divided the commercial kingdom with Fortescue. During the same week the 'On Tour' column of the *Stage* noted 106 attractions, but of these only thirty-nine were plays, the majority of the remainder being described – with appropriate licence – as 'revues'. It is clear that repertory companies provided the playgoer with the lion's share of 'straight' drama, and that the commercial reps contributed a substantial portion of those plays.

Since the kingdoms of Fortescue and Hanson have long since sunk under the tides of theatrical fortune, it may be salutary to attempt some consideration of the phenomenon of weekly rep, noting that as sober an authority as *Who's Who in the Theatre* affirms that 'in 1952 there were over 100 repertory companies in Great Britain, and the majority were weekly reps'.[15] Clearly the audience for a company with a weekly change of programme differed greatly from that for a theatre which offered a three weeks' or month's run. The public at Liverpool, Birmingham or Bristol was drawn from a much wider area and assigned its playgoing a place in a varied programme of artistic experience. The audience for weekly rep was inevitably smaller, less discriminating, and found in playgoing a social and gregarious rather than artistic satisfaction. A shared evening with familiar performers and fellow spectators constituted the basis of their theatrical pleasure. Indeed the familiarity of plays, players and playgoers was an essential of that enjoyment. It could be argued that in the following decade when not only theatres but cinemas fell victim to changes in the entertainment world, Bingo effectively replaced for at least the older playgoer the satisfaction weekly rep had once provided.

Such a comment need not diminish the importance or degree or that satisfaction. But the quality of performance possible within a system of weekly change of programme remains disputable, and in particular the value of weekly rep for the performers. Working for a strictly commercial and often absentee management under conditions of minimum rehearsal and funding could be destructive of talent and ambition. Two witnesses on the subject may be usefully cited and contrasted. When Alec McCowen obtained his first job at Macclesfield in August 1942 ('This confirms your engagement – stage-manager and parts £3 a week. Half salary during rehearsal week. Will let you have a formal contract on arrival if you desire it') he was under no illusions about the quality of the company he had joined. Attempting nearly forty years later to describe his reactions, he found himself quoting Henry James on Irving's *Macbeth*: 'I sat through the performance in a sort of melancholy amazement.' But he remained positive of the value of Macclesfield's training for him as a near-novice:

It was a splendid introduction to the theatre . . . The director taught me everything from tying a cleat to mascaring my eye-lashes. I collected furniture and props from shops and friends of the theatre, and pushed a laden handcart through the hilly streets of the town. There were no dressing-rooms – only a curtained partition under the stage to separate the men and women. As there were no washbasins, I collected two buckets of water from the pub next door for the actors and actresses before the performance each night. I changed the scenery, worked the switchboard, pulled the curtain up and down, and in the lunch hour sometimes sold tickets in the box-office. On Sundays, I cleaned up the previous week's play, swept the stage and helped to paint the flats for the coming attraction.[16]

He was at the time in the middle of his training at RADA. The difference between the two disciplines struck him forcefully, and strikes his reader even more forcefully.

A witness for the prosecution may be found in John Osborne, who joined Harry Hanson's company of Court Players at the Palace Theatre, Camberwell, in the early 1950s. It was a time of low water for Osborne the actor, and for twice-nightly rep, and his reactions demonstrate this:

Hanson's companies were dreaded as the last funk-hole for any actor, but they were not easy to penetrate. If there was a Hanson kind of theatre, there was a Hanson kind of actor, unpersonable, defeated from the outset and grateful to have any sort of job at all. They were apologetic about themselves, if not among themselves. Equity representatives were unknown to speak, fluffs and dries were entered into a book by the stage director and other misdemeanours, if committed enough times, ensured the sack, administered literally according to the Hanson Book. He was the theatre's Gradgrind and his theatres were administered like workhouses of despair . . .

Working in Camberwell was as unpleasant as I had anticipated and the company were docile, like prisoners without heart or spirit. The repertory of plays was vintage Hanson, consitting of pre-1920s melodramas learnt from 'Sides', *Coming through the Rye*, hack adaptations of *Dr Jekyll and Mr Hyde*, *Gaslight*, *Dracula*, *Frankenstein*, *Charley's Aunt* and low, forgotten farces. The audience was noisy and inattentive. Rehearsals were conducted in a guilty kind of haste and the actors were only given moves where not indicated in the script. We committed our lines as if we were sewing mailbags. No one dared fudge them or forget a move.[17]

After three months he was dismissed. 'The Hanson companies operated a policy of spot sacking and I was no doubt selected by the director . . . as being the most replaceable, and to encourage the others.'[18] He may even have deserved it. Clearly there were as many arguments for and against the system of weekly repertory as there were companies. Perhaps the fairest conclusion could be that for the actor weekly rep was a salutary start but an abject end.

THE IMPACT OF TELEVISION

Soon after Osborne's abject end a bombshell hit commercial repertory. The opening of Independent Television on 28 September 1955 provided the British viewer with an alternative service to that already provided by the BBC. More seriously it provided the potential playgoer with alternative entertainment to that offered by his local theatre, whether it housed a repertory company or touring attraction. The result, particularly for the commercial repertory market, was catastrophic. The *Stage Year Books* tell their own story: by 1950 the number of 'theatres with permanent repertory companies' is put at ninety-four, with eleven of these operating under Frank Fortescue's banner and nine making up the court of Harry Hanson.[19] By 1954 the figure is down to sixty,[20] and the following year plumbs the depths at fifty-five.[21] In 1956 the *Year Book* was reduced to whistling in the dark: 'Fortunes may be low at the moment, but like Old Soldiers the Repertory Theatre never dies.'[22]

The corner was turned, according to Hazel Vincent Wallace,[23] founder-administrator of Leatherhead and stalwart of the cause in the 1950s and 60s, with the help of three major changes, all of them specifically aimed to offset the counter-claims of television: the provision of food as an adjunct (or often alternative) to the hasty interval drink in the bar; the opening of the theatre during the day with coffee and culture in the form of exhibitions, talks and club activities as an additional attraction to the nightly performance; and the inauguration in 1958 as part of the CORT jubilee celebrations of a training scheme for theatre administrators. Artistic directors of theatres have always been fed by ambition; their material needs seem irrelevant when artistic satisfaction keeps them working – but administration is less inspiring and often more consistently demanding. Consequently systematic training and a recognisable professional ladder of promotion were deemed essential if this crucial aspect of theatre was not to be delegated to the otherwise unemployed theatre worker.

Another of Miss Vincent Wallace's causes was the replacement of 'repertory' by the term 'regional'. While some element of tradition might be lost in the change, the argument was sound. In the pre-War and inter-War years the word 'repertory' had specific, intellectual overtones, whether for friends or foes. By the 1950s it was devalued, rightly or wrongly, and associated with 'weekly', 'seaside', 'tatty' and other pejoratives. 'Regional' not only stressed the local loyalties of public and programme (never in fact strongly established beyond Manchester at the start and Glasgow in the early years of the Citizens', or Stoke-on-Trent in a later chapter), but emphasised the semi-permanency of those theatres which retained a resident company. In this sense there was a sharp distinction between (say) Birmingham or Bristol, and Windsor, Guildford or Miss Vincent Wallace's own Leatherhead, the last three of course too near London to make a semi-permanent company necessary or perhaps even desirable.

By self-help and Arts Council backing the repertory movement climbed out of the TV-dominated 50s into an age of new buildings. Purpose-built theatres were a feature of the expansive 1960s and 70s. Another was the virtual disappearance of the weekly rep. The Jubilee Report of CORT already cited notes that 'the twenty-three members of CORT in 1952 were almost entirely weekly repertory companies, playing to average houses and a safe and rarely imaginative choice of plays'.[24] The victims of the 1950s were largely the commercial companies, most of them organised in syndicates, who lost not only their public but their homes, the old provincial circuit, in the stampede to stay at home and watch the new wonder-box. Their plight was worsened by the siting of most touring theatres in central locations, appetising to the greedy property-developers, whereas most reps occupied off-centre, improvised accommodation.

An important part of the new, ultimately victorious, policy was the extension of a production's run, largely thanks to Arts Council and local government subvention, to two, three and four weeks, with consequent extension of rehearsal time and raising of performance standards. As the CORT Report just quoted suggests, weekly rep restricted not only preparation but range of play to those (whether well or little known) which could be made ready, if not for Monday's 'paper' public, then with luck for Tuesday's paying audience. *On Monday Next* is the title of a highly successful farce about a repertory company by Philip King, first performed in 1949. As a title it was virtually meaningless by 1959, except in the specialised and restricted world of summer reps at resorts inland and by the sea.

Meanwhile an event of equally great significance had occurred – the opening in 1958 of the Belgrade Theatre, Coventry, the first purpose-built post-War repertory and the first specifically civic theatre constructed for repertory. Local authority had taken up the torch lit by Barry Jackson at Birmingham in 1913 and rekindled by Eric Dance at Oxford in 1938.

7   1958–1983: Renewal, Growth and Retrenchment

ANTHONY JACKSON

THE OPENING of the Belgrade Theatre, Coventry, in March 1958 was undoubtedly a milestone. It was both a culmination – of the post-War renewal of activity already described – and a starting-point. Above all it heralded what was to become a boom in theatre building in Britain and on a scale unparalleled since the Frank Matcham era of the 1890s and 1900s. The figures tell much of the story. Until 1958 no new purpose-built repertory theatre had been opened in the country since before the War. By 1970, however, twenty new theatres had been constructed, fifteen of which were designed specifically for repertory. By 1980 the total, including major conversions of pre-existing premises such as Manchester's Royal Exchange, had risen to forty.[1] And that figure excludes numerous substantial renovations undertaken at other theatres. The expansion was, too, even more a regional than a London phenomenon: no less than thirty-four of the new theatres were situated in the English regions, in Scotland and in Wales. That Coventry rather than London should have been the pace-setter was itself of considerable significance.

The historic importance of the event was fully appreciated at the time – nationally as well as in Coventry. There, as was to be expected, the Belgrade's opening was celebrated as a further sign of the rebirth of a city devastated by war. An international flavour had been added too by the decision to name the theatre after the city which some years earlier had generously donated Yugoslavian beechwood for use in the theatre's construction. The national press shared in the flurry of excitement. British drama had already shown signs of a revival; the prospect of new theatres was seen now as a much-needed complement to the new avenues being explored by such writers as Osborne, Pinter, Behan, Delaney and Arden. Kenneth Tynan, *The Observer*'s influential drama critic at the time, was ecstatic:

To see the curtain rise for the first time in a new theatre is something that happens about once in a generation to people who live in these art-shy islands. It happened to me in Coventry last week, and the mood of thanksgiving is still on me. What came over the citizens? In what tranced moment did the City Council decide to spend £220 000 on a bauble as superfluous as a civic playhouse? They must have known that nobody had built a permanent professional theatre in England for twenty years. They must have heard that provincial theatres were closing in their dozens, dotting the country like so many cenotaphs. Yet five years ago, with no precedent to guide them and bad omens all round them, they made up their minds to build and be damned. It was one of the great decisions in the history of local government.[2]

The independent Trust set up to manage the theatre determined that one of their main goals should be to 'contribute to the strength of the repertory movement, the vitality of which is at the present time one of the most encouraging features of the theatrical life of this country'.[3] The first production, a musical version of Wilde's *The Importance of Being Earnest*, was only the beginning of what was to be an adventurous three-year plan. Under the artistic direction of Bryan Bailey, this was to involve provision of a resident repertory company with fortnightly changes of production, interchanges with other repertory companies and the presentation of companies from abroad, the inclusion of a wide variety of plays in the repertoire but with special emphasis placed upon the encouragement of new plays and playwrights, and the recruiting of a fresh audience of young people. It was an ambitious programme and, while it was never carried out to the extent that had originally been hoped, the Belgrade remained, for the following ten years at least, one of the leaders in the repertory theatre movement – pioneering 'true repertory' for a short period in 1962–3 and, more significantly, giving birth to Theatre-in-Education in 1965. This was no flash in the pan.

The new buildings provided the most obvious signs of change on the theatrical map, but not the only ones, for the change was a profound one which affected the nature, quality and extent of theatre undertaken. Buildings of course are not the be-all and end-all of theatre: it is the companies they house that matter above all. Although the total number of repertory companies in 1980 – around sixty (according to the *British Theatre Directory*) – is close to the fifty-seven recorded (in *The Stage Yearbook*) for 1960, the figures conceal a very real and significant increase in the number of *new* companies doing work that was wide-ranging, of high standard and on a permanent, properly funded basis: companies that in effect replaced the many increasingly precarious commercial and semi-amateur repertory companies that had grown up during the thirties, forties and fifties. The change is put into clearer perspective by the Arts Council Theatre Enquiry Report of 1970 that noted that between 1959 and 1969 the number of repertory companies operating outside London with Arts Council support had almost doubled – from twenty-eight to fifty-two.[4] The extent and rapidity of expansion during these years – at least until the mid seventies – together with the vitality of the work actually done, marks this period as a veritable renaissance in the history of the repertory movement.

But if these developments were for Britain unprecedented, what had led to this remarkable transformation? Did it indeed indicate a long-awaited revolution in the country's hitherto ungenerous tolerance of (some would say its philistine attitude towards) theatre? Did the change reflect an emerging philosophy about the place of theatre in society, or about the importance of the regions in relation to London? Why should such a boom have occurred at precisely the time when television was gaining such a dominant hold upon the general public's leisure habits? And to what extent may the boom have been, as some have feared, illusory, a hot-air balloon that in a less favourable political and economic climate might prove well-nigh impossible to keep air-borne?

In order to clarify the process and the nature of that change and to suggest some possible answers to those questions, it will be necessary to take both a comprehensive, chronological overview of the period and a closer, more sharply focussed look at a selected few theatre companies that have made distinct and varied contributions to British theatre during this period. Hence, this and the following chapter must be seen as closely complementary.

THE PATTERNS OF CHANGE

The complexity of the change that occurred is daunting and it may be helpful to see the period (from 1958) as falling into three main and overlapping phases. The first, marked by the opening of the Belgrade, began in the late fifties and continued in effect until the middle to late seventies. It was a period of optimism and expansiveness, when the repertory movement gained new blood and a new lease of life – and a new belief in the very idea of repertory. Against a background of increasing post-War prosperity, accompanied by a widely shared faith in the necessary and even inevitable improvement of the country's standards of living, it became possible to see theatre as a major means of contributing to that improvement. In such an atmosphere there seemed to many to be genuine public support for and interest in the notion of the arts as a valuable part of any healthy and progressive society and indeed as a necessary complement to the technological transformations that the country was already witnessing. It became possible to persuade both national and local government authorities that the arts were a 'good thing' and that a thriving theatre reaching new audiences could be seen as an emblem of a thriving community. A richer (if not bottomless) public purse was cautiously being opened wider by the year, or so it seemed, and the arts in general and the theatre in particular benefitted. The financial struggles by no means disappeared and not all public funding bodies were equally as generous or as wise in how they chose to spend, but at least the future seemed to promise ever-increasing support for the arts and opportunity to explore new paths. Both preceding and spurred on by the financial support was an optimism among artists themselves about the role that theatre could play in society. Not merely as a ploy to win public money for doing what had already been done for years, but genuinely as a desire to see theatre as a cultural and social centre for the community, new ventures were proposed and accepted that stressed the essentially *civic* nature of the enterprise. Buildings were to be not merely 'playhouses' but venues for arts exhibitions, lunchtime concerts, lectures and poetry recitals, post-performance discussions, educational programmes on examination texts for school children, and not least for the lighter social pursuits of eating and drinking. The cafeteria, restaurant and bar, as well as adding usefully to the theatre's revenue potential, were to be as much part of the 'community forum' idea as the more obviously cultural events. This philosophy animated the plans for all the new main civic repertory theatres from the Belgrade onwards.

In most cases the developments took the form of new or substantially rebuilt theatres for already proven repertory companies – such as those at Nottingham, Sheffield, Birmingham and Bristol – and with a marked increase in auditorium size and technical capability. Sheffield's 1000-seat Crucible Theatre, for example, replaced an older building seating 547. But there were also many completely new ventures inaugurated and buildings provided in such major cities as Liverpool (the Everyman), Manchester (Contact and the Royal Exchange), Newcastle (the University Theatre), Leicester (the Phoenix) and Edinburgh (the refurbished Royal Lyceum); and in smaller though no less enterprising cities and towns as diverse as Stoke-on-Trent, Mold, Scarborough and, for their summer festival seasons, in Chichester and Pitlochry.

But many of these cultural centres appealed as much to the search for prestige of the big city corporations as to their concern for the arts themselves, and it was perhaps inevitable that a certain 'establishment' aura should attach to many of the new buildings. A theatre built to be shown off as a monument to civic pride is not thereby guaranteed to be the ideal venue for the exploratory, risk-taking events that must form at least some part of a healthy arts scene. Nor will it necessarily prove able to reach the community whose local taxes go to support it.

Suspicion of the very notion of 'establishment' repertory theatres, together with a good deal of new thinking about what theatre could and should be doing, a strong desire to experiment with theatre styles and a commitment to reaching new audiences lay behind the beginning of the second phase. The beginning of this phase can be dated from as early as 1964 – a sign of the rapid currents at work – with the setting up of the Everyman Theatre in Liverpool. There was already of course a repertory theatre in Liverpool, and one with a long and distinguished history: the Playhouse. The significance of the Everyman was that it was begun as essentially an *alternative* repertory company, designed to appeal to specific kinds of audience and above all to young people who were really not catered for by the Playhouse. Its work was youthful, experimental, provocative and educational – in its early seasons dividing its programmes equally between presentations of school syllabus playtexts in the afternoons and the more adventurous, adult work in the evenings. And the theatre building itself, a cheaply converted cinema, was, to say the least, non-prestigious – in the early years, theatre on a shoestring – and this was an essential part of its character.

The impetus for the 'experimental' side of the enterprise had come largely from the growing fringe theatre movement, foremost in which was the Traverse Theatre Club founded just one year earlier by Jim Haynes in Edinburgh and quickly becoming the professional power house of the Edinburgh Festival 'Fringe'. Before long Haynes had moved to London to set up the short-lived, but influential, Arts Lab in Drury Lane. Soon, the experimental work being done there and in warehouses, attics and other makeshift theatre spaces in such cities as London, Edinburgh and Liverpool had begun to suggest new directions in both playwriting and acting, directions that were pursued throughout the sixties. Such work needed, it seemed, small, intimate spaces, and many repertory directors recognised that to keep abreast of what was happening, to ensure that new work and new forms were fed into their own work, it was essential to find alternative playing spaces to the main auditoria. By the end of the sixties therefore many repertory theatres had built, converted or were designing their own 'alternative' theatre studios: the Close Theatre Club, next door to the Glasgow Citizens' Theatre, opened in 1965, the Bolton Octagon's Studio in 1967, and the Belgrade's Studio in 1968; while plans for studio theatres were being incorporated into the designs for the Sheffield Crucible Theatre, the new Birmingham Repertory Theatre, the soon-to-be-rebuilt Bristol Old Vic, and – to complete the circle – the shortly-to-be-extended Liverpool Playhouse. The pattern was strengthened even further by the decision of the Royal Court Theatre and both the main national companies to open their own theatre studios – the Royal Court's Theatre Upstairs in 1969, the RSC's The Other Place in Stratford and the Warehouse in London in 1974 and 1977 respectively (and now The Pit in the new Barbican Centre in 1982), and the National Theatre's small, purpose-built Cottesloe Theatre on the South Bank in 1977.

The other, related strand in the Everyman's programme was the work for schools. While it was some years before the Everyman's own work for young people developed beyond the performance of the set texts, the belief that repertory theatres should be actively engaged in work for and with youth was taking a strong hold in the latter half of the sixties. The specialised touring children's theatre companies and Caryl Jenner's enterprising Children's Theatre scheme at the Unicorn Theatre had developed since the War but on a very piecemeal basis and many companies during the sixties had collapsed or were struggling. Apart from Christmas pantomimes and the occasional Shakespeare chosen to fit in with the current O-level examination syllabus, the reps themselves had, with a few exceptions, made very little effort to reach young people. The anomaly of such a state of affairs was highlighted in a seminal Arts Council report on Theatre for Young People published in 1966. The Report, together with the funds that were as a result allocated by the Council to help redress the balance, certainly led to greater consciousness in repertory of this major gap in their provision – and many theatres responded energetically.

Perhaps the most significant development was the formation of Theatre-in-Education (TIE) teams based at a number of repertory theatres (financed by both the local authorities and the theatres themselves), who took educational programmes into local schools using theatre techniques and exploring new ways of using the theatre medium to great effect. Once again, the Belgrade Theatre led, with a pilot venture beginning in 1965 that soon became an important and permanent part of the theatre's function in the city.[5] Other teams were established at the newly opened Bolton Octagon Theatre in 1967, at the Leeds Playhouse in 1969 and by 1970 at the theatres in Edinburgh and Greenwich. And within the following few years

10. *Pow Wow*: a Theatre-in-Education programme devised by the Belgrade TIE Company and presented in Coventry schools in 1973. Photo: Belgrade TIE Company.

teams were also established at the reps in Nottingham, Glasgow, Watford, Lancaster and elsewhere, which in turn influenced the subsequent setting up of new TIE and Young People's Theatre teams by education authorities or as independent companies, both touring and theatre-based. The Young Vic in London (reconstituted in 1970) and Contact Theatre in Manchester (from 1973) are two examples of repertory theatre companies formed specifically to work for young people and operating in and from theatre buildings rather than touring.

The significance of TIE was that it represented a genuinely innovatory development in theatre: one that broke through the traditional boundaries that had tended to separate entertainment from education. TIE teams of 'actor-teachers' (as they soon came to be known) undertook work in class-rooms, school halls and drama studios that dealt with issues and themes of importance to the pupils in ways simply unavailable to individual teachers. *Pow Wow* is one outstanding example of such a programme, devised in 1973 by the Coventry Belgrade TIE Company for the five-to-seven age group and successfully dealing with attitudes to race and to minority groups through the medium of a cowboy-and-indian story. TIE was not primarily seen as an audience-building exercise. It was, though, for the theatres themselves at this early stage a further valuable link between the main house and various sections of the community and further helped to challenge the conventional notions of what theatre was supposed to be. The local theatre might after all have a much needed and obviously *useful* part to play in the community.

Repertory during this period seemed capable of almost anything: the diversity of work done under its umbrella was impressive. It had been an initiator and it had responded to new ideas and methods with remarkable flexibility and often with flair.

The pace of change was accelerated in the late sixties and early seventies by the emergence of a growing number of theatre groups outside the main stream of repertory. From half-a-dozen 'fringe' groups in the mid sixties, there were by the end of the seventies over a hundred 'alternative' theatre companies,[6] most of them receiving some form of public subsidy (from the Arts Council or from local sources), small though that may have been. Their size, scope and working practice varied enormously – there was theatre for local communities, for young people, for women, for 'gays' and for a wide range of political and industrial groupings (for labour clubs, trades union centres and even factory canteens). Most if not all of these companies were committed to some kind of social or political change. Indeed there was in the thinking of many of such as John McGrath's 7:84 Company a serious challenge to be made not only to capitalism but to the repertory theatre system as well which, along with most other 'establish-ment' organisations (including the Arts Council), was seen as consciously or unconsciously bolstering the status quo in society. The very fact that

repertory companies were based in buildings, playing only to those relatively small numbers of people prepared to travel to the theatre, was to the
alternative companies an indictment of their work. In this respect Studio
theatres made no material difference to the role of repertory in the community. Only by abandoning the traditionally held preconceptions of what
theatre was, only by taking theatre to the people in streets, pubs, clubs and
community centres and addressing problems that were of direct relevance
to those people and in ways that would both entertain and stimulate, could
the theatre hope to play any significant part in the life of the community;
only in this way, it was argued, could genuinely new audiences be reached,
working people who would rarely if ever even consider going to the smart
theatres in town.

In many respects the new community theatre companies were claiming
to do what many repertory directors also sought to do. The differences
often lay less in the aims than in the methods of operation. The reps were,
and still are, essentially building-based (even the so-called touring repertory companies such as Prospect and the Cambridge Theatre Company
have been geared almost exclusively to performance in conventional
theatres); the alternative companies by choice are essentially touring
companies taking work to specifically non-theatre, 'community' venues
and in this way fulfilling a substantially different role. None the less, repertory in this second phase of development, at least up to the mid seventies,
was able to encompass and be part of both the alternative and the mainstream; the boundary lines between the work undertaken by many of the
repertory companies and that of the alternative theatre were far from distinct. Indeed a good many of the reps themselves formed their own travelling units that took theatre into the community – just as TIE had gone into
the schools. And in the building itself repertory was able to offer the
dangerous and the safe, the innovative and the familiar. There were many
reps that clung to traditional programmes and rarely took risks. But what
characterised the period as a whole was an enormous and often exciting
variety of work and a plurality of approach.

The third phase is marked by the effects of a faltering economy on the
nation and on the arts especially – and, some would say, by a certain loss
of energy, even a loss of faith in the exciting ideals of the sixties, a slowing
down of the momentum that may not have been entirely due to the effects
of recession. Downturns in the economy were of course nothing new but
the sudden and largely unexpected leap in the world price of oil in 1973
and 1974, together with the serious and debilitating increases in inflation
(by 1975 inflation had reached over twenty-five per cent per year), were
destined to do enormous damage to the willingness of governments to continue the increase in real terms of public spending on the arts. Despite sizeable annual increases in grant to the Arts Council from the Treasury, from
1975 onwards the money available for subsidising theatre has failed

adequately to keep pace with inflation: many theatres have suffered badly from dwindling resources; several indeed have had to close down completely (the Theatre Royal, Lincoln, the Civic Theatre, Chesterfield, and the Lyceum at Crewe are three recent casualties), while many have retrenched, shortened their seasons, kept to safe, well-proven and where possible small-cast plays. Other theatres have found ways of adapting imaginatively and managed to hold on to their artistic integrity and their audiences, producing, still, good, exciting theatre, though in increasingly difficult and financially precarious circumstances. The new buildings already in the pipeline were completed but from 1977 onwards the numbers of new or substantially rebuilt theatres have fallen off sharply. And it is during this third phase that the disadvantages of the prestigious new buildings have fully made themselves felt: they are enormously costly to run, particularly when the prices of all fuels have risen even more steeply than the average rate of inflation. It has been a well-publicised fact that the costs simply of keeping the National Theatre open, quite apart from the mounting of productions, are of alarming proportions,[7] but large newly built repertory theatres, well staffed, comfortably heated, with spacious foyers and sophisticated stage-lighting systems are also immensely expensive. As the resident companies have become increasingly tied down and constricted by the costs of their buildings, so the more innovative and risk-taking aspects of their work have become pared down and sometimes cut all together. Studio adjuncts are being used for performances less and less frequently and in some cases not at all (as for example at the Farnham Redgrave Theatre in the 1980–1 season). Touring community and young people's theatre units based at the reps are becoming scarcer – operating very infrequently (as, at the time of writing, is the case with Sheffield's Vanguard Company), or, for philosophical as much as financial reasons, separating completely from the parent company to become full-fledged, independent companies, as the Bolton Octagon TIE team did in 1977 (subsequently becoming the M6 Theatre Company) and likewise the Liverpool Everyman's educational theatre team in 1978 (which became the Merseyside Young People's Theatre).

By the late seventies it had become clear that the expansiveness and accompanying sense of adventure and purpose, and the ideal of the theatre as the cultural powerhouse of the community, had all taken a severe knock. The idea of the permanent company resident in the community, striven for if attained only at a handful of theatres, has become increasingly in the regions a thing of the past.

As the theatre struggles to maintain its impetus and its standards the mood has inevitably become gloomier, and the general state of mind of most theatre directors at the beginning of the eighties is succinctly expressed by Reggie Salberg of the Salisbury Playhouse: the question now is, not how do we move forward, but how do we stop ourselves from going backward?[8] The disappointment that may be felt at the general state of the repertory movement in the early 1980s may be in part because we expect more from our reps than we did in the 1950s. And that itself may be a mark of the extraordinary achievements of the two decades that followed.

This then has been the general pattern: one of renewal, optimism and excitement, matched by an expansion of the resources available, followed fifteen to twenty years later by the retrenchment, the pulling-in of the reins and the cutting of corners simply to survive. But the cycle is not of course as clear-cut as this summary might suggest. Talk of the 'expansiveness' of the sixties blurs the reality that money for the arts – certainly by European standards – has usually been in short supply. As Giles Havergal (director of the Glasgow Citizens' Theatre) has said, working in the theatre to achieve anything worthwhile has always been a struggle: money to pay actors' salaries has always been tight and making ends meet by the end of the financial year has always been a problem.[9] Funding bodies have moreover been a good deal more generous with grants towards capital projects than towards operating and salary costs and it is the latter that bear most heavily upon the company, its policy and its practice.

A preliminary overview such as this, brief as it is, would not be complete without mention of two further sources of influence upon repertory, especially from the mid sixties: two ventures that, while they do not strictly qualify for the purposes of this study as repertory theatres, are closely entwined in the growth of the repertory movement. The first was Joan Littlewood's Theatre Workshop Company, which became based at the Theatre Royal, Stratford East, in London, in 1953. With its roots in the socialist workers' theatre groups of the 1930s, the company had developed an adventurous policy of presenting foreign plays, the classics and the work of new writers in a style that was vital, energetic and emphasised con-temporary relevance and a strong critical edge: 'Brechtian' in the best possible sense. From 1953 to 1964 the Theatre Royal endeavoured to function as a repertory theatre in London, but never really managed to win the local working-class audiences that it had so earnestly hoped for. Instead, as its reputation grew and its financial viability became more pre-carious (the Arts Council was notably ungenerous to this company), it came to rely increasingly on middle-class audiences travelling into the East End and, even more so as the years went by, on transfers into the West End theatre of such 'hits' as *The Quare Fellow*, *A Taste of Honey* and *Oh! What a Lovely War*.[10] The rough exuberance and the company ensemble method of working and performing did nevertheless have a considerable influence upon the work of directors and actors alike. David Scase (at Manchester's Library Theatre 1954–63 and 1971–83), Peter Cheeseman (at Stoke since 1962), Antony Richardson (at Coventry 1960–5), Alan Dossor (at the Liverpool Everyman 1970–4), Richard Eyre (at Nottingham 1973–8) and Clare Venables (at Sheffield since 1981) are only a few of the repertory directors who have explicitly acknowledged that influence.

The second influence came from George Devine's English Stage Company at the Royal Court Theatre, formed in 1956 essentially as a playwright's theatre to promote new writing. In the late fifties and early sixties, it was the Royal Court first and foremost that acted as a catalyst in the astonishing upsurge that took place in British playwriting. New plays by Osborne, N.F. Simpson, Arden, Wesker, Pinter and British premières of plays by Beckett, Ionesco and Brecht suddenly shook up and expanded the repertoire available to theatres in the regions, and undoubtedly the new lease of life that they gained from the late fifties onwards was in part a result of the fresh blood that was sent pulsing round their veins. The need for that new blood was evidenced by the speed with which *Look Back in Anger* was pounced upon and produced by dozens of theatres up and down the country within a year of its first production at the Court. Such was the pattern for as long as the Court was able to generate so much good new drama. But 1958 also saw the first hints of the role that the reps themselves were to play in that revival of playwriting when one of the plays submitted to the English Stage Company – Wesker's *Chicken Soup With Barley* – was offered by a busy Court to the Belgrade Theatre. Though a largely 'one-off' production by John Dexter, with the promise of eventual performance at the Court if successful, here was a major première by a new writer being given at a regional repertory theatre. That in its own way was a small but significant stepping-stone.

Certain key aspects of the changes undergone in this period deserve closer examination: the new buildings, the ways in which repertory has been financed, the crucial and increasingly influential role of the artistic director together with two particular and inter-dependent features of his theatre's artistic policy, the acting company and the repertoire, and, finally, the audiences themselves.

BUILDINGS

Although bricks and mortar – which take many years to plan and to argue through committees and yet more years to erect – might not seem to be the most sensitive reflectors of the swiftly changing ideas, approaches and fashions of the repertory movement, it is nevertheless revealing to look at the variety of shapes and sizes of the new theatres and at some of the significant features that many of them share. It is a measure of just how extensive and how deep the changes were that so much was reflected so quickly in the buildings alone.

Not surprisingly, the city which first took upon itself the task of initiating a major new theatre venture was one that had suffered the most complete devastation of its centre from wartime bombing raids. Coventry was the first city to embark upon a major replanning of its heartland and the massive task was begun with determination and imagination. A new cathedral was to be built and by the mid fifties Britain's first traffic-free shopping precinct was already taking shape. When the Arts Council decided in 1953 to withdraw from running the Midland Theatre Company based in Coventry the next logical step was for the city itself to provide for its own theatre company and in a building in keeping with the spirit of renewal. The theatre that was at last opened to the public (on 27 March 1958) managed to be both reassuringly traditional in concept – a proscenium stage facing an oblong auditorium with stalls, circle and even side boxes – and expressive of the new building technology and of the new belief in theatre's potential as a cultural centre for the community. The clean lines and the spaciousness afforded by glass and steel, the steeply raked 900-seat auditorium offering an excellent view to every member of the audience and the volume of space allocated to the foyers combined to assert a new positively post-War character to the theatre. 'Enter most theatres', said Tynan, 'and you enter the gilded cupidaceous past. Enter this one and you are surrounded by the future.' His impression of the building is worth recalling further, since it conjures up precisely the mood of excitement and expectation that it managed to generate at the time.

Rather than a museum, it suggests an observatory. The lobbies are long and capacious, like those of a good airport. The auditorium, cherry plush underseat and polished wood overhead, is both resplendent and practical. The sight-lines are impeccable, and the acoustics have a high fidelity bite which makes most West End theatres seem like schools for deafness. The stage is deep. The wings are wide. The opportunity is enormous.[11]

Compared to the traditional Edwardian theatres, or even the Birmingham Repertory Theatre, with which the public would have been most familiar, perhaps the Belgrade's most striking feature was the space devoted to the foyers, the bar and the cafeteria. This was no mere whim, as Bryan Bailey, the Belgrade's first artistic director, clearly pointed out at the opening of the theatre: 'The Belgrade Theatre will be not a playhouse used only during the evening but a centre of theatrical interest and activity for all who love living theatre. The ample provision of lounges and foyers will make the theatre a social meeting place where talks, lectures and discussions can be held.'[12] It would be the headquarters of the Belgrade Theatre Club; there would be a Theatre Bookstall and regular exhibitions and, in order to recruit 'a fresh audience of young people', there would be special productions, matinée performances and an Under-Twenty Club.

Nearly all the purpose-built repertory theatres since the Belgrade have continued to expand upon this pattern until now, in comparison to some of the more recent buildings – such as the Sheffield Crucible (1971), Manchester's Royal Exchange and the National Theatre complex (both 1976) – the foyer space at the Belgrade looks positively cramped. When the

11. The Belgrade Theatre, Coventry, opened in 1958 (architect: Arthur Ling). Photo: Belgrade Theatre. 12. The Nottingham Playhouse, opened in 1963 (architect: Peter Moro and Partners). Photo and copyright: Local Studies Library, Nottinghamshire County Library. 13. The new Birmingham Repertory Theatre, opened in 1971 (architect: Graham Winteringham). Photo: Birmingham Repertory Theatre.

idea was first conceived of building the Manchester theatre within the vast disused hall of the Royal Exchange building, uppermost in the minds of Michael Elliott and his fellow directors was not only the relatively low cost of such a conversion but the enormous enclosed area surrounding the theatre itself that would – and does – provide an extraordinary ambience for meeting, talking, eating and drinking both during the day and prior to the show, and ample space for bookstall, craft fairs, cafeteria and bar space and exhibitions:[13] ingredients considered now to be essential to any self-respecting new theatre. Enlightened self-interest was also at work of course in this and in all such schemes. Once people could be encouraged into the theatre building for purposes other than simply seeing a play the likelihood of improved ticket sales to curious 'passers-by' was also increased; and any enterprise relying heavily on taxpayers' and ratepayers' money needs to *demonstrate* its openness to and involvement with the public.

The auditorium of the Belgrade, however, apart from its comfort and good acoustics and sight-lines, made really very little advance in design terms on theatre auditoria built before the War. The planning of theatre interiors and particularly of the all-important relationship of stage to audience was shortly to undergo more radical change. More especially the proscenium arch was due to be displaced firmly from its absolute hold on theatre architecture. Peter Moro argued in 1962 that in a provincial city where a varied repertoire of plays has to be presented in just one theatre, the case for an adaptable theatre with maximum flexibility of staging was paramount.[14] He produced impressive designs for the Nottingham Playhouse that attempted to combine the intimacy and flexibility of the open stage with the clear focus of the proscenium arrangement – though the adaptability proved not as great in practice as the designs had promised. In 1962 the Chichester Festival Theatre, a full thrust stage inspired by Tyrone Guthrie's Festival Theatre in Stratford, Ontario, excited a good deal of interest and paved the way for the even more positive and adventurous thrust stage of the Crucible Theatre in Sheffield (1971), a design that integrates the stage with the auditorium more happily than is the case at Chichester, no doubt because Guthrie's designer, Tanya Moiseiwitsch, was a consultant at the planning stage. Meanwhile, also in 1962 at Stoke-on-Trent, Stephen Joseph with Peter Cheeseman had bravely committed their newly converted cinema building to full-blooded theatre-in-the-round; and for fourteen years it remained the only permanent in-the-round theatre building in Britain – until the opening in 1976 of the Royal Exchange and in the same year of Alan Ayckbourn's Stephen Joseph Theatre in Scarborough (some nine years after Joseph's untimely death). Joseph's pioneering work to promote theatre-in-the-round had frequently met with bewilderment or indifference but was only a more forceful expression of the growing understanding among actors, designers,

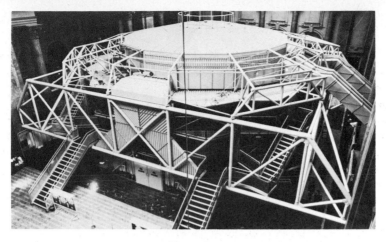

14. The Royal Exchange Theatre, Manchester, built within the vast hall of the old Royal Exchange and opened in 1976. Photo: Kevin Cummins. 15. The Citizens' Theatre in the Gorbals, Glasgow. The ornate façade of the old theatre was removed during renovation in 1977. Photo: Brian G. Donovan. 16. The Everyman Theatre, Liverpool, converted from a disused music-hall and opened in 1964. Photo: Gordon Whiting; copyright: *Liverpool Daily Post and Echo*.

directors – and audiences too – that new theatre shapes were needed to reflect and accommodate the new role that theatre was expected to play. As he argued in 1964, 'the picture-frame stage, no matter how glorious its past, has never had much connection with the drama, and it is now an incubus which is suffocating live entertainment';[15] and again 'the theatre has been, and still is, deprived of suitable buildings in which to present plays. To maintain a steady supply of new plays we must also continually build new theatres.'[16]

By no means all the new buildings were as progressive as the ones referred to so far. Certainly architects were learning to think anew about theatre design and were briefed, more often than not, to provide for as many permutations of actor–audience relationships as practicable – as long as the traditional end-staging was not sacrificed altogether. For many years complete flexibility of staging was striven for but usually within very tight spatial and budgetary limits that almost inevitably resulted in uneasy compromise. The University Theatre at Manchester, 1965, for example, was designed to be used for proscenium, open-stage, thrust and in-the-round performances, and provided with hydraulic lifts to raise and lower a large forestage in two separate sections together with movable sections of seating to facilitate the change-overs. However, while this theatre functions well as an intimate open- or end-stage theatre it is rarely satisfactory in the full thrust arrangement and even less so in the round, because the majority of the audience sit in a permanent bank of seating facing one side of the stage and inevitably exercise the dominant pull upon the stage action.

A later and more successful attempt at flexible staging – more successful because less ambitious – is the design of the Mercury Theatre, Colchester (opened in 1972). A gentle arc of seating in a single tier together with simply modifiable forestage and proscenium side-screens allows for both open-stage and proscenium-stage productions to be viewed with equal ease and without dislocation of the interior proportions of the auditorium. The design proved successful enough in practice to be chosen as the basis for the Salisbury Playhouse (1976) – an example of the sensible application of one solution to the requirements of another similar theatre venture.

As the kinds of drama and types of audience multiplied it became clearer that even the most flexible of auditoria could not possibly accommodate all that directors and actors wanted to do and at least some sections of the public wanted to see. Hence the trend already mentioned towards the provision of Studio Theatres alongside the main auditoria, specifically for the purpose of offering minority interest drama that could not reasonably be expected to fill the main house and which often needed a more intimate, simple staging anyway. Studios of this kind were not confined to the major city reps but became the norm for most of the new buildings after Nottingham – not only at Birmingham, Bristol and Sheffield but

17. The Victoria Theatre, Stoke-on-Trent, converted from a cinema and opened in 1962. Photo: Victoria Theatre. 18. Auditorium of the Belgrade Theatre, Coventry (1958). Photo: P.W. and L. Thompson Ltd. 19. The Nottingham Playhouse: the stage from the balcony, showing the attempt to combine 'open' and 'proscenium' staging (1963). Photo: Local Studies Library, Nottinghamshire County Council.

also, for example, at Derby, Leatherhead and Salisbury. In this way companies that found themselves tied to rather conventional fare in the main house by predominantly middle-aged and conservative-minded theatregoers could at least test themselves out on challenging new work and at the same time woo younger people to the theatre without the risk of antagonising the regular audience.

Mention has already been made of the University Theatre at Manchester, and it is worth recording that many universities have made important contributions to repertory by building theatres not merely for use by university departments and societies but as part of a more general effort to encourage cultural links between town and gown. University theatres that were designed to house, or that soon came to house, professional theatre companies included those at Manchester (where first the 69 Theatre Company and later Contact became based), at Exeter (the Northcott, housing a permanent repertory company from 1967), Southampton (the Nuffield, housing a repertory company from 1975), Leeds (The Playhouse, whose company has operated continuously since 1969) and Newcastle (the University Theatre, which housed first the Tyneside Theatre Company from 1968 and subsequently the Tyne Wear Theatre Company).

The extraordinary explosion of theatre building during these two decades was perhaps all the more extraordinary because of the cost that local authorities and, later, the Arts Council were prepared to help bear. The British theatre had of course lagged far behind the continent in terms of theatre provision,[17] but the speed of the catching up was remarkable – and contained its own penalties. The raising of money to pay for the new theatres was of course never easy and almost every new building was dogged for years by debates and wranglings at local level over cost. But the money was found – a high proportion of it by local authorities who were at last after the War awakening to their responsibility for the provision of cultural amenities, and to the opportunity such ventures offered for them to boost local pride and improve their image where necessary (a very real concern to some Midland and Northern towns that resented the cloth-cap-and-clogs image subscribed to by many in the South).

Most of the first new theatres, in Coventry and Nottingham, for example, and, later, the Forum Theatre in Manchester, were financed totally from local authority funds, supplemented usually by public appeals. But, recognising the momentum for change that had begun and the limited resources of the smaller cities and towns, the Arts Council won a special allocation from the Treasury in 1965 for 'housing the arts', a fund that became an annual source of supply available to local authorities and theatre boards able to submit viable and convincing schemes for new buildings and able to demonstrate adequate local support for the project. The Council would carefully scrutinise every application and allocate

20. The spacious auditorium and stage of the new Birmingham Repertory Theatre (1971), seating 901 – compare with the old Rep Theatre, which sat 454 (see illus. 3). Photo: Birmingham Repertory Theatre. 21. The in-the-round auditorium of the Royal Exchange, Manchester (1976). Photo: Kevin Cummins. 22. The Bristol New Vic studio theatre: built adjacent to and part of the new Bristol Old Vic complex (1972; architects: Peter Moro and Partners). Photo: Derek Balmer.

funds sometimes up to one-third, never more than one-half, of the total cost, so maintaining what it felt to be the all-important balance between state and local government funding. Playgoers themselves were also expected to provide a substantial share of the cost, so providing further evidence of need: public appeals, raffles, jumble sales and other fund-raising events were the order of the day in numerous towns and cities that planned new theatres during the late sixties and early seventies. The example of Bolton is particularly impressive: in May 1966 the decision was taken by Bolton Corporation to approve and grant-aid the building of a new theatre; in August the Octagon Theatre Trust was formed and designs commenced; in October the 'Buy a Brick' and 'Buy a Seat' appeals were launched; by January of the following year enough money had been collected from public funds and public subscriptions to allow work to commence; and in November 1967 the Octagon Theatre – a moderately sized but ingeniously imaginative flexible theatre – was officially opened.

But what was, perhaps inevitably, unforeseen in the sixties when the majority of these enterprises were coming onto the drawing-board, was the escalating inflation and successive recessions that characterised the seventies. Designed and, for the most part, built in an era of seeming plenty – when 'expansion' and 'development' were the inevitable catchwords of progress in so many spheres – these theatres needed considerable sums of money simply to be kept in working order. When the cost of oil, and so heating, quadrupled in price in 1973–4 and when salaries of actors and staff were, rightly, raised to respectable levels around the same time, suddenly it seemed as though the spaciousness and complexity of these theatres were a burden rather than an opportunity. In 1974–5 the operating costs of the new Birmingham Repertory Theatre, that is excluding artists' salaries and set and costume expenses, accounted for sixty-six per cent of the theatre's total budget.[18] When the National Theatre was completed at last in 1976, after decades of planning and debate, and incorporating all the features that seemed already to have been so well proven in the new regional theatres, and on an even grander scale, it opened at a time of peak inflation. While criticism was relatively muted in that opening year, by 1978, when the Arts Council's grant-aid to all theatres was facing yet further curtailment, the voices of protest at the drain on those resources represented by the National's enormous running costs were loud and angry. And when audiences at the regional theatres became choosier about the plays they went to see, following the rapid rise in ticket prices that had taken place, the large 900- and 1000-seat auditoria at Coventry, Sheffield and Birmingham could sometimes look bleak and deserted, even with several hundred people inside. The size of the building had already been a factor in artistic policy: by the late seventies it had become for some directors a millstone.

Given the expense of running any reasonably sized repertory theatre, on

23. The Victoria Theatre, Stoke: the auditorium of Britain's first permanent theatre-in-the-round (showing Peter Cheeseman in rehearsal with the cast of *The Knotty*, 1978). Photo: Don McNeil. 24. The Salisbury Playhouse (1976), based on the design of the Mercury Theatre, Colchester, and showing the successful relationship of open stage to auditorium (architect: Norman Downie, with Christopher Kerley, consultant). Photo: Peter Brown. 25. The Sheffield Crucible Theatre (1971), probably Britain's most successful thrust-stage theatre (designed by Tanya Moiseiwitsch; architects: Renton, Howard, Wood Assocs.). The production being given is of *Aladdin* in 1981. Photo: Sheffield Newspapers Ltd.

top of the cost of providing the building in the first place, it is not surprising that throughout this period the matter of how theatres were funded, by whom and according to what criteria, became increasingly the subject of debate and controversy.

FUNDING

Throughout these two decades the three main sources of income for theatres have been the box office, the Arts Council and the local authorities. There have of course been grants, donations and sponsorship from other sources too – from the regional arts associations, from wealthy individuals and from business firms – but with only a few notable exceptions these sources for the reps have been minimal.[19] What has perhaps been most noticeable during this period is the change in the balance between each of the three main revenue sources: in particular the increasing reliance upon grant-aid from the Arts Council. In 1970 the Arts Council's Theatre Enquiry glowingly reported that the fifty-two repertory companies operating outside London with Arts Council support recovered, on average, seventy-five per cent of the expenditure at the box office.[20] By the end of the seventies the picture looked strikingly different. For example, in 1979–80 at the Bristol Old Vic Theatre with its renovated main building and its two additional smaller auditoria (the New Vic and the Little Theatre), total earned income was £317034, a figure that was easily surpassed by the total grants from all sources of £428 477. In 1963–4, by comparison, before the New Vic had been opened, total earned income had been £51 466, while total subsidy had amounted to a mere £16 500. Likewise at Sheffield the figures for earned income and total subsidy respectively in 1978–9 were £314 294 and £423 891, compared with the position in the early fifties in the old repertory theatre when no subsidy whatsoever was received. Less expensive new theatres, such as the Mercury at Colchester, were in 1978–9 still earning more at the box office than they received in subsidy (£177 806 as opposed to £150 727), but only marginally. (Appendix 3, Table I shows how the shift in sources of income was reflected in the finances of six selected repertory theatres over a twenty-year period.)

Part of the answer lies, obviously, in the increased costs involved in operating the new buildings together with the effects of wage and price inflation, which generally was even more marked in the theatre than elsewhere – because of the heavy reliance upon such expensive materials as wood for scenery and because theatre of its very nature is a labour-intensive industry. Deals involving 'increased productivity', common in industry have limited, if any, applicability to the casting of a play. But part of the answer too lies in the policy of the Arts Council during this period in two main respects, both of which were seen as essential components of the Council's broader responsibility for the arts as laid down in its charter.

The Council's Royal Charter, granted in 1946 and renewed and redefined in 1967, had declared two of its main objects as being 'to develop and improve the knowledge, understanding and practice of the arts' and 'to increase the accessibility of the arts to the public throughout Great Britain'. It was with the first of these objects in mind that the Council had urged its client theatres, as we have seen in the previous chapter, to move away from the treadmill of weekly repertory and towards two- and three-weekly schedules of presentation. It was in fulfilment of the second object that the Council encouraged ticket prices generally to be kept to a minimum and gave particular support to theatres serving areas of the country where theatres were thin on the ground, and the habit of theatre-going had been all but lost.

While many older directors and actors now look back upon the days of weekly rep with some pride at what had been achieved under increasingly trying, if not impossible, circumstances, there was little disagreement during the fifties and early sixties that standards of performance and production were in dire need of improvement. And if there were doubts, they were quickly shed once the impact of commercial television, which began in 1955, had been felt – as the previous chapter has already made clear. The regular, once-a-week, theatre-going audience, tempted now by not only cinema but television and an increasing army of other entertainment facilities as cities and towns rebuilt their centres, had been lost for good. If the theatre was to be able to compete at all the quality of the work presented had to be first rate. The Arts Council which in 1954 had begun making funds available to help theatres with the change-over and to tide them through the difficult periods when audiences were being re-educated to a different pattern, was by 1962 able to report that satisfactory progress had been made right across the country. Leatherhead Repertory Theatre, typical of many, introduced its first two-week run in 1961 and by 1966 virtually all its plays were running for three weeks at a time.

In 1964 the steady year by year increase in government grants to the Arts Council, matching and sometimes inching a little ahead of the rise in the cost of living, received a new and most welcome boost with the appointment of Jennie Lee as Minister for the Arts in the new Wilson government. A White Paper on the Arts was published in 1965, promising at last a *real* increase in money available for the arts as a whole, an increase that by Continental standards did not look especially generous but in British terms represented a significant redirection of policy and resources.

The Arts Council's report for 1965–6 (titled 'Key Year') welcomed the opportunity now afforded arts organisations to budget at last a little above subsistence level, the agreed allocation of money for the long-awaited Housing the Arts fund and the opportunity now to grant-aid the new developments that were burgeoning, in practice or in embryo, across the country. The fruits of this release of further money for the arts were seen in the new theatre buildings, in new theatre companies such as the 69 Theatre Company in Manchester and the Haymarket Company in Leicester (which superceded the Phoenix as that city's main rep in 1973), and in the increased activity of the already existing companies both inside and outside the building: the Theatre in Education and touring units, the Studio work.

But the more the money became available, the more open to criticism the Arts Council became as to how it ought to be spent. One of the most persistent complaints from the regional theatre during this period had been about the balance between the funds available to the English regions, Scotland and Wales and those allocated to London. The touring undertaken by the two national companies, the Royal Shakespeare Company (RSC) and the National Theatre, was infrequent and sporadic (although the RSC has been more evident in the regions of the two). The 'real' national theatre, it was argued, was the network of repertory theatres providing a year-round theatre service across the country. The funds allocated to the 'national' companies were, it was claimed, disproportionate: it was not so much that money should be denied to London but that the regions deserved more. The London-versus-regions argument is one that has surfaced more than once in this century but probably with never so much heat as in the sixties and early seventies. Gradually, as was the Arts Council's way, the balance did begin to shift in favour of the regions. In 1974 the Council was able to claim that since the early sixties, when the four main drama and opera companies accounted for half of total grant-aid, money for the areas outside London had been boosted to such a level that those companies' share of resources was now down to twenty-five per cent. And by 1979 London's total share of grant-aid (in the arts as a whole) was down from fifty per cent in 1969 to thirty per cent, with Scotland and Wales taking a fraction under twenty per cent and the English regions accounting for a little under fifty per cent (though this share includes provision for national touring work throughout the UK).

In Scotland the small but significant increase has helped in establishing the Royal Lyceum Theatre Company in Edinburgh in 1965 and more recently (in 1981) the setting up of the new Scottish Theatre Company to tour Scotland and to encourage new Scottish playwriting. Wales however still lacks a major resident repertory company of anything like national stature and scope. Funds were in fact made available for the formation of the Welsh Theatre Company in 1962, with English-speaking and Welsh-speaking units, to tour the cities and small towns of both North and South Wales. In 1973–4, the two units split into what became the Welsh Drama Company and Theatr Cymru, the latter based in the newly opened Theatr Gwynnedd at Bangor University. But in the words of the Arts Council's Welsh Committee in 1976, 'a feeling of artistic impermanence remained the hallmark of the theatre in Wales':[21] by 1981 the Welsh Drama

Company had disappeared altogether although new theatre companies had emerged with some success in Milford Haven (Torch Theatre) and in Mold, North Wales (Theatr Clwyd). Cities such as Cardiff and Swansea are still without permanent repertory companies. The expansion has taken place, in Wales, rather in the alternative touring and community theatre fields than in repertory. Northern Ireland has its own separate Arts Council, in receipt of grants direct from the Department of Education, which have grown at a similar rate to those for England, Scotland and Wales. The special problems of Ulster have complicated the pattern but despite fluctuating audience attendances the province's main repertory theatre, Belfast's Lyric Theatre (inaugurated in 1951 and transferred to new purpose-built premises in 1968) has rightly been given support and encouragement to continue to make an important cultural contribution to Belfast and its region. Its annual Arts Council grant (£136 500 in 1980–1) compares favourably with grants received by such theatres as the Salisbury Playhouse and the Victoria Theatre, Stoke.

The Arts Council has since the late sixties repeatedly declared that 'the balance of provision between London and other regions' is one of its main concerns and one of its criteria for assessing the allocation of grant-aid – a major switch of emphasis from the period of the 1950s when the Secretary-General gave priority to the subsidy of a few 'centres of excellence'. The most dramatic manifestation of the reality of this concern came at the end of 1980. With government grants still failing to match inflation, the Council decided that, rather than inflict yet another year of debilitating all-round cuts upon all its clients, it was better to 'grasp the nettle' and make total withdrawals of grant-aid from a few selected clients in order to maintain the system as a whole intact. As a result, from 1981–2, three regular theatre companies were denied further grant-aid, one of which was the recently formed Old Vic Theatre Company, formerly Prospect. The main reason given for this denial was the Company's decision to reduce its regional touring commitment in favour of longer seasons in London.[22]

A further cause of complaint voiced about the Arts Council's policy, particularly during the seventies, and increasingly so as the money became scarcer, was to do with the balance between money available for the building-based repertory companies and for the small-scale touring and community companies. In its annual report for 1975–6 (entitled 'The Arts in Hard Times'), the Council's tone had begun to get noticeably grimmer, announcing as it did that a decade of expansion in arts funding was now over – and dissatisfaction with the cutters of the proverbial Arts Council 'cake' inevitably grew. Despite the very real increases in grant-aid to alternative theatre companies, the amounts awarded in relation to the National Theatre or even the Birmingham Rep were still minute (in 1979, about eleven per cent of the total Drama allocation) (see Appendix 3, Table II). And when community theatre was developing fast, and claiming to be providing the kind of theatre service that the reps were for the most part now unable to do, the cry from that quarter was for greater democracy and accountability on the part of the Arts Council. Was the Drama Panel truly representative of the whole spectrum of British theatre? Why could it not be elected? Why were many of its recommendations apparently rejected or modified by Council itself? Why couldn't the Drama Panel be given fuller powers? Why could the discussion and detailed recommendations not be made public? Though the Arts Council, under Roy Shaw, was quick to deny political leanings or any narrow-minded establishment prejudice in its decision-making, the loudness of the voices from many quarters, and the reps included, demanding as a minimum greater openness about the Council's procedures and criteria and greater consultation in the decision-making, did produce increased efforts by the Council to explain itself, clarify its criteria and ensure that as wide a spectrum of interest as possible was represented in its deliberations.[23]

The moves towards greater consultation did nothing, however, to prevent further serious erosion of the money available for the arts under the new Conservative administration (from 1979) nor the decisions in 1981 to withdraw grants completely from three theatre companies, the Prospect (at the Old Vic) and those at Crewe (the Lyceum) and Canterbury (the Marlowe). Each of these companies, according to the Council, had failed to meet one or more of the criteria advanced during the previous year (to do with such matters as the size of their audiences, their creative and artistic quality and the extent of local authority support). Though cuts of some kind were unavoidable, there was much criticism at the time of the apparent lack of adequate advance warning and time for improvement given to the two regional repertory companies by the Council. In the struggle to maintain the repertory system, the Arts Council has constantly urged local authorities to pay a fairer share of the costs of their local repertory theatre. Indeed this 'appropriate balance' factor by 1981 had become another of the Arts Council's main criteria for assessment of grant-aid, and further warnings to theatres were issued underlining this fact. Those theatres whose local authority support continued to be low were given to understand that their future level of central funding could well be in jeopardy. But, though some real increases in local funding were secured, the efforts were bound to meet with limited response since local government itself was coming under increasing pressure from central government to check and even cut its expenditure on all fronts. Theatre directors were, as ever, in a cleft stick.

The principle of funding from many sources has none the less been an important one, and one that most directors would wish to maintain – largely as a way of minimising their vulnerability to the changing political priorities of both national and local government, also of keeping each of their funders on its toes by use of telling comparisons between the levels of grant awarded by different bodies. But there are some notable exceptions to the rule. Manchester's Library Theatre Company, unique in the UK because it is wholly funded by Manchester City Council from its Cultural Services budget, has operated with a fair degree of security since its inception in 1952 and indeed was expanded in 1971 in order to run a second, larger theatre in the southern suburbs of the city, the Forum. At the other end of the spectrum is John Counsell's Theatre Royal at Windsor, which proudly claims to be able to survive with no local government or Arts Council subsidy whatsoever, as it has done since its formation in 1938. There have been occasional grants and donations from private firms, but Counsell's argument is that in an area such as Windsor it should be perfectly possible to function independently of grant-aid, relying wholly upon a carefully planned, broadly popular programme of plays running through the entire year and aiming to recoup costs wholly from the box office.

Has subsidy, though, had any *measurable* effect upon the quantity, quality or kind of work done or upon the impact that can be made upon the community? Subsidy has, for the majority of regional theatres, become a vital part of their operation and it is highly unlikely that theatres operating on the Windsor model would survive as worthwhile enterprises in more than a handful of places outside the West End. Even what remains of the provincial commercial touring circuit has had to be bolstered by substantial Arts Council and local authority money. Subsidy has not only guaranteed survival of most of the regional reps and encouraged improvements in the standard of productions, but it has also helped to depress the real cost of tickets, so ensuring that theatre is kept within the financial reach of a broad section of the population, and it has had a marked effect upon play policy. Research conducted in 1980 into the impact of revenue subsidies upon repertory theatre policy showed that, although theatres were as a result of such subsidy discouraged from 'high levels of activity' (such as the weekly change of bill), there was a measurable increase in the number of 'minority interest plays' presented.[24]

The inter-relationship of income and what a theatre can and does actually do is close and crucial. It is artistic policy – the practical realisation of the ideas and objectives of the theatre within the given financial limits – which must next take our attention.

ARTISTIC POLICY – DIRECTORS, COMPANIES AND PLAYS

As repertory theatres developed, became more complex, made larger claims upon the public purse and endeavoured to fulfil an increasingly vital role in their cities and regions, so the organisation and control of the theatres became correspondingly complex – and fraught with difficulties. The sixties in particular witnessed a series of crises in various regional theatres as methods of organisation were sought that would safeguard both artistic integrity and financial accountability: crises that in retrospect seem to have been the almost inevitable teething troubles brought about by new circumstances. The new publicly subsidised breed of reps in the post-War period were governed by trusts or limited companies – just as many of the pre-War reps had been (in contrast to the individual patronage exercised by such wealthy and dedicated pioneers as Miss Horniman and Barry Jackson). These 'non-profit-distributing' companies, usually formed initially by a local group of theatre enthusiasts and other interested and influential local figures were – and are – managed by an elected board, composed normally of representatives from the business, education and arts communities in the region together with local councillors where local subsidies were involved. It is in law the board that is ultimately responsible for the conduct of the theatre's affairs and the proper accounting of its books. But 'ultimate responsibility' does not mean, necessarily, control of the artistic policy. And it is in this grey area where a good deal of debate and controversy has taken place. Generally the pattern since the late 1950s has been that the board appoints an artistic director to conduct and determine the artistic work of the theatre and direct some of the productions, and an administrator to assist him, with responsibility for day-to-day management and budgeting matters. Occasionally because of local circumstances the appointment has been of a general theatre manager who will oversee both artistic and administrative affairs and appoint a director of plays, as has until recently been the case at Salisbury, Derby and Leatherhead. However the appointments are made it is axiomatic that the chain of responsibility should be clear. The division of responsibilities has in most theatres worked well but between 1966 and 1969 a spate of disagreements on policy occurred between boards and artistic directors, most notably at Stoke, Glasgow and Nottingham, leading to the resignation or sacking of the directors involved. Though circumstances and particular causes differed, the flurry of argument and counter-argument that took place in theatre circles generally and even in the national press did lead to a clear statement from the Arts Council's Theatre Enquiry Committee in 1970. The committee concluded unanimously that 'the artistic control of a theatre should be vested in the Artistic Director. As long as he keeps within his budget, and retains the confidence of the public, the choice of plays and all that is implied in the choice should be his.'[25] It was an important confirmation of what most had assumed should be the case, important because authoritative and a point of reference for any future dispute that might later arise. Few major disputes of this nature have occurred since.

Directors

It was important too that the post of artistic director, a substantially different job from that of such pre-War entrepreneurs as Barry Jackson on the one hand and that of the theatre managers and their play producers on the other, should be seen to carry with it both scope for creativity and sufficient authority to translate that creativity into practice. The size of the task faced by most directors has been enormous and challenging. Without doubt the achievements of post-War repertory have had much to do with the imagination, the personal visions, the 'fire in the belly' of particular directors who have managed to carry through their ideas into practical reality and in collaboration with an extraordinary range of people and organisations: the local council, the Arts Council, accountants, actors, playwrights, designers, administrative and technical staff and the board itself. What the director will finally be judged on, above all, will be his ability to stage a consistent series of lively, high-quality productions and complementary activities in the theatre good enough to sustain public interest and support and to fulfil at least most of the promise made at the start of the season. To be overall director of the theatre and play director as well is usually an exhausting task and one that, single-handed, many directors find difficult or undesirable to sustain in one theatre for more than three to five years. Peter Cheeseman, director of the Victoria Theatre at Stoke-on-Trent almost continuously since 1962, is an exception that proves the rule. At other theatres, such as Manchester's Royal Exchange and Glasgow's Citizens' Theatre, multiple directorships have allowed for a more reasonably paced and longer-term strategy. The directorships at both these theatres have remained more or less constant for over ten years.

More typical of the general pattern, however, would be the professional careers of such directors as Peter James (who has moved from the Liverpool Everyman to the Lyric Theatre Hammersmith via The Young Vic in London and, for a spell of six years, the Sheffield Crucible Theatre); Clive Perry (progressing from the Derby Playhouse via the Leicester Phoenix as its inaugural director, to Edinburgh's Royal Lyceum and finally to a ten-year contract at the Birmingham Rep); and Richard Eyre (moving from the Leicester Phoenix as assistant director, followed again by the Royal Lyceum and later by free-lance directing for British Council tours abroad, television and the 7:84 Company, to his reign at the Nottingham Playhouse, further television work and his current work at the National). The nurturing of talent that repertory can foster, noticed already in Chapter 6, as directors progress from sphere to sphere, is still very much in evidence. And the variety of challenge offered within the repertory system is underlined by the marked differences between the paths followed. Although, for some directors, the gravitation towards London seems to have been irresistible, for others the reverse has been true – particularly when the directorship of a large, well-subsidised regional theatre, with tantalising opportunities to develop a fresh artistic policy, is in the offing. Clare Venables, at one time holding the reins at the Theatre Royal, Stratford East, and now in charge of Sheffield's Crucible Theatre, is a case in point.

What motivates a director in deciding to take up a post in a new theatre? Philip Hedley, currently the director of the Theatre Royal, Stratford East, and endeavouring to build once again a repertory theatre that will serve the East End, no doubt reflects the thinking of many:

There are always six elements for me in making a choice: the city, and if you felt empathy towards that city. Secondly, the place in the town – the Northcott Theatre within Exeter for instance is up a hill so only those with cars can get to it. Thirdly, the shape of the building, the audience–stage relationship. You can't fight some of those concrete monoliths being built nowadays . . . Fourthly comes the money available to run it – though now we're all equally poorly off. Fifth, the theatre board. And sixth, the kind of resident staff you had to accept.[26]

The artistic policy itself will vary, not only from director to director but according to the particular circumstances of the theatre as indicated by Hedley.

Some fifteen directors were interviewed in the course of preparing this book and, though their philosophies and working methods differed markedly one from another, common to them all was a strong – often passionate – investment of personal belief and commitment in what they were doing. While their theatres may stress in their publicity their 'service to the community' (expressed in various ways), there was general agreement that the community was best served by work that the director himself or herself thought important and wanted to do. For David Scase (Manchester Library Theatre) theatre was not about giving the community what he thought would be good for it – as though an arm of the social welfare department – but about the expression of feelings and ideas that he and his associate directors believed to be 'life-enhancing' and that would matter as much to the audience as they did to him: a view shared by Clare Venables (Sheffield Crucible as from 1981), who felt that a personal element in the choice of plays to be presented was essential if they were to be alive and communicative.

Artistic policy then, as expressed in the programme of plays and related activities from season to season, must evolve from an interplay of many factors: the budget available, the catchment area, the actors available and, not least, the imagination and sensitivity of the director. While actors will always (in Britain at least) tend to come and go, the director who is not only a good play-director but committed over a long period to one theatre and its links with the region it serves is worth his or her weight in gold. For this reason above all, theatre Trusts have learned to tolerate individual eccentricities, irrational hunches and occasional failures from their directors: it is in the interest of their theatre in the long term to do so. How repertory policy has developed in the past twenty years may be gained from a brief look now at two key components of that policy: the acting company and the play repertoire itself.

Acting companies

One of the ideals of the repertory movement articulated from the very beginning has been that of the permanent acting company, committed to one theatre, working closely together and developing an ensemble performance style. As previous chapters have shown, most of the resident companies that evolved from the 1920s onwards – the small-scale weekly reps – tended, with a few celebrated exceptions, towards the second or even third rate in their standards of acting and presentation. In the 1960s, however, as the repertory movement revived and expanded the permanent company was given a new *raison d'être* and a fresh impetus. By the end of the 1970s, the resident permanent company had become a rarity.

The importance of the company ideal was articulated with particular force by Peter Cheeseman, who at Stoke-on-Trent has done more than most to sustain the ideal in practice. In 1965, for example, in the theatre's report on its first three years (*The First Three Rounds*), he claimed that 'the most important thing about the new repertory theatres is the fact that all the people concerned in the creation of the plays live in the community to which the theatre belongs'. If theatres were to fulfil their promise of contributing to the life of a whole community, if they were to succeed in breaking down 'the barrier which has grown up between the creative artist and most ordinary people', then they must, he argued, endeavour to connect their work with the outside world through more than just performances in the theatre. The activities engaged in at Stoke, Coventry, Nottingham, Manchester (Contact) and elsewhere in the late sixties and through to the mid seventies – talks, demonstrations, drama workshops for young people, advisory services for amateur groups, performances given in schools and other outside venues – were in some cases nearly as many as the number of performances given in the theatre. And they involved the whole company. This work, maintained Cheeseman several years later, was not only of use to the community but provided the 'contact with the world outside . . . that is necessary unless the artist is to become a mere creature of the theatre, with no relationship with the outside world . . . How can an actor do justice to a world he never comes in contact with?'[27] Actors were needed, then, who were not only good performers but were prepared to participate in the larger task of making theatre relevant to the community, a task that required of them residence in that community. This was of course an ideal and rarely was it possible to keep actors in one place for more than a season at a time – Stoke was one of the leading exceptions – but the shared sense of purpose and the involvement of actors in more than just acting advocated by Cheeseman and others was achieved by many reps in this period and contributed significantly to the vitality of the regional theatre.

British actors have, however, traditionally preferred to 'move on' at frequent intervals – unlike the practice in many Continental repertory theatre systems in which actors may be employed on long-term (sometimes life-long) contracts. A number of directors, too, in repertory as well as in the West End, have preferred to cast each new play afresh, believing, like Michael Elliott of the Royal Exchange, that any play worth doing deserved as near perfect casting as was possible – and that meant employing new actors from production to production, keeping only a few of them from one to the next. This was expensive, in that at any one time two sets of salaries were being paid: one to the company performing in the evening and one to the new actors rehearsing during the day. Well-known actors – often television 'stars' in their own right – would often be engaged where appropriate: this would usually add to the expense still further because of the higher salaries paid, but was often off-set by higher box-office takings. The permanent company however involved only one set of salaries, no extra subsistence payments (a more recent factor), usually no star names, and so – depending on the size of the company – could actually be cheaper. The main difference between the two approaches, however, has been one not of budgetary but of artistic policy. The priority for Elliott has been the highest-possible calibre of acting appropriate to a theatre committed to a largely classical repertoire (Shakespeare, the Jacobeans, Sophocles, Shaw and Ibsen have figured prominently in its seasons). The priority for Cheeseman has been a repertoire of twentieth-century, new and sometimes company-devised plays together with the occasional classic presented in a lively and often non-traditional manner. The one approach stresses the play and 'theatre art' above all, the other stresses the performer and the community event.

As the financial stresses and strains of the seventies began to take their toll, with money available for actors' salaries becoming tighter, the number of performers that could be employed at any one time became reduced – and with it the viability of the permanent company. Where the majority of reps tried to offer a broad range of plays each season it soon became impossible to cast with any degree of credibility from a dwindling number of regular actors. One cannot cast from a permanent company *Three Sisters* requiring five actresses and nine men followed by *Julius Caesar* requiring only two women and a dozen or more men unless one has the resources of the National Theatre or The Royal Shakespeare Company. The predominant pattern was to keep a small nucleus of actors together for half a season or more at a time and 'buy in' for specific plays as required while, for both convenience and economy, programming large-cast plays for the middle of the season only. More recently the nucleus, where it exists at all, has become smaller and held together often for no more than two or three productions at a time. Actors themselves, once they have gained a degree of experience in repertory, will often prefer to be based in London, close to their agents and immediately available for well-paid television work, taking only the occasional venture out into the regions to keep their wits sharpened. The prospect of staying in the regions for a whole season and at paltry salaries rarely appeals now to the experienced actor. In this climate it is the reps in or within easy reach of London, such as the Hammersmith Lyric, Guildford's Yvonne Arnaud, the Leatherhead Thorndike, the Watford Palace and the Greenwich Theatre, that tend to benefit most from the services of very successful actors. Only a handful of major and relatively well-endowed reps outside the London area, such as the Royal Exchange and the Birmingham Rep, can now attract stars at worthwhile rates of pay and with the promise of high artistic standards – and even then only for single productions. Peter James (at the Hammersmith Lyric) believes that *because* of his theatre's proximity to Central London the notion of a permanent company – in direct competition with the major national companies – is just not feasible. The consolation is, he suggests, that 'like any other director, I suppose I have 200 or 250 people who have worked with me before, who represent [a] loosely based company'.[28]

An influential factor in this trend at some of the newer theatres has been the larger performance arenas in which work is presented to the public, which make greater demands upon actors, vocally and physically. Each new production at theatres the size of, for example, the 1000-seat Crucible Theatre, may need to be cast afresh to ensure that actors are not only right for their parts but have the talent, skill and experience to command the new big stages and auditoria. A further factor in many directors' minds has been the sense that audiences now themselves expect more perfect casting (at least in the naturalistic sense) than ever before because of television drama and its meticulous attention to the casting of each role. You cannot get away any longer with young actors playing old men (unless the inappropriateness is a deliberate part of the play's style, be it spoof, pantomime or satire), nor with ageing Juliets. There are only a few theatres, such as the Glasgow Citizens', where naturalism and its accompanying artistic confinements have been shunned as a matter of policy.

The theatres that still endeavour to maintain resident companies tend to be those that are smaller and aim to provide a more specific type of repertoire – such as Stoke, Liverpool Everyman and Manchester's Contact and Library Theatres. Actors in these companies may be young and often lacking in experience but usually compensate for this by their energy, commitment and teamwork.

Further exceptions are of course the two main national companies, the Royal Shakespeare Company and the National Theatre, which can afford to employ actors both young and experienced on long-term contracts and at reasonable rates of pay, often allowing a good deal of spare time to performers not involved in every current production. The benefits of such a system have been demonstrated time and again, particularly in the high quality of the Royal Shakespeare Company's ensemble work in productions such as *Nicholas Nickleby* (1981). But, apart from these exceptions at either end of the scale, by and large it is the independent touring community and young people's theatre companies, generally devising their own material, that now carry the banner of the permanent ensemble company – small though such companies may be.

Plays

If one of the main functions of a repertory theatre is to provide a 'library' of theatrical art (as the early pioneers expressed it), able to bring to the public classic works of the past, recent and new plays and a broad mix of the best in serious and light drama, how far has the new breed of reps gone to fulfil that function?

True repertory, which comes closest to the library or art-gallery model, allowing the public to choose from many types of play which may be on offer within any two-, three- or four-week period, has not proved attractive or possible for many companies without the resources of the National or the Royal Shakespeare Company. The Coventry Belgrade Theatre's experiment with true repertory in 1963 proved unsuccessful, and short-lived. The Nottingham Playhouse, on the other hand, did sustain a full-fledged true repertory system from the opening of the new theatre until the late seventies when costs were proving prohibitive. And at Stoke the flexibility of theatre-in-the-round (and consequent savings in set-changing) together with its permanent company has enabled true repertory to flourish. But these have been the exceptions.

The financial difficulties involved in operating 'true repertory' in a conventional theatre building are well illustrated in Terry Browne's account of the William Gaskill experiment at the Royal Court in 1965–6. A 'permanent' company of twenty-one actors was formed for a six-month period and a repertoire of nine plays (including one double bill) presented. It was an adventurous season ranging from Bond's *Saved* to Middleton's *Chaste Maid in Cheapside* but a financial failure. Not only had many of the plays received unfavourable reviews but the extra stage-management and permanent-company costs incurred in true repertory had proved too burdensome for a season without sufficient guaranteed box-office winners. There had been, Gaskill believed, some positive results, including the 'nursing of *Saved* after unfavourable notices, which would not have been possible in the straight-run system', and 'the beginnings of a regular audience'. But the theatre reverted to short runs once the experiment was over.[29]

Despite the infrequency of the true repertory system, it is true to say that the majority of repertory theatres since the War have felt a responsibility to provide the 'broad mix' in the course of a season, even if only in a simply consecutive 'short-run' pattern, and thus endeavour to satisfy a variety of tastes. Being 'all things to all men', however, is an attribute that has ambiguous connotations, implying either praise or condemnation depending on your standpoint.

The basic outline of an average repertory season, which shows remarkably little sign of having changed in twenty years, is usually made up of the following ingredients:

1 two or three classic, and most likely modern classic, plays (often including a Shaw or an Arthur Miller, and only occasionally a Shakespeare where resources allow); plays that are on examination syllabuses will often dictate the choice;

2 two or three modern comedies and/or 'thrillers' (Priestley, Rattigan and Coward, for example; Alan Ayckbourn's comedies of modern middle-class manners have become a more recent popular addition; Anthony Shaffer's *Sleuth*, for example, or, less commonly now, an Agatha Christie);

3 one or two recently released plays from the West End or the National Theatre (the latest Ayckbourn and Russell's *Educating Rita*, for example, or at the sharper end a Dario Fo political farce, once its drawing power had been proved in London);

4 a new play or an adaptation of a well-known novel or classic play (a dramatisation of *Crime and Punishment* for example, as at the Royal Exchange in 1978);

5 the family play or pantomime at Christmas.

(See Appendix 2 for a comparison of some typical seasons at six selected repertory theatres between 1960–1 and 1980–1.) The variety of permutations upon this pattern is almost endless and exceptions to the rule abound, but it is striking how prevalent the basic outline has been among the smaller and middle-range and even many of the larger-scale reps. Such a pattern, if often wearily predictable, has its rationale and value and will often be the product of acute observation and assessment of audience habits and responses over past seasons. The theatre's geographical location, its audience catchment area, its proximity to London – all these factors must be carefully weighed and pondered and no artistic policy can be shaped irrespective of them, no matter what the personal enthusiasms of the artistic director may be. At Derby, Dundee, and Mold in North Wales, the likelihood of audiences having already seen the latest West End success will be small, which allows a strong chance of the latest Alan Ayckbourn comedy 'straight from the West End' (even though in a totally new production) attracting good business at the box office. On the other hand, while Shaw may still draw large audiences in Salisbury his plays may be a guaranteed box-office disaster at Sheffield or Newcastle. Hence the variousness of the permutations within the broad pattern.

The danger lies of course in that the more a programme from year to year follows a set pattern, the more formula-bound will be the approach to the productions themselves. Once a theatre settles for 'playing safe', the vitality and imagination essential to any worthwhile performance are likely to be in short supply. The complaint voiced by Alan Vaughan Williams in a *Plays and Players* article in 1967[30] – that too many reps present routine and stereotyped West End productions simply to fill a gap or to increase box-office returns and so help finance those 'riskier' but more interesting productions elsewhere in the bill – is echoed in the Theatre Writers' Union report in 1982. While many managements showed a desire 'to produce good and relevant theatre' they also felt impelled by box-office pressures to choose most of their programmes on the basis of 'safe bets'.[31]

Despite the necessary attention to the box office, receipt of subsidy does encourage – indeed requires – some attempt by the theatre to cater for minority tastes and to present work that will involve risk, either because brand-new and therefore unheard of, or because considered too high-brow or challenging in its subject-matter or too innovative in its style. The theatre that continually plays safe and never caters for minority interests will not only be likely to suffer a decline in its own vitality but will run the risk of a critical scrutiny from the Arts Council, which in turn could mean a decidedly smaller-than-average increase in grant-aid. The balance to be struck between adventure and safety presents managements with ever-recurring dilemmas.

Fortunately for the health and vitality of the repertory movement as a whole there has been an impressive number of theatres willing and able to work against the usual pattern – not to ignore local factors but rather to reinterpret them and find ways of integrating them with a more adventurous policy. A few brief examples here will indicate the range of different strategies, and further, more detailed examples will be given in Chapter 8. Following years of decline and a succession of somewhat predictable and unexciting programmes, the Oldham Repertory Theatre was bought by the Town Council in 1977 and, with the aid of the Arts Council, a new company established. The new director, Kenneth Alan Taylor, had worked as an actor in Oldham some years before, knew the nature of the problem well and began to build a new identity and direction for the theatre. Far from following the well-trodden paths, his policy was to present each year a season of seven or eight plays, all of which were to be new or recent work and presented in a style that emphasised the energy, humour and robustness of the kind of entertainment he believed would appeal to the people of Oldham. The policy worked: stage adaptations of Barry Hines' *Kes* and Jack Rosenthal's television play *Spend, Spend, Spend*, Martin Sherman's *Bent* and Richard O'Brien's *The Rocky Horror Show* and premières of MP Joe Ashton's *Majority of One* and Bleasdale's *Having a Ball!*, all amply fulfilled Taylor's faith in the area and the theatre was frequently packed. Other examples of innovation abound: there have been the Stoke documentary plays, the young audience emphases at Contact and the Young Vic, the striking and original reinterpretations of classic plays at the Glasgow Citizens', the several seasons of musicals (ranging from Rogers and Hart to Brecht and Weill to brand-new works) at Manchester's Forum Theatre by the Library Theatre Company, and there have of course been the innumerable seasons of new and experimental plays at studio theatres in towns and cities as diverse as Salisbury, Leatherhead, Birmingham, Derby and Edinburgh.

New writing is the very life-blood of a vital contemporary theatre, and much of the energy in these theatres has properly gone into encouraging the talents of new writers and developing fruitful relationships with other already-proven writers. Resident writers have been employed for varying periods of time at, for example, Stoke (Peter Terson), Nottingham (David Hare), the Liverpool Everyman (Willy Russell and Bill Morrison) and Birmingham (David Edgar), and at Scarborough Alan Ayckbourn is both resident writer and director. There have also been close working associations between writers, companies and directors on particular projects, such as that between Arnold Wesker and John Dexter for *Chicken Soup with Barley* and *Roots*, first seen at the Coventry Belgrade Theatre in 1958–9, and between Trevor Griffiths and Richard Eyre at Nottingham on *Comedians* in 1975. These collaborations have been successful mainly because of particular working relationships that have evolved between individual writers and directors, but it has been important for British theatre that such successful and productive relationships have been fostered as much in the regions as in London. During the seventies indeed most London critics for the national newspapers found that their task took them necessarily to regional premières. The critic who failed to see *Comedians* at the Nottingham Playhouse would already be several steps behind his more alert, regionally minded colleagues. Robert Cushman in *The Observer* noticed the difference between Bleasdale's *Having a Ball!* at the Oldham Coliseum and its London opening at the Hammersmith Lyric in 1981: set in the North, and written by a Northern playwright with Northern audiences in mind, this funny, abrasive play – not surprisingly – worked a good deal better in Oldham than it did in London.[32]

The extent to which regional theatres have been able to encourage new writing has been in part conditioned by Arts Council grant-aid, which from 1952 was first available for the direct promotion of new plays and later in the form of guarantees against loss, writers' bursaries and contract schemes for resident playwrights. From the writer's point of view however conditions were rarely conducive to making a living from his craft. As Elsom observed in 1973,[33] the rewards available to playwrights writing for the repertory theatre are meagre – unless you are a beginner and are content simply to see your work actually performed. New plays from unknown and little-known writers are rarely scheduled for more than three weeks and often less, and they will frequently be scheduled for studio performances, given the small houses that will be anticipated. If the writer is to gain any reasonable income from his play, his only hope will be a London transfer and then, perhaps, a television production. Since Elsom wrote, the situation has not materially improved, and in recent years has actually deteriorated (the number of premières listed in the play-lists of regional theatres for 1980–1, for example, was considerably lower than the figure noted by Elsom nine years earlier).[34]

A worrying trend in recent years has been charted in a report by the Theatre Writers' Union[35] which pointed to the considerable growth in Arts Council money for, and productions of, new work in all areas of theatre between 1975 and 1978, followed by a sharp drop between 1979 and 1981. The highest proportion of new work during these six years, it observed, was presented by the fringe and alternative companies, while within the repertory sector 'new work production is heavily concentrated among a few courageous and imaginative theatres'. The top five network theatres in this period, according to the report – Birmingham, Scarborough, Nottingham, Sheffield and the Liverpool Everyman – had, for example, during 1978–9, taken up over half of the Writer's Contracts awarded to repertory theatres. But even they had cut back substantially by 1981. Also noticed was an increasing number of 'semi-new' plays – adaptations of novels, classic plays and the like – creeping into the repertoire: considered no doubt safer by managements because carrying a 'bankable' title, but offering a narrowing of the scope available to writers.

But how safe now *is* the 'safe bet'? Analyses by both the Arts Council and the Theatre Writers' Union interestingly call into question the common assumption that 'new work empties houses'. While musicals, children's plays and pantomimes not surprisingly achieved the highest average audiences (between seventy-one and seventy-four per cent of capacity) in 1981–2, in the same year premières accounted for twelve per cent of all performances given and attracted as high an average audience as for non-première drama (between fifty-five and fifty-seven per cent).[36] (Appendix 3, Table II shows in diagrammatic form the average audience attendance at each of various categories of dramatic production at the English repertory theatres during 1981–2, together with a breakdown of total audience attendance at those theatres over the whole season.)

Just as the size of the new playhouses has influenced many directors in their choice of casts, so, even more, it has influenced the choice of plays. One of the first to recognise and do much to solve the problem of how to fill these spacious theatres was Peter James while director at the Sheffield Crucible (1974–81). Despite and indeed partly because of the gloomy state of the economy, he planned a series of seasons in each of which there would be at least one 'blockbuster' – a large, expensive, colourful, musical and highly theatrical event such as *Cabaret* and the British premières of *Chicago* and *The Wiz* (in 1977, 1978 and 1980 respectively). As long as the show was done with energy and polish, the cost could be borne by the high audience attendance and possibly too by eventual transfer to London – which is what happened to *Chicago* in 1979 (though James does not see London transfers as any longer a profit-making exercise). In much the same way the National Theatre's recently acclaimed production of *Guys and Dolls* will, through its box-office success, help to subsidise other less popular revivals and new plays. Richard Eyre (first at Nottingham, later at the National), Clive Perry (at Birmingham), Howard Lloyd-Lewis (at Manchester's Forum Theatre) and Richard Digby-Day (at Nottingham since 1980) are directors who share a similar faith in the worth and box-office potential of the musical.

It is undoubtedly significant that the commercial West End theatre has come to rely increasingly heavily upon products transferred from the sub-sidised theatre – not only prestigious productions from the National Theatre and Royal Shakespeare Company but from the regions too. In 1975 the Arts Council annual report noted that productions originated by subsidised companies had begun to form a substantial proportion of the West End fare; in 1980 it was claimed that 'up to half of the productions in the West End today originate in subsidised houses'.[37] And the trend has continued, with regular seasons at the Roundhouse by the Royal Exchange Company, and a steady series of transfers from theatres as varied as those at Sheffield, Bristol and Salisbury, from the Leicester Haymarket and the Glasgow Citizens'. Sometimes such transfers have been negotiated after a particularly successful production has come to the notice of national critics, as was the case with Salisbury's *84 Charing Cross Road* in 1981. Sometimes transfers have been pre-arranged as a way of cutting costs and yet maintaining high standards to the benefit both of the commercial and the repertory managements – a frequent feature of Val May's direction of the Bristol Old Vic, the production of *Conduct Unbecoming* in 1959 being just one example. The dangers inherent in the latter type of arrangement if it becomes a regular practice (the ceding of control over policy, for example, to commercial managements) are, however, plain.

AUDIENCES

Just as one of the declared objects of the Arts Council was to 'increase the accessibility of the arts in Great Britain', so this has equally been one of the over-riding concerns of the regional theatre in the sixties and seventies. Has the repertory movement in this period made theatre more accessible? Have audience numbers increased? Has the social range of the audience widened? Have audience tastes changed markedly since 1958? As Peter Cheeseman argued in 1968 (in *The Stage*), 'Municipal subsidy forces us to justify our existence in a new and critical way.'[38] And the justification had to be not just in terms of the box-office success but in the broader, if vaguer, terms of reaching as wide an audience as possible and of offering something that the audience themselves could perceive and appreciate as worthwhile and important. It was not just a question of justifying the receipt of grant-aid: any director and theatre company with artistic integrity would be deeply unhappy with a consistent run of poor audience figures. Playing to half-empty houses week after week can be depressing in the extreme for artists whose prime skill is that of communication.

There have been innumerable audience surveys, some of more use than others, carried out by theatres throughout the period in question, but clear and indisputable evidence on which to base answers to the above questions is difficult to come by. Certainly, by the early 1960s it had become clear that, while overall audience attendance at theatres had dwindled with the closing down of so many commercial and touring theatres, attendance at the better reps was proving to be healthy. Indeed, as more and more changed from weekly to fortnightly and then to three-weekly repertory, without alarming decreases in the weekly attendance, it must have been the case that more people were attending though less frequently – a pattern that made sense in an age of increased television viewing and fast-changing leisure habits.

Recent statistics suggest that audience figures during the past ten years have remained fairly constant, putting admissions to home-based performances by the English regional and London repertory companies at around three and a half million per year during the 1980–2 period. This compares with admissions in the same period to the National and Royal Shakespeare Companies of about one and three-quarter million and to the West End theatre of around eight million.[39] No figures for any one year can be taken as indicative of the general state of affairs, but the underlying pattern over the preceding decade does seem to suggest a relatively constant picture, with attendances at the regional theatres falling slightly in recent years and those in London slightly increasing. What should be borne in mind, though, is that a constant level of attendance is something of an achievement when viewed against the recent background of increasing unemployment, a slowing down of the increase in average earnings, and an increase in ticket prices above the annual inflation rate. Additionally, as a result of the financial squeeze upon theatre budgets there has been a fall in the number of performances given – especially in the studio theatres – so there has been less theatre on offer anyway.

Whether or not theatres have managed to reach new sections of the population – the working class and ethnic minorities, for example – or simply managed to retrieve the traditional highly educated middle-class audiences that have formed the backbone of repertory support since before the First World War, is a matter of some debate. The alternative theatre companies claim that the reps have by and large failed, have stuck with their traditional customers, and that it is they, the small-scale community theatre companies touring to community venues, that have made the real inroads. Most of the audience surveys done so far have suggested that repertory audiences are indeed in the main still the middle class but that the proportion of young people has increased markedly. There are however enough exceptions to the first element of this 'rule' to justify some optimism that the broadening of the audience that has taken place in certain theatres and at certain times can be extended still further. The role played by the studio theatres, the Theatre-in-Education and community touring units based at repertory theatres, and by all the other many extra activities organised to promote community links, has without doubt been of immense importance – as have the vitality and social awareness of much of the new writing. A survey in 1969 pointed out that, whereas the proportion of people from skilled and unskilled manual working backgrounds in the population was a little over seventy per cent, the proportion of people from this background in the average theatre audience was usually less than ten per cent.[40] The exceptions noted – all too rare but significant none the less – were for performances of Plater's *Close the Coalhouse Door* at the Newcastle Playhouse and of *Clydeside 2* at the Glasgow Citizens' Theatre. At both of these productions some twenty-two per cent of the audience came from working-class backgrounds – no doubt because the plays were both semi-documentaries concerned with the history of working-class struggle and drew upon popular entertainment forms in their presentation style.

Statistics in themselves reveal very little: some attempt will be made in the next chapter to suggest in more detail how some of the repertory companies have endeavoured to win and maintain their audiences and in what ways they have earned that support.

8   1958–1983: Six Reps in Focus

ANTHONY JACKSON

THE six theatre companies chosen for more detailed discussion here are not intended to represent a complete cross-section of the contemporary repertory movement. They have been chosen because they serve to illustrate particularly effectively certain of the characteristics and trends outlined in the previous chapter. Such has been the speed, complexity and variety of the developments of the past twenty-five years that it has seemed more useful to document these developments through focus upon specific theatres than to incorporate all examples and detail into one straightforward chronological account. Each of the ventures described below therefore has been chosen, not because it is 'the best' (though each must certainly be considered among the best of its kind), but because the contribution each has made, to theatre in general and to its own community in particular, has been distinct.

The reasons for including the theatres of Nottingham, Glasgow, Manchester (the Royal Exchange) and Stoke-on-Trent perhaps need very little elaboration. All four have achieved distinction not only in their own region but nationally and internationally. All four serve big industrial conurbations and act as centres for their larger regions as well, and yet each has made its mark in different ways, faced different problems and evolved different approaches to the work undertaken. Equally, the buildings in which they operate vary in size (from Stoke's tiny in-the-round theatre to Manchester's many-tiered auditorium-in-the-round and enormous foyer space) and in shape (from theatre-in-the-round to the Victorian proscenium theatre at Glasgow). (Instead of Manchester or Nottingham one might of course have easily chosen Bristol or Birmingham – equally prestigious and distinguished theatres.) Salisbury and the Liverpool Everyman Theatre are included to complement the other four. The first exemplifies the challenge faced by a theatre serving a mainly rural and widely spread catchment area; the Everyman at the other end of the spectrum was the first of the 'alternative reps', endeavouring to provide in a large industrial metropolis a kind of theatre that would appeal especially to younger audiences not adequately catered for by the 'mainstream' rep in the city centre.

Evolution of artistic policy has differed in relation to the geographical and social contexts of the six theatres, to the level of funding received, and in relation too to the ideas, attitudes and skills of the individual directors who founded or have subsequently made their reputations at those theatres. Whereas the policy at Stoke, for example, has remained consistent through twenty years because of the long stay of its director, the policy at Nottingham has varied in tandem with changes of artistic director.

In each of the mini case histories which follow, then, the object is briefly to trace how the theatre's policy has evolved and how dependent it has been upon a manifold combination of circumstances, personalities and ideas, and to suggest, tentatively, the nature and significance of its achievement.

NOTTINGHAM PLAYHOUSE

Although not the first of the new wave of theatre buildings, the Nottingham Playhouse rapidly assumed a leading position among the regional reps, a position it managed to sustain for some fifteen years from the date of its opening in 1963. Unlike the Belgrade Theatre which had opened just five years earlier, the new Playhouse already had a strong and unbroken tradition of repertory upon which to build. In this respect, 1963 marked a revitalisation and expansion of a going concern, and it is doubtful if the Playhouse would have been able to start work with such energy and sense of direction had it begun entirely from scratch. The Nottingham Theatre Trust had been founded in 1948 by a group of local and influential theatre enthusiasts, with the aim of providing Nottingham with a theatre that could stand comparison with those in Bristol, Birmingham, Liverpool and Glasgow. There was promise of a yearly grant from the City Council together with financial assistance from the Arts Council in converting an old cinema (which itself had housed a small rep company for some years) into a suitable home. Despite an unsteady start the first Playhouse company soon achieved a national reputation under the direction of André van Gyseghem, with successful productions of *The Rivals*, *Twelfth Night* and plays by Shaw, Coward and Rattigan. In the summer of 1949 the Arts Council invited Nottingham to present its *Othello* in a Repertory Theatre Festival held in London, alongside companies from Manchester (The Library Company), Glasgow (The Citizens'), and Bristol (The Old Vic) – a measure of the extent to which the Playhouse's aspirations had been recognised already beyond Nottingham.

From the beginning the policy was to present fortnightly changes of bill as a means of ensuring higher standards than were usually possible in weekly rep. John Harrison took over the artistic direction in 1952 and after him, in 1957, Val May, both of whom continued the policy of high quality productions of Shakespeare, Shaw, Maugham, Anouilh, Coward and Peter Ustinov. The company was also beginning to take on a more regional, indeed national role, with tours for the Arts Council to theatre-less towns in the North East and tours of plays for children in rural Nottinghamshire. These activities, together with the special school matinées, the lunch-hour and Sunday concerts and the Playhouse Club, were all part of the attempt to make the theatre into an essential ingredient of the city's and county's life.

Conditions in the old building were, however, cramped and confining for both actors and audience, although the audience were for the most part unaware of the triumphs and ingenuity that had been achieved on a stage twelve feet deep with no adequate flying facilities and wing space a mere three feet on one side. The new theatre by comparison was to have a stage fifty feet deep with thirty feet of wing space on one side; seating capacity would be nearly doubled, from 433 in the old theatre to 760 in the new, and yet no one would sit more than sixty feet from the stage.

Proposals for a new theatre had been debated and argued over for years by the City Council before a firm decision was taken in 1961 to go ahead. The Council had already committed the profits from its Gas Undertaking, before nationalisation in 1948, to a project of cultural benefit to the city, and eventually agreed to use this fund to finance the major part of the building cost (£328 000), leaving the Theatre Trust to raise the remaining amount (£42 000), which it did. The Gulbenkian Foundation also contributed money for equipment.

Peter Moro's design for the theatre, though not so revolutionary as many claimed at the time, did mark a considerable advance upon that of the Belgrade. The central architectural feature, repeated in numerous ways throughout the building, was the cylindrical shape of the auditorium, which attempted to give some feeling of enclosure and intimacy to the actor–audience relationship, in other respects a conventional end-stage arrangement. (See illustration on p. 105.) It was one of the last theatres to be built with a conventional balcony but this did at least allow for a capacious auditorium on what was a very small site. One regret the most recent director, Richard Digby-Day, had was that no studio theatre had been built alongside when space was available: the site now allows no room for further expansion.[1]

There was initially to be a triumvirate of directors, consisting of Frank Dunlop (who had directed the previous two seasons at the old theatre), John Neville (who had been a member of the old rep company and was now, following several successful seasons at the Old Vic, an actor of national distinction) and Peter Ustinov (the playwright and actor). Little was seen of Ustinov, and Dunlop moved on after a year leaving the mantle solely upon Neville's shoulders. He proceeded to forge, in his remarkable five years at Nottingham, a repertory theatre venture that came to be seen as one of the beacons of the revitalised repertory movement. From the first, Neville saw the Playhouse as an opportunity to do something in the theatre that did not seem to be possible in London. Here was a chance to create a theatre of the quality and excellence of the companies at the Old Vic and the Royal Shakespeare Theatre but to give it at the same time a distinctive regional stamp. It was to be, as he later expressed it, 'a pocket National Theatre for the region'.[2] His policy from the outset was to concentrate upon revivals of classic plays on the one hand and upon contemporary drama on the other and to run them on a full-scale 'true repertory' basis – which, though more expensive than short runs, would he believed be good for the acting company and good for audiences. He was later to claim (in 1967) that the true repertory system had increased the number of people that came to the theatre and so helped to recoup the extra cost involved as well as providing a better theatre service.[3]

Neville's contribution to the opening period of the Playhouse's life was not only as theatre director but as actor too; only occasionally did he actually direct any plays himself. Every season there were usually at least two or three outstanding productions that managed to set new standards on the repertory stage, and in many of those it was Neville's acting that generated the excitement and set the pace. In roles as far apart as, for example, Richard II and the homosexual barber in Charles Dyer's *Staircase*, he demonstrated the extraordinary range and depth of his acting. Neville was concerned too that the Playhouse should be part of Nottingham and contribute to it in a variety of ways – hence the innumerable late-night performances, poetry and jazz sessions on Sundays (in which Neville would often take part), and the touring versions of the classics for schools.

The audiences were won over. Attendances in the first four to five years averaged eighty per cent, and this in a theatre nearly double the size of the old rep. Clearly the Playhouse was becoming a landmark on the theatrical map that the national critics could not afford to ignore. For a year, too, the Playhouse had become responsible for running the newly opened Newcastle Playhouse, until a newly constituted Trust was able to take it over fully in 1968.

But at the apparent height of success Neville dropped his bombshell. By March 1967 he had, he said, become so disheartened by the failure of his attempts to win more financial support from the city and, most of all, the Arts Council, that he would resign his directorship in fifteen months' time. For a year and more controversy and speculation reigned. The Arts Council agreed to make some further improvements to the grant-aid offered, but it soon became apparent that the argument was as much between Neville and the Theatre Board as between Neville and the Arts Council. At one stage Neville offered to withdraw his resignation but the Board refused, and Neville quickly became something of a *cause célèbre* among the theatre profession. Clearly, a good deal of bad feeling and misunderstanding had grown up between Neville and the Board, the minutiae of which need not concern us here. What is interesting however are the larger issues that the controversy brought into the open: the level of funding that a major and developing regional theatre could expect from national and local funding bodies; and the proper relationship between a theatre board and its artistic director. Neville argued in the press and elsewhere that his stand was a philosophical as well as a practical one: that a lot of noise had to be made about the needs of regional theatre, and about what Neville saw as the Arts Council's timidity in doing little more than increasing the grants of existing clients by *x* amount each year to allow for inflation but always avoiding any major reassessment of the theatre's needs in the light of new paths being pursued. As Neville himself recalled some years later, when the Playhouse was opened it was generally thought to be imperative that it should not fail, 'because it was a pattern, a blueprint, a signpost for the future of regional theatre in this country'.[4] It was therefore doubly important that, having proved itself so far, the theatre should be allowed to pursue the logic of its developing role, a role that had to become 'vital to the wellbeing of the people who are working hard in this region to put this

26. John Neville in the Nottingham Playhouse Production of *Richard II*, 1965, directed by John Neville and Michael Rudman. Photo: Local Studies Library, Nottinghamshire County Library.

country back on its feet'. It was for Neville therefore time for 'a really quite massive reappraisal of thinking in terms of regional theatre' by the Arts Council and local authorities as well as those involved in running theatres. Certainly the financial set-up in Nottingham demanded reappraisal and the almost-daily debates in correspondence, leader and feature columns of the local press are testament to the success with which these matters were being aired. It became clear, for example, that viewed from one angle the theatre in Nottingham was subsidising the finances of the city rather than vice versa. In 1966–7 the city council gave the theatre a grant of £22 000 while receiving in return from the Playhouse an annual rent of £27 000.

On the second issue, the view of Jo Hodgkinson, as the Arts Council officer sent to help resolve the gathering crisis, is that Neville had taken too much of the burden and the control of the enterprise onto his own shoulders, rejecting the wishes of the board when they did not agree with his own.[5] Neville, on the other hand, argued that the artistic director once appointed should be given a free hand as long as he could keep to his budgets: was not the director likely to understand the nature and requirements of his task more clearly than a board of well-meaning non-professionals who were, he felt, insufficiently accountable to Nottingham playgoers?[6] Neville left in 1968 but the board, which it must be said had generally had good relationships with its previous directors in the old smaller theatre, also made changes to its constitution to reflect a wider representation of interests, including those of the playgoers themselves.

The director appointed to replace Neville was Stuart Burge. His task was a difficult one. With a good deal of the theatre profession by now highly antagonistic towards the Playhouse Trust and its board, the paramount need was to save the theatre from a slide towards mediocrity or even extinction. Mutual confidence between the Trust and the theatre profession needed to be built again, artistic standards maintained and audiences kept. All three Burge managed to do with considerable dexterity. Coming from the Bristol Old Vic and with experience behind him both as an actor and as a director in theatre and in television, Burge made it clear that he would endeavour to continue to expand Neville's artistic direction and that it would be his function 'to guide the Board in matters of professional policy'.[7]

His opening production was the rarely performed *King John*, followed by Jonathan Miller's production of *School for Scandal*, a revival of Plater's *Close the Coalhouse Door*, the drama-documentary about miners first seen in Newcastle, and then the première of Peter Barnes' savage satire of the British class system, his critically acclaimed *The Ruling Class*. On this latter production Barnes worked closely with the director throughout rehearsals, so beginning his own association with the Playhouse of many years. True repertory was maintained and the schools work expanded to include primary as well as secondary-level children; adult tours were also increased as a way of exploiting good productions beyond their usual twenty or so performances. The artistic quality of the productions and the national reputation of the Playhouse were maintained and indeed strengthened during Burge's five-year reign, with guest productions by Miller and other notable directors, a Playhouse season at the Old Vic, a memorable *Waiting for Godot* which included Peter O'Toole as Vladimir, a new version of the *Lulu* plays by Barnes – and substantial increases in grant-aid from both city and county councils. But the audience attendance figures slipped from their hitherto high level – perhaps inevitably once Nottingham people had taken the new theatre for granted and with the increased competition from new theatres in Birmingham, Leicester and nearby Derby.

Burge left to return to television in 1973 and was succeeded by Richard Eyre, until 1972 director of the Royal Lyceum Theatre Company in Edinburgh and with several recent productions for the 7:84 Company to his credit. He brought with him David Hare as resident dramatist and literary manager, and so began another prime five-year phase in the life of the Playhouse. Eyre was keen to breathe new life into the theatre and in so doing to reverse the slide in audience attendance: the approach had to be lively, bright and not too esoteric or remote. He was, he told the local press in 1978, a passionate believer that theatre should entertain in the fullest sense of 'giving relevance to our lives, with clarity, joy, vitality and a social conscience'.[8] As Eyre recalls, his first season had to make a strong statement – it had to be very good by any standards and it had to take risks.[9] Hare and Howard Brenton had already written a play with the Nottingham Playhouse in mind – *Brassneck*, a hilarious, boisterous and controversial play about local government corruption. This, together with *Taming of the Shrew* and an adaptation for Nottingham of McGrath's Liverpudlian *Soft, or a Girl?* formed the spearhead of the new season.

Eyre's period at Nottingham became characterised by his determined policy to bring new playwriting to the Playhouse, and for a few years critical attention turned naturally to Nottingham as the source of adventurous new plays. Eyre was in fact responsible for approximately fifteen major premières. In 1974, for example, there was Brenton's *Churchill Play*; later, Adrian Mitchell's *White Suit Blues,* Ken Campbell/Davd Hill/Andy Andrews' *Walking like Geoffrey,* Stephen Lowe's *Touched* and Trevor Griffiths' *Comedians.* The latter – a funny, provocative, disturbing essay on modern humour and the social attitudes that lie behind the jokes – has now achieved the status of a modern classic. Opening to critical acclaim (although not to packed houses) in Nottingham in February 1975, it eventually transferred to the Old Vic.

The policy worked. Not only was a remarkable number of exciting new plays presented, but audience figures were up too – by ten per cent in

1973–4 – and at a time when rumours were rife that a quarter of the country's repertory theatres would have to close because of the increasingly grave financial crisis faced by the arts world. Eyre maintained the true repertory system, and worked at building a permanent company who would 'regard the Playhouse not as a jumping off ground or a stop-over on the M1'![10] Alongside the main house work, too, the Theatre in Education company *Roundabout* became firmly established as one of the leading companies of its type in the country.

Following in the footsteps of his predecessors, Eyre left after five years – like Burge, for television – and was succeeded for a short while by Geoffrey Reeves in 1978 and then by Richard Digby-Day in 1980. But with a worsening economic recession requiring economies that made exciting, full-blooded productions increasingly difficult to mount, coinciding with an initial uncertainty of artistic direction, the Playhouse had lost much of its momentum. True repertory had been phased out by 1979 and as audience attendance fell the theatre slipped deeper into debt. Digby-

27. *Brassneck*, by Howard Brenton and David Hare: Nottingham Playhouse, 1973, directed by David Hare. Photo: Local Studies Library, Nottinghamshire County Library.

28. *Comedians*, by Trevor Griffiths: Nottingham Playhouse, 1975, directed by Richard Eyre. Photo: Local Studies Library, Nottinghamshire County Library.

Day's aim in 1980 was therefore to bring back audiences to the Playhouse at a time when 'the cost of theatre-going is such that we must assume that even our most regular patrons will be choosy'.[11] That meant, he argued, offering 'a wide variety of entertainment', 'a totally attractive experience to the widest possible range of audiences' – including late-night foyer performances and craft fairs. His first season set the tone: it included the musical *The Boyfriend*, *Mrs Warren's Profession*, *Stevie* (the one-woman show about poet Stevie Smith – presented on Monday nights only in the absence of a studio), *A View from the Bridge*, *Old King Cole* for Christmas and Sondheim's *A Little Night Music* – proven modern classics, musicals and no risky premières. The contrast with the Eyre period just a few years earlier was marked, but in Digby-Day's view necessary. It was no use, he insisted, going out for 'one audience' any more: 'It's important not to be imprisoned in one age group or one ideology. Theatre is about change and alternatives.'[12] There is now no longer a permanent company and there are co-productions being arranged with other theatres, such as the Northcott in Exeter and the New Shakespeare Company (at the open-air Regent's Park Theatre in London), which allow more money to be spent on the productions while cutting costs by giving them fuller, and probably deserved, exploitation.

The policy has indeed done much to restore the fortunes of an ailing Playhouse. Audiences have begun to return, if slowly, and the financial position has improved, but it has been, as Digby-Day himself admits, at some cost. The role of the Playhouse, from the Neville era onwards, as a powerhouse of new ideas and new plays – a regional theatre with a national reputation – has fallen into the shadows while a local base has begun to be, it is hoped, rebuilt. 'Let's get the audiences back first and then start doing new plays'[13] has been Digby-Day's priority. The recent oscillations in the fortunes of the Playhouse and the current struggles to maintain standards and audiences in the face of a tightening financial straitjacket are in a sense symptomatic of the fortunes of the British repertory movement as a whole during the late seventies and early eighties.

THE CITIZENS' THEATRE, GLASGOW

The achievement of the Citizens' Theatre throughout the seventies provides a dramatic example of the resourcefulness, initiative and imagination of which the repertory movement is from time to time capable. One's first visit to the Citizens' involves making adjustment after adjustment. Situated in the Gorbals district of Glasgow – on the other side of the river from the city centre, amidst the hideous high-rise flats which have now replaced most of the nineteenth-century slums that used to characterise the area – the theatre presents a bleak and uninviting prospect, shorn of its once ornate facade and looking more like some ancient aircraft hanger than a theatre. But once inside the contrast is astonishing – rich scarlet walls and carpeting in the foyer and a beautiful, intimate, red and gold Victorian auditorium. After plans to build a new Citizens' Theatre as part of a large cultural centre in the city fell through, the local authorities gave money for massive refurbishing of the old theatre in 1977, and the interior colour scheme was designed by Philip Prowse, the theatre's resident designer/director. It is another world inside and the contrast is a consciously contrived hallmark of the current Citizens' style which extends into the concept of virtually all their productions. The theatre may be there to explore and shed light on the real world but the stage itself is not the reality outside: the attempt is never to mirror slavishly the world outside but to illuminate it through artifice. The idea itself is not particularly original but it is remarkable how few of the regional theatres have managed to break away from the naturalism of both style and content that dominates so much of the mainstream of British drama. The Citizens' is prepared to take risks, sometimes in quite outrageous ways and with both new and classic works, and its willingness to *assert* artifice, rather than disguise or apologise for it, has characterised its production policy ever since 1970 when the new régime began. It has also earned, as Cordelia Oliver observed in 1979, 'an international reputation for unusually imaginative and interesting work'.[14]

Prior to 1970 the Citizens' had had an uneven history not dissimilar to that of many reps founded during or shortly after the War. Like Salisbury, it had benefitted from the financial support of CEMA during the War years. It was, however, essentially the product of a particular combination of talent, vision and determination in the person of James Bridie, who must take most of the credit not only for its foundation but for its early sense of direction. Aiming at the establishment of 'a fully professional Scottish National Theatre', Bridie began operations at the small Athenaeum Theatre in 1943, and after two seasons transferred to the Royal Princess's Theatre in the Gorbals on a ten-year lease.[15] When the lease ran out, Glasgow Corporation secured the theatre for the company for a small rent.

From the opening production in the Gorbals building – Priestley's *Johnson over Jordan* – until the late sixties, the policy remained close to Bridie's original intention: to present the best of British and European drama and to encourage new plays by Scottish writers. On average, one or two new Scottish plays were indeed given every season, though Bridie's own are the only ones to have survived beyond their time. Arden's *Armstrong's Last Goodnight* – a play set in sixteenth-century Scotland though not by a Scottish author – was premièred at the theatre in 1964.

By 1960 however the content of the repertoire had already shown signs of the change occurring throughout British theatre with the production that year of three one-act plays by Ionesco. There was evident need for the opportunity to take risks with contemporary plays that were important but might not attract large audiences and many of which required more intimate and informal staging than was possible in the Victorian auditorium. In an enterprising move Michael Goldberg, the chairman of the board, proposed, and himself injected a good deal of money into, the purchase and conversion of premises next door into a studio theatre. The scheme was approved and the Close Theatre in 1965 became one of the first studio theatres to be opened as part of a repertory theatre complex. Its first season began with a double bill of Genet plays and continued to present an adventurous programme of recent, new or otherwise unconventional drama from Britain, Europe and the USA until it was unfortunately closed for good by a fire in 1973. One indirect consequence of this permanent closure and the lack of money to rebuild has probably been to strengthen the imperative felt by the current directors to ensure an experimental and adventurous attitude to work presented in the main house. (In 1981 the Tron Studio Theatre, a new small-scale independent theatre venue for experimental and new work, opened in the city centre – in effect a replacement for the Close.)

The late sixties at the Citizens' were however marred by a rapid succession of directors, and murmurings of dissatisfaction with the Theatre Board became an outcry in 1969 when it refused to renew the contract of the most recent director, Robert Cartland, who had been appointed only the year before. Audiences had dwindled, largely because of the deteriorating neighbourhood but partly because of an insufficiently appealing artistic programme. The newly appointed director in 1969 was Giles Havergal, until then director at Watford, who was asked to plan a more broadly popular programme.

The groundswell of discontent with, and within, the board culminated in 1969 in several major changes in its constitution which were to have important and long-lasting effects. Several of the 'old guard' on the board left, a new chairman was elected, William L. Taylor (a lawyer and one-time Labour leader on the city council), and by 1970, stemming mainly from his initiative, there was a freshly constituted board that included officially appointed representatives from the city and regional councils, the two universities, the Royal Scottish Academy of Music and Drama and the Glasgow School of Art, together with elected representatives from the Citizens' Theatre Society: the playgoers. There was one further significant shift. Whereas Bridie, as chairman of the original board, had instigated a committee-run theatre with powers to approve and vet the play-list, the new board recognised the changed circumstances and vested responsibility for artistic policy in the director. Final approval of the season's plays is still subject to board approval but the authority and judgement of the director are given proper acknowledgement. This, together with the increased democracy and spread of interests in the board's constitution, has led to a far healthier and more harmonious relationship between board and director. And since that change there has been no major upset to interrupt the theatre's artistic development.

The real beginnings of the current distinctive Citizens' style came in Havergal's second season. The direction of the theatre was to be a multiple one, consisting of Havergal himself as director of productions and, occasionally, actor, Philip Prowse (who had worked with him at Watford) as designer/director and Robert David MacDonald as dramaturg/playwright: three individuals who shared common, if not identical, artistic goals and who have proved themselves capable of working well together. In addition to giving the direction of the theatre an increased range of talent and easing the burden from the shoulders of one man, this arrangement reflected the Citizens' concern with 'total' theatre in which design, acting, writing and directing were all seen as equally important, integral features.

It was from the 1970–1 season onwards, too, that the Citizens' became a 'company theatre' – at least so far as financial constraints allowed. A company of eighteen actors was formed, all of whom were paid the same, most of whom were young (though many such as Michael Gwilym have gone on to make major reputations for themselves at the Royal Shakespeare Company and elsewhere). The organisational hierarchy was minimised (the names of *all* theatre staff are listed in every programme alphabetically, whether director or wardrobe assistant). Even though a permanent company proved impossible to maintain, the theatre was soon able to draw regularly upon a sizeable pool of actors who were keen to work in the Citizens' style, prepared to play large roles and small: as close an approximation to a permanent ensemble as it was possible to get.

A third strand in the new policy was the concern to widen the social range of the audience and increase audience sizes from the low levels of the late sixties. In 1975 the special low-price scheme was introduced in which all seats in the house were sold at fifty pence. By 1980 the price had risen to ninety pence but still, in comparison to average seat-prices elsewhere, remarkably low. The thinking behind this – which the box office figures substantially bear out – was that far from reducing the theatre's income such a policy actually would generate more by drawing people in who might otherwise not have risked coming to see a show not familiar to them. One measure of this (but only one) is given in the results of an audience survey conducted in 1976 which showed that not only were audiences much younger than the average of the population but that they were in fact 'younger even than is usual among theatre audiences generally' (forty-three per cent of audiences were under twenty-one, for plays as varied as *Hamlet, Sailor Beware* and *Thyestes*).[16] Between 1969 and 1979, moreover, average attendances almost doubled.

What really gives the Citizens' its *raison d'être* however is the repertoire itself and the quality of the theatrical experience offered. While there had been many notable new plays premièred at the Citizens', the artistic policy is less to do with new plays *per se* and more to do with finding production styles that will make every performance, whether of a classic or a contemporary play, a new, eye-opening experience for the audience. Much of the creative energy has been directed to fresh interpretations of the classics, particularly Shakespeare and other Elizabethans and Jacobeans. The first Havergal production of *Hamlet* (in September 1970), for example, was an attempt to present the play 'as a disaffected youngster's view of the generation gap'[17] stunningly and expressively staged: the set a box within a box and almost everything including costumes in black. It outraged the tastes and preconceptions about staging Shakespeare of many adults (there were, Havergal recalls, thirty days of letters to the press about it – the biggest arts scandal in Glasgow since the Picasso exhibition in the thirties!),[18] and schools cancelled their bookings – but youngsters were excited by it and came on their own in droves.[19] As the years went by the style became more assured and often more daring. The company seemed most in their element with productions of Genet, the early Brecht, Büchner, Edward Bond and the Jacobeans. The production in 1975 of *Thyestes* for example sought to

29. *Thyestes*, by Seneca: The Citizens' Theatre, Glasgow, 1975, directed and designed by David Hayman. Photo: Mike Henderson.

disprove the common notion that Senecan tragedy was unstageworthy. Director David Hayman set his production in tribal Kenya and filled the stage with a gloomy mist from which at the opening of the play the dim figures of Masai warriors and the sound of drum music emerged. The translation of Seneca into ritualised tribal antagonisms caused bewilderment and excitement as the contrasting reviews of the production testify. Whatever the final judgements, it proved without doubt that a stunning, vivid presentation could be given of a play probably not performed professionally since the Jacobean period.

Some of the triumverate's most interesting and ambitious work has been the direct product of their own artistic collaboration – notably the plays written by MacDonald and directed and designed by Prowse, with Havergal in the cast: *Chinchilla* (on Diaghilev) in 1977, and *A Waste of Time* (an adaptation of Proust's *Remembrance of Things Past*) in 1980. Both were investigations in different ways of the many-faceted relationship between art and life and the design played a creative role in both in communicating the experience at the core of the plays. The setting for *A Waste of Time* consisted of a series of gilt picture frames enclosed one within another from the proscenium arch inwards: 'It is life in a picture-frame', commented Ned Chaillet of *The Times*, and it helped to clarify Proust's 'obsessive transformation of life into art'.[20] The use of the large mirrored background in *Chinchilla* similarly suggested the artist's obsession with his own image as well as the mirroring of life which was the function of his art. The play was, according to MacDonald, not an essay in biography, 'not an exercise in backstage nostalgia, but a backstage drama of what life in the theatre is really like';[21] or, in the words of Michael Coveney (in *The Financial Times*), the real business of this 'relentlessly aphoristic text' was 'to pinpoint with much glee the jealousies, quarrels and personal rivalries endemic to any cooperative artistic endeavour'.[22] The mirror was there to reflect not merely life but the art of the stage itself as it unfolded before its audience.

It is often said that the Citizens' is in essence a designer's theatre and the acting as such the weakest link. There has on occasion been more than a grain of truth in this, as many of the reviews of particular productions suggest. What, on the other hand, is also true is that rather different criteria are used than is usual when casting is done at the Citizens'. 'Stage presence', 'watchability', ability to work not only in an ensemble but as part of a dynamic stage picture are key qualities that are sought.[23] Voice seems sometimes to receive lesser attention – which accounts for some of the criticisms made. But equally, on innumerable occasions, the acting has been expressive in a fuller, more bodily sense than is usual on the British stage. Robert Cushman probably catches the experience of many in this comment upon a Goldoni production at the Citizens': 'I generally begin in Glasgow by finding the playing hopelessly inadequate to the sophistication demanded of it, and then adjust as the evening proceeds and the production creates its own world.'[24]

A further complaint, voiced less now than in the past, has been that there is no longer any effort made to nurture new Scottish playwriting talent. MacDonald is of course a Scottish playwright but is in no need of nurturing, having established himself now as a writer of national stature (the Citizens' production of his *Summit Conference* (1978) was recently revived, with new cast, for a West End run). Part of the reason for the lack of commitment to Scottish playwrights is that the directors see their commitment to pursuing artistic worth and a particular kind of theatrical experience as having a higher priority. Coupled with this is the fact that most of the new plays received by the Citizens' from aspiring Scottish writers have been wedded to the naturalistic mode that has now been shunned at this theatre. Whatever the loss involved in the new policy there can be little doubt that it has been far outweighed by the gains. As Havergal explains,[25] repertory will work at its best only when there are people who are prepared to be 'odd-balls', to go against the tide. He believes that the standards set by the National Theatre and Royal Shakespeare Company have had a dulling effect upon those in regional theatre who feel the most they can do is provide second-rate, small-scale versions of what the national companies offer. Only a handful of reps, he claims, such as Stoke, have dared to commit themselves wholeheartedly to work

30. *Chinchilla*, by Robert David MacDonald: Citizens' Theatre, Glasgow, 1977, directed and designed by Philip Prowse. Photo: John Vere Brown.

that is genuinely exciting and peculiar to their theatre, their audience and their own directors' creative imaginations. There can be little dispute about the Citizens' rightful claim to be one of those few.

SALISBURY PLAYHOUSE

Glasgow and Nottingham are essentially metropolitan reps, their catchment area is mostly the city, the suburbs and the numerous satellite towns that look naturally towards the city centre for their share of professional arts in the region. Salisbury Rep – formed in 1945 as an Arts Council-run theatre following the successful operation of a wartime regional theatre there from 1943 – has a life-span similar to that of Glasgow and Nottingham, but its role has been different in significant respects. Salisbury is a small city by any standards (pop. 35 000), notable for its cathedral and its proximity to the army garrison and as a good base from which to tour the rural south of England. Its value as a theatre centre, from the first, lay less in its playing to the citizens of Salisbury than in providing an 'outgoing' regional service to the whole of a widely spaced and largely rural catchment area – that is, to Wiltshire, Berkshire, Hampshire and even to Somerset. In the early post-War years, the experiment proved disappointing in both financial and audience terms and when Southampton eventually got its own theatre in 1951 the Arts Council took the not surprising decision to withdraw from management of the Salisbury Rep. Southampton made far more sense as a regional centre that could also rely on substantial support from local audiences (which Salisbury was never able to do) and the Arts Council wanted to withdraw anyway from direct funding (the Southampton theatre was to have its own Board), so the Salisbury Theatre was handed over to a new locally formed non-profit distributing company. The new Salisbury company, the Arts Theatre Company, struggled on with an unchanged policy, still running two operations, one at the theatre and the other geared to regional touring, but made ever-increasing losses. The crisis was reached in 1953 when losses had become such that touring had to stop and a plea for greater support was issued to the city and in particular the playgoers – as a result of which the theatre was saved from bankruptcy and audience attendances began to creep up again. Also in 1953 the theatre changed its name from the Arts Theatre to the Playhouse (considered less highbrow-sounding).[26]

With the fortunes of the theatre at last showing signs of recovery the then theatre manager, Michael Wilde, moved on elsewhere. His replacement, in 1955, was Reginald Salberg, whose experience of managing a theatre in Preston and running his own company in Hull, his general business acumen and his rare ability to combine a love of theatre with a 'sixth sense' about what in practice would work in a given social context, were to prove invaluable to the Playhouse for more than twenty years. When he took over as theatre manager – and at Salisbury it has until recently been the manager, not an artistic director, who has carried responsibility for policy – plays were still being performed with only one desperately inadequate week's rehearsal (and even then only daytime rehearsals because of performances in the evenings). His primary concerns were therefore to lift the standard of performances and to ensure stability and growth. He began, for example, to experiment with alternative large and small cast plays and found that in this way at least a quarter of all the forty or so plays in the season could be given two weeks' rehearsal. Recognising that touring was too expensive an operation he went out to entice audiences from the region into Salisbury by systematically contacting organisations within a thirty-five mile radius and encouraging party bookings. Coach parties have been a significant feature of Playhouse audiences ever since. Advertising was increased and many company members became involved in talking to Women's Institutes and such-like groups throughout the area.

As a result the next twenty years saw steady progress in establishing the Playhouse once again as the region's theatrical centre. From 1960 an increasing number of plays were run for two weeks and within a further seven years a three-week run had become the norm. Such was the success of Salberg's managerial policy and the reliability and general improvement of standards that by 1976 many plays were being given a four- or even five-week run when it was judged that they would have sufficient audience appeal – *Cowardy Custard* ran for five weeks in 1976, and played to eighty per cent capacity. Indeed John Bavin in his history of the playhouse asserts that each increase in the length of run has brought about an increase in audience attendance – attributable, he suggests, at least in part to the fact that it is 'easier to find a dozen or so plays with audience appeal, rather than having to find forty-eight each year'.[27]

By the early 1970s the need for a new building had become paramount. The company had been housed since its origin in 1943 in the old Picture House, itself a converted chapel built in 1869. Bavin has described the 'cramped and slum-like conditions in which the actors work',[28] and in 1965, now that the theatre had become well established and audiences had shown that it was wanted, the planning for its replacement was at last given the green light. From drawing-board to completion took many years but the outcome proved worth waiting for. The new playhouse, designed by the architect of the much-admired Mercury Theatre in Colchester (Norman Downie with Christopher Morley as Consultant) opened in 1976 on a site still close to the city centre. The auditorium seats 516 (compared with 400 in the old building) in a single raked tier with excellent sightlines and an adequate open proscenium stage. A studio theatre, seating approximately 100, was added together with extensive workshop facilities.

Salberg had announced that once the new building had opened he would retire as theatre manager but remain as a part-time consultant and Roger Clissold, director of productions since 1970, was appointed artistic director. Clissold saw his main task as being to continue and to develop the policy that had served the theatre so well and for so long – and audience attendances remained high. Only in one respect was there any switch of emphasis and that was in the considerably increased attention to new plays. Whereas in the old theatre experimental drama had been necessarily confined to Monday nights when there was no performance of the main show, now the Studio allowed a more regular and more adventurous pro-gramme (beginning in February 1977 with *Kennedy's Children*) both of modern drama and of small-scale shows, poetry readings and theatre workshops for young people. Work for young people had in fact been an important aspect of the company's work since 1965 with the formation of 'Stage 65', a still-thriving young people's group who meet regularly to develop their own theatre work under professional guidance, often towards performance in the theatre. The following year, too, saw the start of a regular pattern of schools tours by members of the professional company, under the direction of Clissold (at that time a trainee assistant director at the Playhouse). In 1967, the 'Theatrescope' company was set up with a specific brief to tour not only schools but arts centres and other venues in the region, presenting a wide range of plays and documentaries on contemporary issues, and occasional Monday night performances in the main house. Specifically for schools, 'play days' on the set texts were organised, usually involving a demonstration in the morning of various critical and theatrical problems of interpretation followed by a complete performance in the afternoon. All this activity was continued and extended in the new playhouse.

The play policy at Salisbury offers an interesting example of the way in which a repertory theatre serving a predominantly rural area and audi-ences conservative in their tastes can none the less provide a programme that both caters for those tastes and attempts to extend them. Richard Findlater, in an article for *Time and Tide* in as early as 1961, noted at Salisbury 'the catholicism of a good rep's range' and the 'changing appetites of its audience'.[29] Top of the box-office ratings, he discovered, were *A Taste of Honey* and *Man for all Seasons* (both ninety-nine per cent capacity), with *Pygmalion*, the pantomime and *The Boyfriend* close behind (all ninety per cent), and even as demanding and disturbing a play as *Long Day's Journey into Night* played to average houses of sixty-six per cent – leading him to conclude that 'Audiences have grown increasingly more adventurous in the last few years.' Miller, Shaw, Shakespeare and Anthony Shaffer are frequently to be found in the repertoire, together with 'safer' but by no means unworthy plays such as *Victoria Regina* on the one hand and the 'riskier' recent and new drama such as Nichols' *Privates on Parade* and the première of *84 Charing Cross Road* on the other. Salberg himself has learned that, far from there being simply one homogeneous audience for theatre in the area, there are in fact three quite distinct audiences: those who come to see *Not Now Darling*, those for the classic or modern-classic play and those for the more adventurous *Privates on Parade* type of drama – a characteristic confirmed by Clissold, one of Salisbury's longest-serving play directors.[30] The programme for each season – now as much as in the past – has to be planned carefully with each of these potential audiences in mind. The fact that the resulting programme closely resembles the formulae adopted by many reps should not disguise the care, thought and backlog of experience which are invested in that choice.

From the late sixties onwards, when runs became normally three to four weeks in duration and the number of plays reduced to eleven in any one season, the pattern has usually included: the Christmas pantomime, a classic (e.g. Shakespeare), a modern classic (e.g. Shaw), a comedy (from Molière to Coward), a 'middle-of-the-road' drama (e.g. Priestley or Rattigan), a thriller, a modern 'avant-garde' play, and a première. Whereas the pantomime, however, would run for six weeks, the avant-garde plays would usually be scheduled for a shorter two-and-a-half-week run and slotted in at the end of the season so as not to upset the normal rehearsal schedule. The avant-garde has never proved a box-office attraction in Salisbury, but in this way the responsibility that the management has felt towards new and recent work, and towards the smaller but significant audiences that do exist for it, can be met. This positive attitude to programming that might seem on the surface to be formula-bound has clearly paid off in terms of audience support. In 1976, the year in which the Playhouse moved to its new home, Salberg proudly recalled the contrast between the theatre's 'position of near despair' in the early fifties and its recent achievement, able now to run most of its productions for four weeks with attendances over the previous years averaging eighty per cent of capacity.[31]

The remarkably successful *84 Charing Cross Road* – handsomely staged in 1981 with the aid of a commercial sponsor (Benson and Hedges) – is not untypical of the Salisbury repertoire. Adapted from the best-selling novel by Helene Hanff, which was itself based on the exchange of letters across the Atlantic over a period of twenty years between herself and a London antiquarian bookseller, it received critical acclaim for its 'civilised', 'delightful' qualities, its 'amusing and moving moments' and its perceptive account both of the developing relationship between two distant people and of the different worlds they inhabited.[32] Though technically a new play, it hardly broke new ground in form or in content, but nor was it the product of a management determined to stay still and play merely to known tastes. Its transfer to the West End was deserved and not unexpected.

The Playhouse's most recent director, David Horlock, who took over the reins from Clissold in 1982, has endorsed the policy that has clearly worked so well in the past. The programme has to be, he argues, a developing one but which builds at the same time upon the strong tradition of theatre-going that now exists in Salisbury: the fuller and wider the programme of plays the better for both company and audience. He quotes with satisfaction, for example, the recent playing of Sherman's *Bent* (a disturbing drama about the treatment of homosexuals in Nazi Germany) in the Studio in tandem with the *Reluctant Debutante* on the main stage.[33] This concern with the gradual but positive extension of the repertoire has been the consistent hallmark of the Playhouse's approach.

One measure of the success of the Salisbury policy and particularly of the high level of activity it has involved was provided by a recent audience survey[34] which revealed that, in 1979 as a whole, 341 performances were given in the main auditorium and 135 in the Studio; there were forty-seven performances on tour in Wiltshire and Hampshire and a further eighty-eight in London with the transfer of *Under the Greenwood Tree* and *Old Herbaceous* to the West End. Box office and other earned income accounted for over sixty per cent of total income – a much higher percent-

31. *84 Charing Cross Road*, by Helene Hanff, adapted and directed by James Roose Evans: Salisbury Playhouse, 1981. Photo: Peter Brown.

age than is earned by most theatres. Over fifty per cent of the audiences travelled more than fifteen miles each way to the theatre, and over thirty per cent of audiences were parties – which means that ticket prices have to be kept as low as possible to help compensate for the increased costs to patrons of transport.

Despite the Playhouse's standing as one of the most successful regional reps, funding from the local authorities has remained a continual disappointment. The Arts Council generally prefers to have an equal partnership in theatre provision between itself and the local authorities, whereas in Salisbury Arts Council support accounted in 1981 for eighty-four per cent of the theatre's total subsidy. Both the city and the county had contributed generously to the costs of the new building but, as the theatre management argued in 1980, 'having been given the means to build this splendid and much loved theatre, we must plead for the funds to run it!'.[35] Some small increase was received in subsidy from the local authorities in the following year, but it is to be hoped that their contribution in the future will more adequately reflect the contribution that the Playhouse itself has made to the life of the area.

THE VICTORIA THEATRE, STOKE-ON-TRENT

In 1965 Peter Cheeseman claimed that a new kind of theatre had been springing up in Britain, with new aims and ambitions: the 'community-based repertory theatre' with a permanent professional company of actors living in the town and 'a creative life closely linked to the area it serves'.[36] If this was so, there can be little dispute that Cheeseman's own venture at the Victoria Theatre, Stoke-on-Trent, stands as the forerunner and one of the foremost of this new breed of reps. Beginning life in 1962, the Victoria has maintained over twenty years a continuity and consistency of policy that have established the theatre firmly in its community and as part of its cultural and social fabric. Cheeseman, again in 1965, articulated his belief in the need for a theatrical art that 'must spring from our contact with this community' and pinpointed four major conditions that he felt had to be fulfilled to this end:

1. Actors and actresses must stay together in Stoke as long as possible, so that they get to know one another, the community, and the feelings of the people who come to the theatre;
2. Writers must work as closely as possible with us so that they get to know us, the theatre and the audience;
3. I must stay here as long as I am useful to the theatre and the place – an active lifetime if possible – and I certainly plan to;
4. We must all work together sympathetically and sensitively as a group of artists, ready to respond in a positive way, but as artists, to the needs and demands of the community.[37]

Remarkably, those conditions have been fulfilled to a degree that even

Cheeseman might have doubted possible. If the momentum has been lost in recent years, this has been due not to a loss of faith in the ideal nor to any failure to translate those ideals into working practice, but more to an economic climate that has stymied the natural and logical expansion of the work and, above all, the move into a new, larger and more fitting building – plans for which have been on the table for many years. Nevertheless, for the past two decades, in a converted cinema desperately short of space and technical resources, the theatre has built an international reputation for its new plays, its documentaries, its ensemble acting, its commitment to theatre-in-the-round and above all its role as a genuinely community theatre.

The theatre actually had its origins in the pioneering work of Stephen Joseph – vigorous advocate of theatre-in-the-round, director and teacher extraordinary – who had formed his Studio Theatre Company in 1955 to play in Scarborough in the summer and tour theatreless towns around the North of England at other times of the year. Four years later, Newcastle-under-Lyme (next door to Stoke-on-Trent) was included in its schedule and before long the borough council gave its support to the company's plans to set up a permanent theatre-in-the-round in the town. The policy was for a variety of plays but with an emphasis upon new work by young writers working with the company (Alan Ayckbourn's *Mr Whatnot*, for example, was premièred in 1963). Joseph stressed the paramount import-ance of 'writing plays with a company in mind, of writer and company being close together, of writer and audience being known to each other, of the writer being imbued with the experience of acting as well as writing',[38] and this was a principle that Cheeseman worked to put into practice in later years. Joseph's dedication to theatre-in-the-round stemmed from his belief that it led invariably to the increased contribution of the audience to a performance because they were more intensely aware of what the actors were doing. In the face of television entertainment, theatre-in-the-round offered something distinct and profound: drama in its essentials, not reduced by trappings. 'The actor', Joseph claimed, 'is the most important person in the theatre. The audience is essential. The writer is useful (par-ticularly if he is a member of the company).' The director was important for his directing but even more so because 'he will set the whole tone of the theatre's work, [and] he will be the more important the less he directs each actual play'.[39] This emphasis upon the vitality and communicative power of the performed event was one to which Cheeseman – who was appointed manager of the venture when it began – wholeheartedly subscribed. It was all the more unfortunate therefore that yet another Board-versus-Director clash took place within four years of the start of the Stoke enterprise, with Joseph and Cheeseman on opposing sides. Cheeseman, though in name the theatre manager, had become by 1966 in effect the artistic director of the theatre while Joseph, with tongs in fires elsewhere, monitored from a distance. In distressing circumstances Joseph, suffering from terminal cancer at the time, together with his small board of directors, had rejected the efforts of Cheeseman and others to give the theatre a stronger local base by enlarging and including more local representatives on the board. Cheeseman was sacked; local support for his case grew and before long the Studio Theatre Company was officially wound up and a new company, the Stoke-on-Trent and North Staffordshire Theatre Trust, formed, with strong local representation and a new degree of security assured; and Cheeseman was immediately appointed, formally, artistic director.

From there onwards the enterprise continued with renewed strength and direction, and the company's reputation for new work grew year by year. Writers who were encouraged to work in close association with the company included Peter Terson (the Vic's resident playwright, 1966–8), Tony Perrin, C.G. Bond and Bill Morrison.

But the company is probably best known for its documentaries. These company-researched presentations have provided the main link that was sought between the theatre and the people of Stoke, Newcastle and the surrounding towns that constituted the Potteries. And it is the form that has brought together most clearly the company's concern with new work and with ensemble playing. Perhaps the most distinctive feature of the documentary – and that which in Cheeseman's eyes separates it from the play – is the reliance upon *primary* source material, put together collectively by a team of people drawn from the company: not the product of one writer who takes ideas suggested by company improvisations, but the result of the combined efforts of director, writer, actors, designer and secretarial team in researching and compiling and shaping original documented material into theatrical performance. Whether it be a show about the present or about recent or more distant history – about the current crisis in the local steel industry, about the building of the railways or about Stoke in the Civil War – the principle remains the same. All the words spoken must be authentic: the words actually used by the historical or contemporary figures depicted or by contemporary historians, with only the most minor alterations allowable for the sake of clarity. 'If there is no primary source material available on a particular topic', argues Cheeseman, 'no scene can be made about it.'[40] No doubt Cheeseman's study of history at university in Sheffield had much to do with his enormous respect for historical authenticity. *The Knotty*, for example, Stoke's third documentary (about the building of the local railway), required research by the team into books, original documents, diaries, letters, newspaper articles, plus tape-recorded interviews with former railwaymen who had worked on the old North Staffordshire Railway. The research process took six months or more, involving first the director and the resident writer (Peter Terson); then a research group of actors and actresses not involved in the rehearsal or performance of the play prior to the documentary (deliberately a small cast play) took over specific areas of research and joined in the general discussions about the shape and storyline the material was likely to take. A rehearsal period of three to five weeks then tested and developed ideas in theatrical terms – sometimes with the further help of some of the railwaymen themselves – until the final structure and script were arrived at.[41]

Despite the seemingly dry and laborious method employed, the documentaries in performance have nearly all been immensely successful and popular. Rather than dramatised history lessons they have been (in Cheeseman's words) the celebration of a community's stories,[42] and as such have struck chords of recognition in those many in the audience connected in some way with the events, traditions or people depicted and the issues raised. Perhaps the most obvious illustration at work was *Fight for Shelton Bar* (1974), which dealt with the imminent crisis in the area brought about by proposals to close down the nearby steelworks. The story told was always updated night by night by a speech from a member of the works' action committee, and on a number of occasions the performance was followed by a debate in the auditorium. *The Knotty* too proved to be an extraordinary success and has been revived four times since its first presentation in 1966.

The national and international interest shown in these documentaries has been considerable, although Cheeseman makes no claim to having invented the form, which he readily acknowledges has its origins in the American 'living newspapers' of the 1930s by way of Joan Littlewood's work before and after the War. Despite the general interest shown, moreover, the documentaries have been above all of and for the people of Stoke and North Staffordshire. Indeed Cheeseman believes that it has been through these productions that local people have realised that 'we were serious about our attachment to the district', such has been the extent of audience response.[43]

There have been to date nine documentaries, the latest of which was *Miner, Dig the Coal* in 1981, together with numerous revivals of the more successful ones. But the theatre's general output and activity level, quite apart from the documentaries, has also been impressive. It is a year-round theatre, playing forty-nine weeks per year with only a three-week break in June. Plays are performed in true repertory – easier at Stoke because of the virtual absence of set-changing required by in-the-round staging. And the repertoire has been varied, notable recent successes having been, for example, a company adaptation of *Pinocchio*, Dario Fo's politically-barbed farce *Can't Pay, Won't Pay*, and Shakespeare's *A Midsummer Night's Dream*. The latter production, directed by Nigel Bryant in 1982, was typical of Stoke at its best, relying not on elaborate costume or set but on the liveliness and inventiveness and pace of acting and direction: a production set out of period that had, in the words of one critic, 'non-stop energy, burning creativity and a delightful taste for the outrageous'.[44]

For a number of years in the early 1970s the 'Vic' maintained a Community Office – in the main a separate project financed under the government's special 'Quality of Life' scheme; there has been, until the financial cut-backs recently intervened, an advice service available to groups in the area who might want help with amateur theatre work or talks from theatre staff; and there were, between 1973 and 1976, frequent and highly successful tours by the Vic Road Show to pubs, clubs and community centres in the area. Only a skeletal form of this 'extra-mural' service now remains. There has also (as we have already observed in Chapter 7) been the persistent endeavour to maintain a genuinely permanent, resident acting company: for Cheeseman an essential component in his concept of a theatre of and for the community. Without such a company indeed the company-researched documentaries would have been all but impossible. But holding a company together against an array of competing pressures has proved increasingly difficult. The scheme devised to encourage and reward actors prepared to stay with the company for a period of years – an incremental salary structure based on years spent with the company – has

32. *A Midsummer Night's Dream*: Victoria Theatre, Stoke-on-Trent, 1982, directed by Nigel Bryant. Photo: Victoria Theatre.

33. *Pinocchio*, by Warren Jenkins and Brian Way: Victoria Theatre, Stoke-on-Trent, 1982, directed by Mark Dornford-May. Photo: Gerald Wells.

had to be abandoned for lack of money, and the size of the regular company has been reduced.

The heyday may seem to be over. Cheeseman has over the years, and with the invaluable aid of his staff (notably of his administrator from 1966 to 1974, Vivian Nixson), achieved miracles with a minimum of resources. But the failure of grant-aid to match inflation has meant a smaller company and a smaller number of plays in the repertoire each season. The need for a new theatre building, though, is manifest. The achievements at Stoke compare with those (if they do not surpass them) at any other regional theatre and the commitment to the area is astonishing in its continuity. While some would argue that the excitement of the 'Vic' lies in its very 'shoestring' quality – its tininess, intimacy and seeming ordinariness in contrast with the vitality of so many of its productions and the ingenuity, innovation and stimulus necessitated by those very conditions – it is also clear that many of the steps forward the theatre has wished to take (such as improvement of audience comfort, catering services and, not least, backstage facilities) have been frustrated by lack of adequate premises.

At the time of writing, a site for a new theatre has been allocated (close to the present Vic and to the boundary between Stoke and Newcastle), architects have been briefed, detailed plans drawn and capital funds for the building voted by three major local authorities (Newcastle, Stoke and the County of Staffordshire) and by the Arts Council. A public appeal is underway and the opening of the new building planned for 1986. The design is for a 600-seat theatre-in-the-round, retaining the present theatre's compactness and intimacy but allowing for much greater flexibility both in the staging of plays and in the presentation of such other events as concerts and recitals. It is to be hoped that one of the few reps in the country genuinely to have earned the title 'community theatre' – and ironically one of the few to have been by-passed in the wave of spending on new and renewed theatre buildings in the sixties and seventies – will at last get the facilities and resources with which to develop and sustain its community role.

THE MERSEYSIDE EVERYMAN THEATRE (LIVERPOOL)

If 'rep' tends to be associated in the public mind with the conventional, with a predictable programme of 'safe' classics and recent West End successes spiced with the occasional 'risk', then the Everyman might seem to require a whole new category. 'Alternative rep' might be one. From its very beginning it was conceived as something different, and the taking of risks came to be its *sine qua non*.

As with the commencement of all new ventures it was a particular combination of circumstances, individuals and timing that lifted the project off the ground. The founders of the company were themselves all recent graduates of Birmingham University sharing a common experience of student drama which was to give the enterprise its initial characteristic stamp – Martin Jenkins, a Liverpudlian who had done work at Stratford and the Nottingham Playhouse, Terry Hands, who had just finished an actor-training course at RADA, and Peter James, who had likewise completed a postgraduate course at the Bristol University Drama Department. In 1964 Jenkins managed to persuade a prominent local councillor and solicitor, Harry Livermore (now Sir Harry), of Liverpool's need for a new kind of theatre, one that would provide first and foremost a programme for young people and in particular regular school matinées of plays on the GCE examination syllabus. Though there were to be evening performances for adults too it was undoubtedly the 'school service' element that enabled Livermore to obtain grants from Liverpool City Council both to help set the project up and to pay for the matinées themselves. In a remarkably short period of time the Everyman was in business. Livermore set up a board of directors that was to prove, under his chairmanship until 1974, and that of his successor Alan Durband, immensely responsive and supportive through some trying periods. Premises were found in the form of a building on Hope Street adjacent to the university area, once a chapel, later a cinema and at that time housing a beat club in the cellar. (These were the days of a thriving popular music scene in Liverpool, with the Beatles having shot to fame only a year earlier.) For twelve months, theatre and club shared premises, which meant that theatre performances in the evenings had to be restricted to Mondays, Tuesdays and Wednesdays. None the less, a rough-and-ready thrust stage was built into the auditorium, designed by Jenkins, and productions relied – as Terry Hands has said – almost entirely upon the acting.[45] Scenery, inescapable in proscenium theatre, was to be virtually non-existent.

Liverpool at this time was probably ripe for such a venture. Not only had the Beatles put a new gloss upon the city's international reputation, but it had become the focus for many young folk musicians, poets and artists. And Sam Wanamaker's adventurous 'New Shakespeare Theatre' – though short-lived and driven to close for financial reasons several years earlier – had paved the way for a Liverpool theatre committed at least in part to new drama. The well-established Liverpool Playhouse meanwhile was providing worthy but only occasionally exciting productions of the conventional repertory fare (Shaw, Sheridan, Wilde, Priestley, Shakespeare) together with occasional forays into more recent and abrasive drama (*The Fire-Raisers* and *Luther* in 1962–3, *The Hostage* and *The Entertainer* in 1963–4). There was clearly room for a theatre of a different kind appealing more directly to newer and younger audiences.

On the face of it, the choice of plays for the evening performances in the first season did not look especially different from those at the Playhouse – *Henry IV, Part 1, The Servant of Two Masters, The Caretaker, An Enemy of the People*, for example. The changes in the content of repertoire were to come later. What was different was the noticeable emergence of an Everyman 'house-style': acting that had, in the words of Liverpool theatre critic and historian of the company's first ten years, Doreen Tanner, 'a unique collective personality . . . moulded by coherent direction and able to shape plays to its own purposes'.[46] The actors employed were generally young, capable of playing at breakneck speed and compensating for lack of experience by their energy, vitality and ensemble performances. There were also the regular school matinées coupled with frequent visits by members of the company to schools and other interested organisations to talk about the work together with many extra activities and events, such as poetry readings, organised in the theatre. Energy and adrenalin were key requirements for any member of the company.

The first six years were marked by determination, enthusiasm and the willingness to improvise. With the departure of Jenkins because of ill-health during the first gruelling season, the Everyman was led by Terry Hands until 1966(when he left for the RSC), and later by Peter James; and gradually its unique house-style began to gain a wide-spread reputation. If the artistic achievements were only rarely outstanding – though they did occur, in, for example, *Hedda Gabler* (1966) – what was emerging strongly was the verve, vigour and freshness of the acting, the ensemble playing in a variety of plays, and the concern to bring immediacy and contemporary relevance to all the plays tackled, from *Agamemnon* (underlining the Vietnam War parallel) to the mini-skirted modernity of *As You Like It*. It was in fact with the latter production (in 1967) that the company first achieved any form of national recognition – the London critics all enjoyed it – and their first full houses.

Audiences hitherto had been disappointingly thin, but the city council was sympathetic and agreed in 1966 to pay the whole of the Everyman's rent, which enabled the company then to take over the building fully and perform plays for the whole of the week. In the year of James' taking over as artistic director, the theatre gained a new full-time and highly able administrator in the person of John Gardner, and learned of the success of their application for grant-aid to the Arts Council. From then on the company was able to look forward with a degree of confidence and develop a high level of professionalism in its work. In that watershed year too came the production of a company-devised, musical documentary about the opening of the new Catholic Cathedral across the road, *The Mersey Funnel* – funny, irreverent, lively and naive, and above all a first step towards the local, musical-documentary style that was to become the Everyman's forte in later years. By the end of the 1967–8 season, attendances at the evening shows had risen by twenty-four per cent and in the afternoons by fourteen per cent.

The theatre's work for children, which ran in parallel with the adult

34. *Soft, or a Girl?*, by John McGrath: Everyman Theatre, Liverpool, 1971, directed by Alan Dossor. Photo: Everyman Theatre.

evening programme, evolved even more dramatically. The limitations had soon been realised of bringing school children to see the set play, and before long visits *to* the schools by actors were being organised, prior to the matinée performances, to talk about the play in question. By 1969, Paul Harman, originally an actor with the Everyman who had left to work with TIE companies in Coventry and Watford, had returned with a specific brief to develop the young people's work further. From education *about* theatre, the emphasis switched to education *through* theatre and in 1973 a three-year grant from the Gulbenkian Foundation was given to finance a joint project between the Everyman and Liverpool's Educational Priority Area organisation, under Eric Midwinter. For this period the 'Everyman Priority' team became based in one of the EPA schools and worked intensively with children in the underprivileged urban areas of Liverpool. Complementing this work, there was also a youth theatre group at the theatre for teenagers interested in learning theatre skills and putting on the occasional production in the theatre.

1970 saw the beginning of a new phase in the Everyman's history with the departure of Peter James to work as assistant to Frank Dunlop in setting up the new Young Vic Company in London (a company that was established, if not on the identical model of the Everyman, at least strongly influenced by its achievement in providing a young people's theatre) and the appointment of Alan Dossor as his successor. Dossor had already guest-directed at the Everyman (*Loot* in the previous season) and had worked with Cheeseman at Stoke and as a director at the Nottingham Playhouse, and he brought with him a more explicit commitment to work that would tackle political and social issues and offer perspectives on matters of specific concern to the area. A great admirer of Joan Littlewood's work, he asserted from the start that he was 'not interested in plays that did not relate to the community outside'.[47] Audience figures, though they had improved, were still disappointing, and one of Dossor's primary tasks was to try to build a regular and a wider audience.

His second production was a new documentary play with music about the well-known local personality Bessie Braddock, a Liverpool Labour MP active in the forties and fifties, called *The Braddocks' Time* – a clear pointer to the direction he wished the theatre to take. The production had its weaknesses and played to only thirty per cent houses, but it impressed John McGrath (founder of the 7:84 Company) enough to write some short plays for the theatre – collectively titled *Unruly Elements* – and then, in 1971, a rock musical about Liverpool and the generation gap called *Soft, or a Girl?*[48] The plot of this later play was a simple one, concerning two air-raid wardens from the Second World War who find themselves blown forward in time and their astonishment at the world thirty years on. But it was, for Dossor, the moment of 'breakthrough':[49] a form of theatre that accommodated political comment, local interest, popular music and exuberant comedy, and packed the theatre. Shows based on this recipe – sometimes by one author, sometimes, as at Stoke, emerging from the company itself – have subsequently become a common and expected part of the Everyman repertoire. Three of the most recent and successful examples have been Chris Bond's production of the company-devised *Love and Kisses from Kirkby* in 1978 and in the 1981–2 season Bob Eaton's musical biography, *Lennon*, followed by Brian Jacques' nostalgic look at Liverpool in 1950 ('just before they pulled it all down', as the publicity for the show put it), *Brown Bitter, Wet Nellies and Scouse.*

Dossor's account of the main features of the company's work during this peak period at the Everyman (up to his departure in 1975) stressed 'the tremendously important role the writers have played, John McGrath and the others . . . I've tried to give them as much freedom as possible, and they have stayed with the play, come down and watched rehearsals and worked with the company.'[50] Other writers who worked with the company during this period included Chris Bond (also a graduate of the Stoke venture, later to become artistic director of the Everyman), poets Adrian Henri and Roger McGough, Adrian Mitchell and Willy Russell. Russell, hitherto a local teacher, had been inspired by McGrath's *Unruly Elements* to try his hand at playwriting (an interesting further link in the chain of influences), and it was his own documentary musical about the Beatles, *John, Paul, George, Ringo . . . and Bert*, in 1974, that marked the next high point in the Everyman's fortunes. Its overwhelming success in Liverpool – due to Russell's authentic evocation of what had seemed like an era together with his suggestion of the bitter rewards of success and, not least, to Barbara

35. *Brown Bitter, Wet Nellies and Scouse*, by Brian Jacques: Everyman Theatre, Liverpool, 1981, directed by Bob Eaton. Photo: Everyman Theatre.

Dickson's brilliant rendering of the songs – led to a transfer to the West End later the same year.

But the local, musical documentary format was only the most obvious manifestation of the Everyman's style: the classics, such as *Measure for Measure*, and modern plays as diverse as *Murder in the Cathedral* and *The Caucasian Chalk Circle* (with an updated Liverpool-based prologue by McGrath) were also given with an unerring sharpness and clarity of direction. Mike Stott's controversial comedy *Funny Peculiar* was given its première at the Everyman (in 1975) before it too went on to the West End.

The next and most recent phase in the Everyman's history began with the rebuilding of the theatre itself, which had long been in need of renewal – a project financed, significantly, almost entirely by the theatre's supporters. From January 1976 to October 1977 while rebuilding was in progress the company went on tour (there had been a community touring unit of the company, Vanload, operating since 1973), presenting shows at clubs and pubs in Merseyside and further afield. Chris Bond, having acted and written for the company often in the past, took on the artistic direction of the company for the first year in the new building and kept the 'house-style' intact – aided by the fact that the new theatre had been a successful remodelling of the old, retaining its special 'personality' and flexible open staging but vastly improving backstage and front-of-house facilities. One of the highlights of that first season was undoubtedly the première of *Flying Blind* (set in contemporary Northern Ireland) by the new resident writer at the Everyman, Bill Morrison. Since then the fortunes of the theatre have oscillated. The next director was Pedr James, an accomplished television director who tended to do television-type plays with a consequent loss of the expected Everyman brashness, outgoingness and verve, and of audience support. As a deliberate and well-calculated act of policy, the appointment then followed of the extraordinary Ken Campbell – renowned for his rumbustious and hilarious 'Road Shows' at Stoke and elsewhere, and for his 'Science Fiction Theatre of Liverpool' which he started in 1976 in a local makeshift coffee-bar theatre. It was this venture which had inaugurated the National Theatre's Cottesloe Theatre the following year with a five-play science fiction cycle, *Illuminatus!* Campbell's production of *The Warp*, a ten-play cycle written by Neil Oram in collaboration with Campbell, presented in weekly episodes, was his most striking and innovative contribution to the Everyman before, not totally unexpectedly, he too moved on. He was succeeded in 1981 by Bob Eaton, himself an Everyman company member in previous seasons and with experience too as actor, writer and director at Stoke.

Two recent developments signify the change that has overtaken – and been largely the creation of – the Everyman. The first was the separation of the young people's theatre unit from the main company that took place in 1977. Once the Gulbenkian funds for the 'Priority' project had ended,

36. *John, Paul, George, Ringo . . . and Bert*, by Willy Russell: Everyman
Theatre, Liverpool, 1974, directed by Alan Dossor. Photo: *Liverpool Daily
Post and Echo*.

it became clear that there was a need for a professional young people's
theatre company that the Everyman's own resources were unable to
satisfy. The theatre's origins in work for schools had been left far behind;
its main thrust now was as a lively alternative to the mainstream rep in the
city centre and its appeal to young audiences incidental: important but not
exclusive. Paul Harman therefore left to set up the Merseyside Young
People's Theatre with a more specific schools brief and funding from the

local education committee to go with it. (The Everyman, however, still sustains its flourishing youth theatre group for local teenagers.)

A more recent – and ironic – development was the major change which took place in 1981 in the direction of the Liverpool Playhouse, bringing with it an implicit acknowledgement of the debt Liverpool owed to the Everyman. Upon the resignation of the actor-director, William Gaunt, and following a fine (and financially rewarding) production of Willy Russell's *Educating Rita*, the Playhouse board appointed a four-man directorship to bring new life back to the rep – all four of whom were Everyman graduates: Chris Bond, Willy Russell, Bill Morrison and Alan Bleasdale. And the plays chosen with which to open their first season (1981–2) could easily have been the programme at the Everyman: a revival of Bleasdale's *Having a Ball!* (first seen at Oldham; as drama critic Robin Thornber has described it, 'a black comedy about vasectomy and nuclear nerves'),[51] two adaptations by Chris Bond, *A Tale of Two Cities* and *Dracula*, together with a new play for the Upstairs studio theatre, *Blood on the Dole*, by local writer, Jim Morris. Whether or not Liverpool can cope with, or wants, two theatres committed to modern plays and new writing (or rewriting) is an open question. Bob Eaton, with as much enthusiasm for Alan Ayckbourn as for the musical-documentary, believes firmly that there is room for both theatres and that the change offers unusual opportunity to develop between them a livelier and more genuinely complementary programme for Liverpool audiences than has ever been possible before. Whatever the future direction of these two theatres, there can be no doubting that Liverpool theatre has in the past fifteen years undergone a sea-change, and for that the Everyman must be held primarily responsible.

THE ROYAL EXCHANGE THEATRE, MANCHESTER

Just as John Neville claimed for the Nottingham Playhouse in the mid sixties the status and function of a 'national theatre for the region', so in the mid seventies the founders of Manchester's Royal Exchange Theatre aimed to make their venture in effect the 'national theatre of the North'.[52] Since the opening of the theatre itself in the vast hall of the old Royal Exchange building, it has attracted the funds, resources and personnel to mount a successive series of productions many of which, without doubt, have compared with productions seen anywhere in London for the high quality of their casting, direction and presentation. Within a matter of only a few years, the Exchange had succeeded in establishing itself as one of the few genuinely major regional theatres, and with an international reputation. To date, some nine of its productions have transferred to London and *The Dresser* (which opened in Manchester in 1980) began a run on Broadway in October 1981. The aspirations of the artistic directors have led to a distinctive kind of theatre. Aiming for the highest possible standards has inevitably carried with it certain values and emphases which have clearly been reflected in the repertoire and ethos of the theatre and provide a strong contrast with the work of Manchester's other theatre companies.

Like Liverpool, Manchester is the centre of a massive industrial, commercial and residential conurbation, although the city centre itself has suffered from urban decay and a shift of population into the suburbs and satellite towns. Given its strategic location and its surrounding population of over three million within a thirty-mile radius, together with its historic part in the early development of repertory, it is surprising that until the late sixties Manchester supported only one small repertory theatre, the Library Company. By the mid seventies, however, the city was able to boast three permanent theatre companies, one of which (the Library) was operating at two separate theatre buildings. And at the fringes of Greater Manchester, there was now Bolton's Octagon Theatre (opened in 1967), as well as the longer-established Oldham Rep. It was certainly Manchester's role as a regional centre that helped clinch the argument for investing Arts Council,

37. *The Duchess of Malfi*, by Webster: Royal Exchange Theatre, Manchester, 1980. Cast: Helen Mirren, Mike Gwilym, Bob Hoskins; directed by Adrian Noble. Photo: Kevin Cummins.

city and county council money in the ambitious Exchange venture. What is it, though, that distinguishes the Exchange from the other nearby reps?

The Library, though it had tried to cater for all types of drama before the arrival of its competitors, now more appropriately concentrates in its small 300-seat theatre in the basement of the Central Library, upon small-cast and mainly modern plays, often plays with a social orientation and a good deal of 'grit' (the plays of Arthur Miller and Dennis Potter, and recent successes from the Royal Court, are not untypical). At its larger (500-seat) Forum Theatre in the city's southern suburbs, however, the emphasis is upon plays and shows with more popular appeal, exemplified by the whole season of musicals staged with great success in 1980–1. Contact Theatre Company, based at the small University Theatre, is geared very specifically to young audiences, being officially designated a young people's theatre company', and having a brief both to present plays at the theatre (often new work and often the plays of Brecht) and to operate a schools touring service and a broad range of youth and community theatre activities.

The fare offered at the Exchange has in contrast tended to have a classical and literary emphasis. Notable and characteristic productions have included *The Rivals* (1976), *The Lady from the Sea* (1978), *Waiting for Godot* and *The Duchess of Malfi* (both 1980) and *Philoctetes* (1982), and several new adaptations of novels such as *Crime and Punishment* (1978). They have been carefully and expensively cast, drawing 'stars' such as Helen Mirren, Leo McKern, Max Wall and, on frequent occasions, Tom Courtenay. The choice of plays may not be particularly adventurous (although *Philoctetes* could hardly be considered a safe bet at the box office) and even the new work has been of a kind that could have been written at any time during the last thirty or so years, lacking in the abrasiveness of much contemporary writing. The productions themselves may too lack the rough energy of much contemporary performance. But the theatre has likewise managed to avoid the conventional formula of repertoire planning. The directors clearly have their own enthusiasms and penchants and have not been afraid to reflect these in the choice of plays each season. And it has been a clear and stated part of their policy to avoid following the pace and the fashions set by the London theatre, even at the risk of sometimes appearing old-fashioned. Ronald Harwood's *The Dresser* serves as a useful example of the Exchange at its best. A new play but set in 1942, it dealt with the slipping fortunes of an ageing actor-manager (played by Freddie Jones) and the oscillating relationship between him and his dresser-cum-slave (Tom Courtenay) as the disintegrating world outside seems both to reflect and to intensify the stresses and strains of the backstage world that we witness. Michael Elliott's direction and the playing of the two main roles caught the humour and the sadness in the situation brilliantly and were served handsomely by the theatre itself, a point that was underlined at the time by critic David Mayer: the

38. *The Dresser*, by Ronald Harwood: Royal Exchange, 1980. Cast: Freddie Jones, Tom Courtenay; directed by Michael Elliot. Photo: Kevin Cummins.

play was 'so imaginatively staged in the Exchange's arena that I am at a loss to imagine how its spatial qualities can be preserved when the play makes its inevitable transfer to a West End proscenium play house'.[53] (The production transferred almost immediately to the Queen's Theatre, Shaftesbury Avenue – and did indeed, as it was also to do on Broadway, lose something of its imaginative staging in the process.)

There has certainly been an impressive number of finely wrought and often deeply satisfying productions. And they have been presented in a theatre building that must stand as one of the most innovative and exciting pieces of theatre architecture in Britain of this century: a purpose-built theatre-in-the-round that appears to hover like some enormous metallic spider in the vast space of the Royal Exchange: glistening twentieth-century steel and glass in a domed and pillared Victorian hall covering three quarters of an acre.

Although this theatre was built relatively late in the post-War resurgence of repertory, the seeds of the company itself were sown and its links with Manchester forged many years earlier. It was by no means a totally new venture: rather the product of a series of discontinuous but close collaborations between a number of individuals who shared similar views, aims and approaches. The beginnings can in fact be traced as far back as 1954 with the opening of the Piccolo Theatre Club in the premises of the by-then-defunct Chorlton Repertory Theatre in Manchester. There was just one season but it brought together some notable talents in the form of Frank Dunlop (director), Richard Negri (co-director and designer, later the resident designer at the Exchange and the designer of the new theatre itself), James Maxwell, Rosalind Knight and Eric Thompson (actors) and Caspar Wrede (director), nearly all of whom had trained at the influential Old Vic Theatre School under Michel Saint-Denis. All, with the exception of Frank Dunlop, were to become closely associated with the Exchange. The theatre company survived only one full year but had quickly achieved a reputation for lively, inventive and intelligent productions under the most restricted of conditions. In 1959 many of the group came together again, joined now by Michael Elliott, to form the 59 Theatre Company and presented a season of five plays at the Lyric Theatre, Hammersmith. The season, which included Elliott's production of *Brand*, was critically well received but financially disastrous.

For the next nine years this informal grouping of individuals worked together only occasionally – one opportunity being provided during Elliott's period as artistic director of the Old Vic before it became the temporary home of the National Theatre Company in 1963. The real opportunity to form a new company on a more permanent basis however came in 1968. Believing that London was too constricting an environment in which to evolve the kind of theatre that mattered to them, Elliott, Wrede and others were looking for a base in the regions when, fortuitously, it became clear that the Century Theatre Company, a North-West touring company based at Manchester's University Theatre, was intending to withdraw from the city. In 1968, the new 69 Theatre Company was formed (the title chosen to echo that of 59) and became based at the University Theatre, where for the next five years they presented twenty-one productions, seven of which, such as the revival of R.C. Sherriff's *Journey's End* and Jack Good's rock musical version of Othello, *Catch My Soul*, transferred to London. The quality of their work was beyond doubt. But although the company's arrival in Manchester was seen as a major and welcome new contribution to the city's cultural life, the arrangement was never likely to be a perfectly satisfactory or permanent one. The aspiration of '69' was essentially to develop into a major regional theatre. Delightful though the University Theatre was as a playing space, it was small (seating 300) and had to accommodate for a substantial period of each year productions by the university societies and the drama, language and literature departments. It was not surprising therefore that the company should begin looking after only a few seasons towards alternative, larger and more permanent facilities in Manchester. Its prestigious and often 'star-studded' productions certainly attracted audiences from far and wide and a national reputation, but, again not surprisingly, drew criticism from those who felt that the company was using the theatre merely as a tryout for London transfers and showed no real commitment to the needs and interests of audiences from the immediate locality, whether it be the campus or the surrounding working-class and largely immigrant populations of Rusholme and Moss Side.

It could indeed hardly be said that the company was offering a community theatre service, but the criticisms voiced were symptomatic of the company's own dilemma. Until adequate premises could be found the very discontinuity of their operation at the theatre together with its location some two miles away from the city centre was bound to restrict their activity and reinforce the impression of impermanence. None the less there was a scale, quality and stylishness of production brought to Manchester that had rarely been seen in the city in recent decades – apart from the increasingly rare tours of commercial, RSC or National Theatre productions to the two main commercial theatres, the Opera and Palace (both of which were highly unsuited to straight drama because of their size). And the argument for a major new theatre in Manchester – to complement, not compete with, the Library Theatre – had been most effectively put by demonstrating at least some of the possibilities in practice.

In due course, a solution was found. With the help of grants from the Arts Council, the city and the recently formed GreaterManchester Council, the go-ahead was given for Richard Negri's exciting design for a new theatre in the Exchange to be translated into reality. The company moved out of the University Theatre in 1973 – and was replaced almost immediately by the newly formed Contact Company: the product of a scheme conceived by Professor Hugh Hunt of the University's Drama Department with financial help from the University, the city and the Arts Council, a scheme that was to make far more appropriate use of the campus location and proximity to the inner-city suburbs. Following three years of irregular, occasional productions, first in a temporary tent-theatre in the Exchange and later in Manchester Cathedral, the 69 Company became officially the Royal Exchange Theatre Company in 1976, coinciding with the opening of the theatre itself. The company's core was its multiple directorship: Michael Elliott and Braham Murray (who had joined the company in 1968 from Century) – resident artistic directors; James Maxwell, Richard Negri and Caspar Wrede – artistic directors. From this point onwards the company was able to develop its clear commitment to Manchester and region: productions are now staged continuously from September to July and in addition to the main repertoire there is an extensive programme of occasional lunchtime and late-night performances of contemporary drama, lectures, chamber-music recitals, folk and brass band concerts, the annual amateur theatre festival each summer, and, in the foyer, craft fairs and exhibitions as well as the usual bar, cafeteria and restaurant facilities.

It is perhaps the theatre building itself that demands one's attention: Elliott has expressed the belief that 'the vast majority of the theatres we have built in this country since the war have proved partial or total failures because of a confusion or absence of purpose'.[54] Negri's conception for the Exchange Theatre was not, though, of an aesthetic idea but of 'an experience, and an envelope that would not only make possible but enforce that experience on the actor and the audience'. And in words that echo those of Stephen Joseph, some fifteen years earlier, Elliott justifies the choice of theatre-in-the-round: 'Why are we in the round? Because we believe that theatre is a happening, and that what happens among people has more effect than what happens the other side of a peep-hole.' The excitement felt by the theatre's directors has been shared by critics and audiences alike. The concentrated enclosure of the space can be both claustrophic when required and releasing. The mêlée of faces opposite can give a feeling of community, and can fade into nothingness (aided by the seven-sided shape of the auditorium, such that no one row of audience squarely faces another). The challenge it offers directors and designers is immense, and when overcome – more often than not through trusting to a stark simplicity of staging (as in Adrian Noble's splendid production of *The Duchess of Malfi*) – the results can be stunning. Equally, the disappointment felt at productions which fail to meet the challenge (either through timidity or through over-ambitiousness) is intensified by the sense that they have failed the building as much as the audience.

The multiple directorship certainly gives continuity and consistency to the policy and a proper opportunity to work and plan at a steady pace. But there is not and never has been a permanent company of actors. Plays are cast individually, although the Exchange prides itself on the number of excellent and well-known actors (Tom Courtenay and Trevor Peacock, for example) who are happy to return to the theatre because they value the high standards set and, not least, the unique acting experience that it offers. For Elliott it has been a matter of artistic principle, and not of economics, that plays should be given the strongest possible casts and not compromised by the inevitable limitations of range that will be found in the size of a permanent company that could be afforded by a regional theatre (see Chapter 7, p. 120). The frequent return of actors from season to season for perhaps one or two plays at a time does, in his view, allow for a steady building of common understanding between directors, actors and theatre space, and for the theatre to 'breathe', to benefit from new blood and avoid the staleness common in some European companies that remain static for decades.[55]

If the success of a theatre can be measured in terms of audience support, then undoubtedly the Exchange has triumphed just as the Nottingham

Playhouse did during its first five years, playing in 1980–1 for example to eighty-two per cent of its capacity; and there is little sign of any marked downward trend. While the company has clearly amply justified the effort and money invested in the new theatre building by the strength and quality of the majority of its productions, criticism has been levelled at the relative narrowness of its repertoire and the middle-class ethos of its house-style. (A recent *Guardian* review described the Exchange as 'southern and chic and orientated towards success').[56] An audience survey in 1981 certainly confirmed the tendency for the Exchange to draw higher proportions of its audience from the well-heeled Cheshire suburbs than did Contact or the Library, and for its audiences to be older (the proportion of eighteen- to twenty-four-year-olds among the audience was twenty-eight per cent at the Exchange, thirty-seven per cent at the Library and forty-one per cent at Contact).[57] But in its defence it must be said that the Exchange, whatever its limitations and whatever its artistic leanings, does provide high-quality theatre of a kind that is rarely available anywhere else in the North West and which complements remarkably well the programmes offered by the other two theatres in Manchester: this surely is a pattern of provision that makes eminent sense in a conurbation the size of Manchester. And unlike so many of the new theatres of the post-War boom, the auditorium at the Exchange still manages to retain the extraordinary sense of occasion, intimacy and expectation that not only marks good theatre design but provides an ever-present springboard for theatrical adventure in the future.

At the time of writing plans are afoot to launch a mobile theatre unit to tour the North, to be called the 'Young Exchange', with a repertoire of new and recent plays. The aim is to provide what is described as a 'job creation' scheme for young actors, funded by sponsorship and public appeal, and the mobile theatre itself will be a smaller, 400-seat version of the main Exchange arena. The plans, already well advanced, are a healthy sign that the Exchange is not allowing itself to rest on its laurels.

9 The Repertory Movement: Summary, Assessment, Conclusion

ANTHONY JACKSON

THE PURPOSE of this chapter is to draw together the main threads in the development of Repertory – both as an idea and as working theatre practice –and to take stock of what the repertory movement has achieved: its strengths, its weaknesses, its contribution to British theatre as a whole.

The general chronological outline should, we hope, be clear. Clear too should be the enormous distance that has been travelled since the very early years of the movement, leading to the establishment now of the regional repertory network as the main provider of theatre in Great Britain at large – indeed in most areas outside London the sole provider. The fostering and financial support of this network, moreover, has at last become recognised as a responsibility of both national and local government – even if the level of that support remains a bone of contention. In the light of this broad achievement, then – the nature and implications of which will be reviewed in more detail shortly – have the goals been reached? Has the repertory *movement* as such run its course? Arguably, the answer is yes. The pioneering, the polemic, the concerted campaigns, the struggle to establish a non-commercial and non-London-centred theatre against the enormous odds of a quite different theatre system, which have characterised repertory ventures for over half a century, are of the past. A different kind of campaigning may now be needed: to do with preserving what has been achieved and extending its reach. But that is a new and relatively uncharted phase. What is especially important in this transitional period is to underline and to assess what has been done till now.

In order to suggest the achievements and shortcomings of the repertory movement over the 75 or so years of its history, it may be useful to look primarily at those key elements of the 'repertory idea' that were articulated in the earliest days of the movement, which became repeatedly underlined, expanded and reinterpreted as the decades passed and which may act as some kind of measuring rod of what was done and of the changes that have taken place. Those elements may be summarised as: the establishment of a *repertory system* of presenting plays (whether the short-run or 'true repertory'); the offering of a high quality and *varied repertoire* of plays,

173

together with the promotion of *new drama and dramatists*; the improvement in *standards of acting and staging*; the securing of *civic or state patronage*; and the forging (or reforging) of the vital links that must exist between a *theatre and its community* – to which should be added the notion of *de-centralisation* of the theatre from its persistent and often unhealthy London-centredness.

THE REPERTORY SYSTEM

From the very beginnings of the repertory movement, the theatre reform that was sought had to involve, in the view of most of its proponents, the establishment of theatres capable of presenting a wide range of good plays in productions that were available to the public frequently and regularly and not simply run for as long as they could attract an audience. In one respect, these would be the stock theatres of old, but would draw more explicitly upon the repertory theatres of the Continent for their model. The argument was given special emphasis, as we have seen, by use of the analogy drawn time and again with the existence of publicly endowed museums, art galleries and libraries. Theatres ought to be provided in every major town or city expressly to cater for a wide range of tastes; the best of the whole gamut of Western drama, past and present, should be made available on stage as the common heritage of all – just as literature is available to all on the shelves of public libraries. The early campaigners – Archer, Shaw, Barker and others – based their argument on a number of assumptions: that plays constituted an important part of our cultural life and needed to be seen rather than read if they were to be fully appreciated; that play productions could be mounted and 'stored' and re-presented in constant rotation so that at least the successful productions were easily and regularly available over a period of years – the 'true repertory' system; that money could be found to fund a highly expensive operation of this kind; and that audiences could learn to understand and respond to such a system. The faith that such a system was possible and worth striving for stemmed from growing familiarity, from the end of the nineteenth century onwards, with Continental theatre practice, and was confirmed as leading British directors such as Barker and Basil Dean visited theatres in France and Germany before the First World War.

There was, however, never the money to give true repertory a fair trial, let alone build the kind of theatre needed to house it, until after the Second World War. And even then, although true repertory was tried for varying lengths of time at a number of theatres, by and large the expense and complexity of the organisation required proved beyond the majority of reps. Only the two national companies and, in contrast, Stoke's small Victoria Theatre, have shown a long-term commitment to the system, the reasons for which have already been outlined.

But, as Barker pointed out in 1907 (referring specifically to his venture at the Court), the *short run*, though not true repertory, was 'the next best thing'.[1] And the Court compromise in fact established what was to become the norm for repertory thenceforward, with plays running consecutively, usually for a week at a time in the early years, though sometimes longer, with only the occasional return of a popular production to the bill. Has the short run served well? By and large it has proved to be a simple system to operate within the usual tight financial constraints, and has generally been understood by audiences. Certainly, once plays came to be given in three- to four-week runs instead of weekly, with the consequent improvements in performance standards, the only cause for complaint would seem to have been the loss of popular productions from the programme which might otherwise have remained in the repertoire throughout the season. The short-run system is relatively cheap to operate, keeping to a minimum the costs of stage management involved in frequent set-changing. And it does allow companies to plan their seasons economically, employing actors only as and when needed: some theatres may engage a small nucleus of a company for a season (or, now, more often half a season), augmenting as and when necessary for larger-cast plays, such as the Christmas production or the school Shakespeare; or, alternatively, each successive production may be cast completely anew. True repertory usually necessitates maintaining a permanent company and keeping actors on the payroll at times when they may not be required to perform. What is lost of course, in the current version of the short run, is the continuity and sense of company identity that go with true repertory, together with the genuine variety and flexibility of programme that can be offered to its audience. Studio theatres, however, where they exist as part of a repertory theatre complex, can and often do offer a measure of variety and flexibility within the straight short run system.

THE REPERTOIRE

What of the plays themselves, the range of plays offered in the repertoire? Despite the reputation that repertory often tended to find pinned upon it, from the days of the Court and the Gaiety onwards —one of a theatre for intellectuals with emphasis upon the gloomy side of life, or, alternatively, one with a missionary, overtly educational stamp – the records show that there was a more varied and a lighter diet generally available than as was usually supposed. Indeed, as Barker had protested in 1910, foreseeing the objections that many might have to his vision of the repertory theatre of the future, 'No, this does not open up an arid, educational prospect' – modern comedy and romance should be equally part of the repertoire, so long as 'truthful'.[2] A theatre that is aiming to break new ground and at the very least to bring intelligence and a social conscience to its repertoire is perhaps bound to appear earnest, targeted at the well-educated middle class and lacking in the immediate popular appeal for which star-studded commercial productions were clearly designed. But in those early years, alongside Ibsen, Euripides, Galsworthy and Shaw (if Shaw is to be classed as a 'serious' in the sense of a 'demanding' playwright), were also to be found the lighter comedies of St John Hankin, Houghton, Brighouse, Arnold Bennett, Harold Chapin, and even on occasion Pinero and Wilde.

Persistently and certainly right up to the present, the influence of Shaftesbury Avenue has made itself felt in the programme: a recent success in the West End will come with a distinct crowd-pulling cachet. During the twenties and thirties many reps came to rely heavily upon the well-tried popular West End hits irrespective of the worth or variety that they contributed to the season; a trend that was counter-balanced, as has been shown, only by the adventurousness of the programmes at Birmingham, Oxford and Cambridge. In more recent decades, with subsidy to be justified, the 'balanced' programme' has become a requirement, though interpreted in different ways. West End successes still underpin many of the average repertory theatres' programmes, but such has been the change undergone in the West End that such underpinning no longer implies quite the predictable formula that it used to. Shaw, Coward, Priestley recur as they always have done, and so does the statutory classic or two; but the modern repertoire now also includes many of the playwrights whose work was first seen in the reps, in the two national companies or even in the alternative theatre: playwrights as various as Alan Ayckbourn, Alan Bleasdale and Dario Fo. Family entertainment of one kind or another at Christmas remains a permanent feature.

The most variable factor on the other hand is the number of premières of new British plays or of new or newly translated foreign plays – the activity that ought to be at least one of the measures by which the worth of any rep should be judged. Without new work, without the taking of risk, the fare offered by the average repertory programme would be little more than the juggling with innumerable permutations of a well tried, safe and static reservoir of plays.

NEW DRAMA

The concern with the development of new drama was central to the repertory movement from its earliest discernible beginnings. The theatre was about plays and new plays were the life-blood of a thriving theatre. The commercial, profit-orientated stage had inhibited new writing and new writers by being wedded to the long run, to mass appeal and to the star system. Artistic talent has to be nurtured and should not be subject at every turn to the crude criteria of market forces: artists must (as George

Devine in the fifties was to assert so persuasively) have the right to fail. Worthwhile plays may have only limited appeal and audiences sometimes need nurturing as much as do writers.

If a measure of the vitality of theatre can be said to be the quality and adventurousness of its new plays, to what extent has repertory aided or influenced new writing? Before the First World War the reps at Manchester, Glasgow, Liverpool and Birmingham, together with the ventures at the Court and the Duke of York's, were committed, virtually by their articles of faith, to the promotion of new drama – both of recent European writing and of new British playwrights. Certainly the new writers encouraged by this early phase of the repertory movement constituted an impressive fund of talent: Galsworthy, Hankin, Barker, Masefield, the Manchester 'school' of Brighouse, Houghton and Monkhouse. Shaw, too, owes a good deal of his success to the presentation of his plays first at the Court and subsequently in Jackson's various seasons at Birmingham and Malvern. Between the wars it was Birmingham that stood out above all as a theatre whose policy was consistently to enlarge the repertoire, by promoting new, recent or old but newly discovered plays, both home grown and foreign (by Shaw, Drinkwater, Philpotts, Georg Kaiser and the rediscovered Henry Fielding for example). The shorter-lived ventures at Oxford and Cambridge also made major contributions – especially in further opening up the notoriously insular British theatre to influences from Europe and America (Chekhov, for example, at Oxford, and Toller, Pirandello and the early O'Neill at Cambridge). By and large, however, the West End was still the thriving centre of theatre in Britain and exerted an enormous and mainly conservative influence upon the type of writing able to achieve commercial success.

The dramatic resurgence of the post Second World War period, from the mid fifties onwards, coincided interestingly with the renaissance of the regional reps. One was not the direct cause of the other, but both were certainly part of the same renewal of confidence and optimism and the determination to pioneer new paths that lay behind the formation of Theatre Workshop and the English Stage Company, the opening of the Coventry Belgrade and, more generally, the increase in subsidy for the arts and the boom in theatre building outside London. The new writing fostered so effectively at the Theatre Royal, Stratford East and the Royal Court was quickly taken up by the reps; and soon it was the reps themselves that were, with the help of Arts Council grants, initiating new plays. Major writers such as Ayckbourn, Barnes, Wesker, Edgar, Russell, Bleasdale, Griffiths, Brenton and Hare began or were nurtured in the regional reps, while certain of those theatres, such as the Liverpool Everyman, the Nottingham Playhouse, Stoke's Victoria and the Oldham Rep, prided themselves on a conscious 'new plays' policy. Opportunities for risk-taking increased with the building from the mid sixties on of theatre studios for experimental or small-scale new work, and Arts Council aid widened to include play-wrights' bursaries and writers-in-residence schemes, which have been taken up by some though by no means all reps. If there has in recent years been a noticeable falling off in the interest shown generally in new writing – for economic reasons primarily, since there seems to be no dearth of new writers – and a discernible shift of initiative away from the reps to the alternative companies, repertory can at least claim a good deal of credit for what has been a quite remarkable renaissance in British playwriting over twenty or more years.

ARTISTIC STANDARDS

The raising of standards, not only of playwriting but of acting and production across the whole range of plays available on the contemporary stage, was a major thrust in the arguments put by the advocates of repertory in the early years. And it has remained a recurring theme of the repertory movement ever since, although the diagnoses of what was in need of improvement and the cures proposed have changed much over the decades. The early pioneers and polemicists were distressed by stultifying acting conventions, typecasting, the star system and by the debilitating effects of the long run. Theatres run on the Continental pattern, however, would maintain permanent companies staying together long enough to develop an ensemble method of working in which every actor would be expected to play a variety of roles large and small; there would be opportunities to develop skills through experience and (ideally) through training provided by the theatre itself (of the kind that Barker saw at the Dusseldorfer Schauspielhaus in 1910); staleness in a role would be avoided by the variety of the repertoire ('Repertory theatre acting', observed Barker during his visit to Reinhardt's Deutsches Theater, 'is remarkable above all things for spontaneity and resource . . . supreme virtues [which] . . . come easily and naturally, and indeed . . . of sheer necessity to a repertory company'[3]); while the playing of a production over a long period, though not nightly, would allow an actor to deepen his grasp of his character. Freshness, spontaneity, depth and intelligence of interpretation and unity of company effort – these were the priorities in the kind of theatre experience that repertory would, it was hoped, provide.

Permanent companies on the scale envisaged by Barker, however, were not to emerge in Britain until the sixties, and even then only at a handful of theatres. The common pattern at the Court was, as we have noted, the employment of a nucleus of actors, irregular and small though it may have been and with many additions and substitutions from play to play, which did at least provide a base for some degree of continuity and for the building of a very limited 'house style'. It was a pattern that, unsatisfactory as it was, now looks uncommonly similar to the pattern adopted by many reps in the early eighties. In 1904, use was made of actors regularly in work in the West End; in 1983, use is made of actors who wish to return to London regularly to be available for work, if not in the West End then in television. But from the Manchester Gaiety onwards, through the inter-War period and into the fifties, the weekly or two-weekly run system generally meant the retention of small 'stock' companies, augmented for particular productions when necessary, which could at least develop something of a company spirit. Such companies, faced with the constant series of different, weekly, challenges, would have received a useful training in adaptability and often achieved by necessity a high level of teamwork. But the pressure to get productions staged rapidly and with inadequate rehearsal time meant that typecasting remained the rule and generally that artistic merit was sacrificed to expediency.

In the twenties and thirties a few companies – the three or four major reps and the Old Vic Shakespeare Company in London–did manage to rise above the constrictions imposed by weekly repertory and to achieve standards that were comparable to and often surpassed those of the West End. But not until the arrival of subsidy were the Old Vic/National Theatre, the Royal Shakespeare Company and the major-league reps of the sixties and seventies able to employ regular companies of any size who could *as* companies rehearse fully and develop a true ensemble approach through a season or more. The highly influential Old Vic Theatre School (1947–52) under Michel Saint-Denis without doubt did much to pave the way for the acceptance of ensemble – as did Joan Littlewood's Theatre Workshop company, following a more Brechtian approach in contrast to the Stanislavskian orientation of Saint-Denis. As the British actor began to discover at last the value of ensemble work, so the emergence of a number of ensemble companies was increasingly reflected in the types of production staged – notably in the Stoke documentaries, the Everyman documentary-musicals, the large-cast classical revivals and satiric extravaganzas of Barnes and Brenton and Hare at Nottingham. It would be misleading, however, to suggest that such work was typical of repertory as a whole. Indeed, despite the strong growth of interest in ensemble, for most companies there was little sustained work of this kind possible given the restricted budgets available for actors' salaries. More recently, as we have seen, the permanent company has become the province only of the large national theatres on the one hand and several small assertively regional theatres (such as the Victoria at Stoke, the Everyman and Manchester's Contact) on the other. Elsewhere there has been a loss of faith in the value of a permanent company when resources such as those enjoyed by the National Theatre are not available. It is moreover a common view among directors and actors alike, contrary to the arguments rehearsed seventy years ago, that, for the actor, membership of such a company could actually be a constriction, both in artistic and in career terms: the longer he stays with the company the less the challenge to his own artistic development. Does Continental theatre practice in this respect offer a goal to be aimed at? It would seem not. While the actor on the European stage may enjoy the security and other benefits of a long-term contract with his company, the British actor by and large, especially in repertory, prefers to be mobile. Long-term contracts would, it is often said, lead to complacency, a stultifying cosiness and a lack of challenge. A further, perhaps more negative factor, already noted, is that many directors now under the spell, in part, of television practice, increasingly tend to cast each play anew, aiming for the most suitable casting character by character rather than at the development of ensemble playing. All of which goes hand in hand with the general lack of willingness to explore beyond the confines of television naturalism.

Except for the national companies and for a few pockets of resistance in the reps, then, the permanent company is no longer part of repertory practice, and arguably valuable experience available thereby to the actor is being increasingly denied. One of the functions that repertory has long performed has without question been that of a training-ground for actors. Today, however, while he may have been better trained at drama school than hitherto, the young actor will be fortunate to be employed with a company for two or three plays at most – unless he is with an alternative company or one of the few company-orientated reps. Consequently the opportunity he has to develop with other more experienced actors over a season or more and through a variety of roles has become rare. Of course repertory has for too long suffered from being thought of *merely* as a training ground for the West End, National Theatre or RSC, film or television, and it has been the aim of many of the major regional ventures of the sixties and seventies to pull repertory into the 'national league'. This aim has been wholly commendable and indeed an essential component of the repertory movement. But the increasing trend at many theatres, with an understandable concern for box-office success, to do no more to further this aim than employ current television 'stars' in the hope that they will at least 'pass muster' in the production seems somewhat short-sighted – and ironically not dissimilar to some of the less satisfactory aspects of the 'stock' system of old. The sacrifice then of the permanent company may be more of a loss in the long term than many imagine. One can only hope that when (and if) more funds are made available they will once again be directed towards the building of permanent resident ensemble companies – an improvement that may be less immediately noticeable to the general public than the opening of a new building but of equal long-term importance if the theatre is to be able to offer what television cannot.

A further concomitant of the repertory movement has been the emergence of the artistic director. It was always of course a *sine qua non* of the repertory idea that productions be staged with the highest standards of stage management, costume, setting and lighting, and the 'producer' of plays (as he used to be known) only really emerged as a distinctive force in the British theatre with Granville Barker's work at the Court. But the notion of a producer-manager was one that evolved in practice rather than from theory. Barker had at the Court, it so happened, managed and directed plays. What then gradually became characteristic of the new repertory theatres as they began to find their feet was the closer involvement of the director of plays in the over-all artistic direction of the theatre. Miss Horniman had allowed her first play director at the Gaiety a relatively free hand in the choice of plays, though subsequently Casson and others were to suffer from her direct interference. Basil Dean at Liverpool took upon his shoulders from the start the work of both play-directing and over-all artistic direction, subject to the approval of the theatre trust – a practice that has today become the norm; he did, however, come unstuck by insisting on *Hannele* against the Board's wishes. At Birmingham Jackson's control, like Miss Horniman's, was total (and not without reason since it was his money that kept the venture in being); unlike Miss Horniman, however, he did involve himself frequently at the production level, notably in set design for which he was of course exceptionally qualified.

Whilst the reps between the wars were financially dependent upon either the beneficence of one controlling figure or the more mundane box-office income, then the director remained by and large the putter-on of plays and little more. Terence Gray at Cambridge was one of the very few exceptions to prove the rule: a director of productions who also had total artistic control of his theatre and brought to the movement something of the pre-eminence, even autocracy, associated with practice on the Continent. It was after the Second World War, hingeing upon the advent of subsidy, that the artistic director became fully established in the repertory theatre. Ultimately responsible to the theatre trust, he has none the less become the one figure who can both influence and embody his theatre and its policy. The impresario may have become a thing of the past (at least in repertory), but the power of the artistic director, once he has won the support of his theatre board, can be considerable. And while there may be arguments for increasing *and* for decreasing that power (depending upon the circumstances of each particular theatre), there can be no doubting that it is upon the director's vision, skill, tact and inspirational qualities that the special achievements of so much of the repertory theatre movement have depended.

PATRONAGE

Subsidy of some kind has been a regular feature of theatre ever since the dramatic festivals of Athens were financed by the wealthy citizens appointed as *choregoi* by the state. It was a variety of forms of church, guild, state and private patronage that sustained the English theatre through its flowering in the medieval and Renaissance periods, and only midway through the seventeenth century, following the closure of the theatres under Cromwell, did it cease to receive direct subsidy from crown and aristocracy. Henceforward, the theatre had to make its own way, paid for only by its immediate patrons, the audience. The box office remained virtually the sole means of income available – save for the beneficence of such as Annie Horniman and Barry Jackson – until the Second World War. And yet, as we have seen, in the early years of the century subsidy of some form was found to be essential to the proper establishment and running of a major repertory theatre, whether of national or regional variety.

The difficulties that arose at the Abbey between the Company and their benefactress, and indeed those that arose in the post 1918 period at the Gaiety and the Birmingham Rep all testified to the need for endowment of a more secure and adequate kind, free from the personal whims or over-stretched generosity of individual patrons. The struggles, lasting decades, waged by advocates of the National Theatre and by Barry Jackson at Birmingham and others in the regions for proper funding provision from state or city bear witness to the difficulty with which nineteenth-century attitudes to the performing arts were countered. Barker put the problem down to an essentially English, deeply ingrained Puritanism, and proceeded tactically to frame his arguments in suitably Puritan terms.[4] St John Ervine, in 1924, pointed to the decline in the standard of both drama and the repertory movement itself after the War as indisputable evidence of what happened to cultural expression when neither state nor private patronage was available to free it of the stifling circumstances of a *laissez-faire* economy: municipalities had an inescapable duty to provide the patronage that a flourishing dramatic art inevitably required.[5] Again and again Continental examples were appealed to; and the final acceptance, during and immediately following the Second World War, of the principle of subsidy for the arts did nothing to diminish the use made of invidious comparisons between European and British levels of subsidy. Even as late as 1982, when Arts Council and even local authority grants had reached a level that bore no comparison with the minute, tentative allocations made in the forties and fifties, the Parliamentary Select Committee on the Arts was at pains to draw attention to the enormous disparity between public expenditure on the arts in most Western European countries and that in Britain: Germany's eighty-five public theatres, for example, were expected, in 1980–1, to earn no more than fifteen per cent of their total expenditure at the box office, the rest being found from public subsidy.[6]

None the less, subsidy for the arts has grown in Britain, at least until the mid seventies, at an extraordinary rate and has facilitated, if not actually promoted, the rebirth of repertory. As expectations rose faster than the subsidies provided, however, it was to be expected that the debates about patronage would intensify. What should be the right balance in the apportioning of money to theatres in London and to theatres in the regions? Should the building-based theatres receive so much more than the touring community theatres? Should the priority of the Arts Council be to 'raise or spread' – improve and maintain standards in the major centres of excellence or achieve the most equitable provision across the whole country? (The Arts Council's dilemma and how the Council's approaches to it were changing are well summarised by Roy Shaw in the Annual Report for 1975–6.) When public money was spent it did at least mean that the strategy of theatre provision could now be put into the arena of public debate, and that was thought by many to be only to the good. The shifts in strategy – in, for example, the apportioning of funds more recently in favour of the regions, in the provision of new and further resources to the 'fringe', experimental and community work and to new writing – may have proved relatively small but they have been significant: the arguments for reassessment and change were put and had noticeable, if slow, effect.

What have been the most significant effects of subsidy upon the repertory system? The positive and negative aspects might be summed up as follows – first, the beneficial effects:

1. help has been given for the move away from weekly to three-weekly changes in the programme, which has allowed an increase in rehearsal and playing time and, consequently, in the standards of production and performance;
2. prices of admission have been kept artificially low and enabled the theatre to stay within the reach of a wide sector of the population;
3. new or renewed buildings and facilities have been provided by both Arts Council and local authority money;
4. new writing has been promoted by a variety of incentive schemes;
5. new kinds of theatre activity have been enabled (touring units, young people's theatre teams, youth and community workshops, etc.);
6. well-deserved but 'risky' revivals (especially of the less well-known classics) have been encouraged;
7. there has been an increased degree of security and continuity provided, allowing for forward planning and the development of a coherent artistic policy.

Several of the above, and especially the last, have unfortunately become less applicable with the more recent 'pruning' of the Arts Council's Treasury allocations.

Negative effects might be listed thus:

1. dependence upon a single body (whether the Arts Council, a regional arts association or a municipality) for all or the bulk of a theatre's subsidy

can make that theatre's future vulnerable to changes in political control, or even to the whims and manoeuvrings of different 'power-blocs' within the funding body: withdrawal or severe reduction of subsidy by that body will be likely to be traumatic, and probably fatal;

2. a large subsidy, even if perfectly justifiable, can induce the attitude that a production team can buy its way out of troubles rather than solve them by creative ingenuity;

3. the system of subsidy, in aiming to ensure accountability and efficiency, is inevitably bureaucratic: it may often, therefore, fail to be as flexible, open and fair as many would like, or as sensitive to new initiatives, or as accountable to its *clients* as it should;

4. reliance upon funding bodies makes theatres themselves more tied up in administration, with less time and personnel available for creative work.

Certainly the benefits outweigh the disadvantages; and many of the weaknesses in and anxieties about the system as it exists at present result from underfunding rather than the reverse – a point on which the 1982 Parliamentary Committee report was emphatic.

Some (such as Elsom in his 1971 study) see the increased scale of funding from the mid sixties onwards as being of undoubted benefit in the short term but as a long-term liability: it raised too many expectations, started too many ventures that could not be adequately financed in later years and made companies over-dependent upon government funds (with all the inherent dangers already noted of such a position).[7] While there is undoubtedly some truth in such an analysis it must also be made clear that the extra funds encouraged but did not create the new work and the new companies. Rather they afforded creative artists, in repertory as much as in any other theatre field, at least a period of a few years in which to develop new ideas and new approaches in practice – an opportunity without which the repertory theatre would certainly have remained in a constricted and even cocooned state, appealing to a diminishing segment of the population and having to cede most of the adventurousness and new blood to the alternative touring companies, so sealing the split between the two sectors in a damaging and possibly irreversible way. At least the years of expansion helped to open up the repertory movement to vital new approaches and ideas and encouraged innovation and adventure within it that any temporary decline or treading of water will not easily erase now or in the future.

The Parliamentary Committee report on arts funding already mentioned was also concerned to underline the importance of 'plural funding'[8] – the funding of companies from more than one source, apart from box-office income (business sponsorship being one of the alternative sources recommended and increased local authority support a further priority). But plural funding is important not only as a means of generating more money for the arts (the Committee's main rationale), but equally because of the greater security, the reduced vulnerability to changes of mind by one funding body, and because of the lesser likelihood of any attempt by that funding body to assert control over the theatre's own artistic policy. The risks of censorship when all the theatre's money comes from one source are heightened enormously, as the experience of theatres in Eastern Europe would seem to confirm. And although official state censorship was abolished in the UK in 1968, censorship, as is well known, can take many forms and come from many quarters.

Since the 1900s the case for subsidy has remained as strong as ever. The implications of the size, allocation and form of that subsidy have, however, gained a complexity that its original proponents could never have envisaged. What is indisputable is the inevitable requirement of substantial subsidy if the regional theatres are adequately to perform their role in the community.

THEATRE IN THE COMMUNITY

In 1971 John Elsom, in his survey of theatres outside London, asked what exactly was meant by the oft-quoted claim that 'theatre should serve the community',[9] and the problem of defining the theatre's role in society remains. Matthew Arnold believed the theatre to be 'irresistible', a necessary and inevitable part of the nation's culture that simply needed 'organising' to ensure that its contribution to that culture could be effectively unshackled and channelled for civilised ends. Archer, Barker, Shaw, Basil Dean, all in their various ways endeavoured to amplify and develop Arnold's assertions and to test them in practice. Following the First World War St John Ervine lectured and wrote on the 'organised' theatre (describing his lectures as 'a plea in civics'), and Barker wrote of the 'exemplary theatre' – both visions of theatre that in their different ways asserted the moral, social and educational value of dramatic and theatrical activity. Advocacy of both national and municipal theatres was increasingly based on the premise that theatre was 'good for you'. Not only was Shakespeare advanced as indisputable proof of its value and its central place in our heritage, tied in intimately with our sense of national identity; for Barker and others, the 'normal' theatre that was sought now was to be justified as much in terms of the moral health of the nation as of intrinsic aesthetic value. Again Barker's writing is seminal. His 'normal theatre' was a theatre captured 'in the interests of the average man', a theatre that, being by its very nature 'a sociable art, bringing people together', was 'most apt for the expression of modern life' – that could be both free from state censorship and make for 'righteousness'.[10] Theatre, then, was important not only because it brought to life the major works of art from the past and so helped to pass on the culture of new generations, but because it offered insights into and ways of approaching the contemporary world too. It could entertain, uplift *and* educate. Hence national and local authorities were urged again and again to see the provision of publicly funded theatre as in the long-term interests of society, as a duty not a bonus (hence, again, the public library analogy so often drawn).

Though the terminology has changed, the main thrust of such arguments is still central to contemporary debate about the place of theatre in our society. To some extent, the argument has been won. For three decades after the end of the Second World War, the notions of theatre as a civic institution, as a cultural focus for the community, as an expression of local identity and pride, became accepted – as the increasing scale of public funding and municipal theatre-building demonstrated. To a large extent, too, theatre's value in these respects was proved by the volume and wealth of creative activity generated: not only by the plays but by the variety of other cultural events inside the theatre and out. But the debates as to the most important or most useful function theatre ought to perform continue. Should it provide a 'social service' in the sense of reflecting public taste, giving people what they want; should it have a social mission, political, educational or otherwise, responding to perceived needs rather than apparent wants; or should it be the venue for an aesthetic experience that cannot be encompassed by the criteria or obligations associated with other social services or public utilities? Repertory has always been characterised by its endeavour to offer a wide range of theatre to its audiences, but does this mean that it has to be all things to all men? Just as society has changed profoundly from the *relatively* settled era of Edwardian England, so the homogeneity of audiences has, as a factor to be relied upon, all but disappeared, and a pluralistic but coherent artistic policy is an increasingly difficult end to achieve. Should the artistic director simply trust to his own intuition as to what will work and be right for his audience (whoever that might be), or to a personal vision of what his theatre might be and hope that he can take his audience with him – or indeed find new audiences who *will* go with him?

The repertory theatre system stands at present poised between the enormous national companies on the one hand, inevitably at several removes from people in the country generally, and the local, community touring groups which seek their audiences in non-theatre venues (the pubs, community halls and the like) on the other. In this context it has become in the seventies and early eighties the subject of a debate that differs markedly from the debates of the early years of the repertory movement. While the received opinion had for decades been that the regional theatre was a means of improving understanding of and access to the cultural heritage for everyone, an increasingly voluble and articulate (if small) body of opinion began more recently to argue that, organised as it was, this theatre was bound to be only an extension of the 'establishment', able to do no more (and no less) than undertake a form of cultural imperialism, imparting the values of the dominant middle-class ideology to those who came to listen, and enshrining thus the status quo.[11] It was a provocative and in many ways useful challenge. How we see our theatres, and how, therefore, we justify our public expenditure upon them, are questions that need constantly to be asked and the answers constantly re-thought.Such issues have indeed – and partly in response to such challenges – much exercised the Arts Council in recent years. It is undeniable that our regional theatres, whatever their intrinsic value, do reach only a small percentage of the population. This recognition has led, first, the Arts Council formally to urge theatres to do more to educate their actual and potential audiences about theatre – to increase public awareness and understanding of what they have to offer – and, secondly, the Parliamentary Committee on the Arts to recommend increased efforts on the part of both funding bodies and arts organisations to seek a broader audience, especially with a view to attracting 'a greater proportion of the lower income groups and those who do not normally patronise these arts'.[12] The broadening of and greater responsiveness to theatre audiences is possibly one of the most pressing items now on the agenda for the regional theatres.

Certainly the repertory movement in the sixties and seventies made considerable if sporadic strides towards both audience building and the promotion of theatre as an educational medium. The TIE teams at Coventry, Bolton, Leeds and elsewhere that burgeoned in the late sixties, the documentaries at Stoke and Liverpool and the various 'out-reaching' community units at numerous other reps have all been important developments because they pushed back the boundaries of what theatre could do: they involved and excited new audiences *irrespective* of any audience-building effects that they may also have had. Likewise the *deliberate* audience-building strategies (from subscription schemes, ticket discounts for students, old-age pensioners and the unemployed and lotteries to 'theatre appreciation' units touring schools and elsewhere prior to the opening of a new production) have been energetic and often imaginative. But with only occasional exceptions the inroads have not been deep. It is perhaps not surprising that as less money becomes available theatres should retreat from the adventurous policies that characterised at least some of the work done a decade and more ago: playing safe is one strategy for survival. But, new audiences can and have been reached – as repertory as well as the alternative theatre have proved – and the theatre that fights shy of reaching out, of trying to learn about its potential audiences, that tries to play for and retain only one type of audience, will risk being left high and dry as society, its tastes and its needs, continues to change.

The bodies entrusted with direct responsibility not only for the running of the reps but for their proper functioning in the community are of course the Theatre Trusts, and a word should be said at this point about their role in the development of the repertory movement.

THEATRE TRUSTS

If one feature of the growth of repertory has been the emergence of the artistic director, another has clearly been the disappearance of the repertory impresario and the corresponding rise and, now, universal sway of the theatre Trust. Although Miss Horniman, Barry Jackson and Terence Gray might figure more prominently in the records, it was the leading citizens of Liverpool who established and sustained the Liverpool Rep and the burghers of Birmingham who came to Jackson's aid when in 1934 he declared that he could spend no more of his own money on the Repertory Theatre. With the injection into the regional theatre of Arts Council and ratepayers' money from the late 1940s these Trusts were widened to admit spokesmen from those bodies who provided the cash and other representatives of the community (although the Arts Council itself does not require direct representation, only the right to send an observer to all board meetings). Of course some friction between the tune-callers and the pipe-players was inevitable, especially in the early stages as both money and expectations grew at an unprecedented rate and when the rules of the game and principles involved had still to hammered out. But the record of the repertory movement is remarkable more for the discretion with which its paymasters have given rein to their artistic directors than for such comparatively isolated quarrels as John Neville's with the Nottingham Board in 1967.

It may be noted that the idea of theatrical government by Trust (now responsible for dispensing millions of pounds to bodies such as the National Theatre, the Royal Shakespeare Company, the Royal Opera House and the English National Opera) was almost wholly the creation of the repertory movement.

If the Trust system, operating through boards with memberships often of no more than fifteen, fails adequately to represent the community as a whole at policy-making level (and what system could be devised that would wholly succeed?), at least it does ensure some degree of artistic independence for the theatre from those who foot the bill. The 'arms length' principle which operates at Arts Council–government level applies, rightly, at local level too. It is, it must be said, a principle that can be all too easily eroded and one that at national and local levels alike needs to be jealously safeguarded.

DECENTRALISATION

The repertory theatres have been especially a regional rather than a London phenomenon: their geographical location and local base have been part of their *raison d'être*. Initially seen as replacing the old local 'stock' theatres with something of higher quality, in more recent decades their position has taken on a more strategic significance. When new or expanded theatres have been proposed, an influential factor has always been the likely competition with other repertory theatres in the vicinity, and the Arts Council in its funding allocations has certainly taken into account the theatre's geographical position, the extent to which it contributes to and plays a complementary role within the over-all network. No national plan preceded the growth of the rep system – as did the systematic decentralisation of the theatre in France in the 1960s (with the establishment of the regional Maisons de la Culture). But nationwide accessibility to the arts has become an integral part of the Arts Council's thinking and has, for example, influenced the readjustments made in the balance of grant-aid in favour of the regions during the past two decades.

Interestingly, the process that has taken place during the course of the post-War period has been what many have seen as one of 'Europeanisation'. Just as inspiration and the models for repertory in England at the turn of the century had come largely from France and Germany, so the emerging pattern of theatre in Britain in the post-War decade has been largely on European lines (though identical to no one specific country's system). A national theatre based in the capital and heavily subsidised in accord with its prestigious position; a less well-subsidised though often more adventurous 'State' theatre with a more obvious regional presence (i.e. the RSC); in the regional capitals and other major cities, the major repertory theatres subsidised at least in part from government funds, seen often as microcosms of the national companies but generally not carbon copies of them, often offering programmes and employing methods endemic to the particular theatre or region. This similarity if not equivalence between the British and many Continental patterns has contributed to the strength of the British theatre: the reps have developed (to use Michael Elliott's phrase) as 'independent centres of growth', providing range, richness, vitality.[13] That the pattern has flourished less well in the early eighties is due more to general economic problems than to anything inherently wrong with the system. It should also be noted that this Europeanisation has been gradual, almost accidental: it has *not* meant the systematic implanting of a foreign breed upon an inadequate or ailing home variety; rather the pattern has evolved as the result of many indigenous circumstances and other outside pressures. Certainly the example of Continental practice has been one (witness the number of times that Arts

Council reports have introduced the shaming comparison of funding levels elsewhere with our own). Others include the general post-War process of rebuilding and renewal and the accompanying trend towards civic enterprises; the demands of a rapidly changing, mobile, multi-ethnic population; the reassertion by the regions of their right to a fairer share of the nation's resources. Hence, the differences that exist between the European pattern and the British are as numerous as the similarities.

Perhaps a further strength of the repertory system is that, while decentralised and able to foster those 'individual centres of growth', it is compact enough (at least within England, Scotland and Wales) for there to be a good deal of mobility of personnel between one theatre and another, which in itself has helped to promote a valuable cross-fertilisation of ideas, skills and experience. It is a process that has likewise applied across the boundary lines between the subsidised, alternative and commercial sectors.

Repertory *has*, then, contributed to British theatre's sense of itself in that it has provided the basic network of the nation's theatre, without which it would be wholly London-based and deprived of much of that new talent in writing, acting and direction which found its opportunity in the regions. Repertory has provided the decentralised nurturing of artistic strength and individuality and the focus for local cultural growth which has given British theatre the vitality and variety for which it has become so internationally renowned.

How will Repertory survive the eighties and beyond? How will it respond to the increasing challenge of the home entertainment industry and the correspondingly higher expectations and greater sophistication of audiences, with regard to performance standards, production techniques and the seemingly limitless choice of programme available at the press of a button? Will the prestige theatres built in the expansive days of the sixties prove manageable still in the cost-cutting eighties? It would of course be foolish to speculate in any detail. Theatre – and regional repertory at least as much as any other – has shown signs of finding what, in a video age, it can do that television cannot: in, for example, the highly stylised work at the Citizens', in the local documentaries at Stoke, the Everyman and elsewhere, in the rediscovery of the musical and its potential as a vibrant, colourful, spectacular, stage-filling event, and in the 'out-reach' of the TIE and community touring units. And whatever the sense now of stasis or retrenchment, whatever the gloomy forecasts of a continuing erosion of public subsidy of the arts, the role of the regional repertory theatre will continue to be essential if the cultural life of the nation is to be maintained and in any way enhanced. In a world of increasing reliance upon high technology, when the pace and style of our lives will be subject to accelerating change, when more and more time will be spent by more and more of us in front of visual display units of one kind or another, when traditional forms of employment will become ever scarcer, then the *need* for the arts – for both recreational and educational purposes – will surely become inescapable. The regional repertory system, uniquely placed as it is to respond to those changing patterns and needs, if not always as *ready* to respond as it might be, has a vital part to play.

We may indeed have seen the end of a further phase of the repertory movement. In recent years, with only a few exceptions, the initiative for new and exciting developments has been with the heavily subsidised national companies on the one hand and the generally under-subsidised 'alternative' companies on the other. The end of a movement does not matter; the end of movement does. The reps have arrived, the system has been established, the nation has the framework of a theatre service. But the reps also stand in danger not only of being squeezed by current economic pressures into playing forever safe but of thinking there is nowhere further to go other than to attract better levels of subsidy to enable them to go on doing the same kind of thing. If the challenge of the future is adequately to be met, the reps cannot afford to leave all the experiment, ingenuity and 'outward-goingness' to the smaller touring groups and the RSC, or until times get better.

If the term 'repertory movement' no longer seems completely appropriate to describe the range, comprehensiveness and apparently established order of the present British regional theatre system, it may nevertheless still have some value as a timely and useful reminder of the 'alternative' roots and pioneering ideals at the beginning of the century from which that present system grew.

The Repertory Movement: A Chronology

1879	Shakespeare Memorial Theatre opens at Stratford-upon-Avon
1883	Frank Benson's touring Shakespeare Company formed
1889	Théâtre Libre (Paris) visits London
1891	Grein's Independent Theatre (London) formed
1894	Poel's Elizabethan Stage Society formed
1899	Stage Society (London) formed
	Yeats and Lady Gregory found Irish Literary Theatre (Dublin)
1904	Miss Horniman opens Abbey Theatre in Dublin: Abbey Theatre Company, the first repertory company in British Isles
1904–7	Vedrenne–Barker seasons at Royal Court Theatre (London)
1904	Archer and Barker complete *A National Theatre: Scheme and Estimates* – privately circulated; published 1907
1907	Miss Horniman finances trial season at Midland Hotel, Manchester
1908	Miss Horniman buys and redecorates Gaiety Theatre, Manchester, and sets up first English repertory company. First season on tour
1908–17	Manchester Repertory Theatre Company at Gaiety and in London for special seasons (Gaiety sold, 1921)
1909–14	Glasgow Repertory Company at Royalty Theatre
1910	Repertory season at Duke of York's (London) – Barker and Frohman
1911	Trial season at Kelly's Theatre, Liverpool, leads to Liverpool Repertory Theatre at Star Music Hall (renamed Playhouse 1917), directed by Basil Dean (until 1913): first theatre in country to be run by public board (of 'citizen-governors')
1913	Birmingham Repertory Theatre, purpose-built, opens under Barry Jackson
1914	Repertory season under Muriel Pratt at Theatre Royal, Bristol
1915	Foundation of Plymouth Repertory Company by George King
1919	Sheffield Repertory Company (amateur) founded
1921	Foundation of Scottish National Players
1923	Oxford Repertory Company under J.B. Fagan at 'Old' Playhouse
	Opening of Little Theatre, Bristol
	Foundation of Hull Repertory Company under A.R. Whatmore
1926	Opening of Festival Theatre, Cambridge, under Terence Gray
1927	Northampton Repertory Company established at Theatre Royal
1928	Sheffield Repertory Company opens permanent theatre (later named Playhouse)
1929	Barry Jackson founds Malvern Festival
1930	Barker rewrites and publishes *A National Theatre*

1931   With opening of Sadler's Wells for opera, Old Vic given over exclusively to drama

1932   New Shakespeare Memorial Theatre opens (old one burnt down, 1926)

1935   Jackson hands over Birmingham Rep to local Trust – theatre now in effect belongs to city
York Repertory Company established at Theatre Royal
Perth Repertory Company founded

1938   Windsor Repertory Company permanently established at Theatre Royal
Oldham Repertory Company founded at Coliseum
New Oxford Playhouse, Beaumont Street, opens

1939   Dundee Repertory Company founded

1940   CEMA (Council for Encouragement of Music and the Arts) formed with grants from Treasury and Pilgrim Trust – in 1942 financed entirely from the Treasury (Ministry of Education)
Old Vic bombed – Company continues at Burnley, on tour, and from 1942 at New Theatre, London

1942   Old Vic Company established at Liverpool Playhouse

1943   CEMA restores and reopens Theatre Royal, Bristol
Glasgow Citizens' Theatre gives first production at Athenaeum

1944   CORT (Conference of Repertory Theatres, later Council of Repertory Theatres and Council of Regional Theatre) founded

1945   Glasgow Citizens' moves to Princess's Theatre in the Gorbals
Salisbury Repertory Company founded

1946   Arts Council of Great Britain, established under Royal Charter, takes over from CEMA
Bristol Old Vic Company founded at Theatre Royal
Guildford Repertory Company founded
Kidderminster Repertory Company founded
Midland Theatre Company founded (based at Coventry)

1947   Foundation of Library Theatre Company at Manchester – in 1952 Library Committee assumes direct control
Ipswich Repertory Company founded

1948   British Theatre Conference, London
Unicorn Theatre for Young People, London, founded
Nottingham Repertory Company founded

1949   Chesterfield Repertory Company founded

1950   Old Vic Theatre reopens – unofficial 'national theatre'

1951   Pitlochry Theatre Festival (summer only) established
Derby Playhouse opens
Leatherhead Theatre opens
Canterbury Repertory Company established

1953   Theatre Workshop established at Theatre Royal, Stratford East

1955   Lincoln Repertory Company established at Theatre Royal

1956   English Stage Company formed at Royal Court, London

1958   Belgrade Theatre, Coventry, opens –first new repertory theatre to be built since the War

1961   Prospect Productions (touring repertory company) formed

1962   Welsh National Theatre Company formed – based in Cardiff but tour-
ing because no permanent theatre building
Chichester Festival Theatre opens (linked initially to National Theatre
productions)
Victoria Theatre, Stoke-on-Trent, opens
Old Vic becomes home of new National Theatre Company

1963   Phoenix Theatre, Leicester, opens
Nottingham Playhouse (new building) opens

1964   Everyman Theatre, Liverpool, opens (as young people's theatre)

1965   RSC season starts at Aldwych, London
Crewe Theatre opens
Watford Civic Theatre opens
Edinburgh Civic Theatre at Lyceum opens
Studio Theatre at the Glasgow Citizens' opens
First TIE company at Belgrade Theatre, Coventry

1967   Octagon Theatre, Bolton, opens
Northcott Theatre, Exeter, opens
Studio theatre at Coventry Belgrade opens

1968   Tyneside Theatre Trust established at Newcastle Playhouse
69 Theatre Company formed at University Theatre, Manchester

1970   Young Vic, London, opens
New company at Citizens', Glasgow, formed

1971   Crucible Theatre, Sheffield, opens

1973   Contact Theatre Company, Manchester, formed
Haymarket Theatre, Leicester, reopens as the city's main repertory
theatre

1976   New National Theatre building opens on South Bank
Royal Exchange Theatre, Manchester, opens
New Salisbury Playhouse opens
New Stephen Joseph Theatre-in-the-Round at Scarborough opens

1977   Oldham Coliseum reopens
Liverpool Everyman reopens – rebuilt theatre
Withdrawal of Arts Council grant from Chesterfield Civic Theatre;
end of rep company

1979   Wolsey Theatre, Ipswich, opens

1981   Scottish Theatre Company (touring) established
Withdrawal of Arts Council grants to, and subsequent demise of, Old
Vic Theatre (Prospect) Company, Crewe Lyceum Theatre and Canter-
bury Marlowe Theatre

1982   Royal Shakespeare Company moves into its two new theatres in The
Barbican Arts Centre in the City of London

1983   The Young Exchange Company formed in Manchester, as a branch of
the Royal Exchange Theatre
Go-ahead given for a new building for the Victoria Theatre, Stoke-on-
Trent

Sample Repertory Programmes

*[An asterisk * indicates a première]*

PROGRAMMES FOR 1910, 1930 AND 1950

Gaiety Theatre, Manchester: 1910

Director: B. Iden Payne

27 December 1909	*Much Ado About Nothing*	William Shakespeare
7 February	*Before the Dawn*	L. Kampf
	Mother To Be	Basil Dean
14 February	*The Silver Box*	John Galsworthy
	Makeshifts	Gertrude Robins
21 February	*The Voysey Inheritance*	Granville Barker
28 February	*Trespassers Will Be Prosecuted*	M.A. Arabian
	The Talleyman	Edward Parry
	The Purse of Gold	J. Sackville Martin

[7–26 March, Company toured Barrow-in-Furness, Kidderminster, Dublin and Birmingham]

28 March	*Candida*	G.B. Shaw
	The Subjection of Kezia	Edith Ellis
	Red Ria	Gertrude Landa
4 April	*The Critic*	R.B. Sheridan
	The Talleyman	Edward Parry
11 April	*Subsidence*	F.E. Wynne
	Mother To Be	Basil Dean

[18–30 April, Company toured Glasgow and Edinburgh]

2 May	*The Critic*	R.B. Sheridan
	The Searchlight	Mrs W.K. Clifford
9 May	*Widowers' Houses*	G.B. Shaw
	Marriages Are Made In Heaven	Basil Dean
16 May	*Cupid and Commonsense*	Arnold Bennett
23 May	*David Ballard*	Charles McEvoy
	Reaping the Whirlwind	Allan Monkhouse

[30 May–4 June, Company toured Cambridge]

6 June	*The Amateur Socialist*	Kingsley Tarpey
	The Choice	Allan Monkhouse

[13–19 June, Company toured Oxford]

29 August	*Dealing in Futures*	Harold Brighouse
	Effie	Basil Dean

5 September	*The Fantasticks*	Edmond Rostand
	The Man of Destiny	G.B. Shaw
12 September	** Gentlemen of the Press*	H.M. Richardson
	The Talleyman	Edward Parry
19 September	*The Return of the Prodigal*	St John Hankin
	Makeshifts	Gertrude Robbins
26 September	*Independent Means*	Stanley Houghton
	* The Master of the House	Stanley Houghton
3 October	** The Cloister*	
	Emile Verhaeren (first performance in English)	
	The Searchlight	Mrs W.K. Clifford
10 October	*When the Devil Was Ill*	Charles McEvoy
17 October	*Candida*	G.B. Shaw
	The Point of View	Gertrude Robins
24 October	*Justice*	John Galsworthy
[14–19 November, Company toured Oxford]		
21 November	** The Younger Generation*	Stanley Houghton
	* Miles Dixon	Gilbert Cannan
28 November	*Dealing in Futures*	Harold Brighouse
	The Master of the House	Stanley Houghton
5 December	*The Tragedy of Nan*	John Masefield
	The Talleyman	Edward Parry
12 December	*The Vale of Content*	Hermann Sudermann
	Makeshifts	Gertrude Robbins
24 December	*The School for Scandal*	R.B. Sheridan

Northampton Repertory Theatre: 1930

Director: Herbert Prentice. Designer: Osborne Robinson

6 January	*The Prisoner of Zenda*	from Anthony Hope
13 January	*Ghost Manor*	R.J. McGregor
20 January	*Betty at Bay*	Jessie Porter
27 January	*Bella Donna*	J.B. Fagan
3 February	*The Younger Generation*	Stanley Houghton
10 February	** The House of Crooks*	A.L. Bruyne
17 February	*Hay Fever*	Noel Coward
24 February	*It Pays to Advertise*	W. Hackett and R.C. Megrue
3 March	*The Witch*	John Masefield
10 March	*The Good Die Young*	Murray McClymont
17 March	*Mary Rose*	J.M. Barrie
24 March	*It's a Gamble*	Harold Brighouse
31 March	*Easy Virtue*	Noel Coward
7 April	*The Circle*	W. Somerset Maugham
14 April	*Outward Bound*	Sutton Vane
21 April	*Sherlock Holmes*	from Conan Doyle
28 April	*Passing Brompton Road*	Jevan Brandon-Thomas
5 May	*This Woman Business*	Ben Levy

12 May	*Dear Brutus*	J.M. Barrie
19 May	*The Naughty Wife*	Frederick Jackson
26 May	*Fanny's First Play*	G.B. Shaw
	[scene from] *King John*	William Shakespeare
2 June	*Mrs Moonlight*	Ben Levy
9 June	*The Marquise*	Noel Coward
16 June	*The Joan Danvers*	Frank Stayton
23 June	*Her Husband's Wife*	A.E. Thomas
30 June	*Mr Pim Passes By*	A.A. Milne
4 August	*Spring Cleaning*	Frederick Lonsdale
11 August	*Diversion*	John van Druten
18 August	*Skin Deep*	Ernest Enderline
25 August	*The Soul of John Sylvester*	Eric Barber
1 September	*And So to Bed* [two weeks]	J.B. Fagan
15 September	*Water*	Molly Marshall-Hole
22 September	*The Last of Mrs Cheney*	Frederick Lonsdale
6 October	*Misalliance*	G.B. Shaw
13 October	*A Hundred Years Old*	S. and J.A. Quintero
20 October	*The Moving Finger*	Patrick Hastings
27 October	*Canaries Sometimes Sing*	Frederick Lonsdale
3 November	*The Witch*	John Masefield
10 November	*Ask Beccles*	Cyril Campion and E. Dignon
17 November	*March Hares*	H.W. Gribble
24 November	*The Letter*	W. Somerset Maugham
1 December	*Murder on the Second Floor*	Frank Vosper
8 December	*The Young Idea*	Noel Coward
15 December	*Good Morning, Bill*	P.G. Wodehouse
22 December	*The School for Scandal*	R.B. Sheridan

Bristol Old Vic Company: 1950

Directors: Allan Davis (to June); Denis Carey (from September). Designers included Hutchinson Scott

[11 June 1949–5 January 1950, theatre closed for safety alterations]

5 January	*As You Like It*	William Shakespeare
21 February	*Tartuffe* Jean Baptiste Molière, adapted Miles Malleson
	L'Impromptu de Versailles	Molière
14 March	*Captain Carvallo*	Denis Cannan
4 April	*The Admirable Crichton*	J.M. Barrie
25 April	*Julius Caesar*	William Shakespeare
22 May	*The Provok'd Wife*	Sir John Vanbrugh
5 September	*The Lady's Not For Burning*	Christopher Fry
26 September	*The Good-Natured Man*	Oliver Goldsmith
17 October	*The Merry Wives of Windsor*	William Shakespeare
7 November	*Blind Man's Buff*	Denis Johnston
28 November	*The Magistrate*	Arthur Wing Pinero
21 December	*Puss in Boots*	John Phillips; music by Clifton Parker

PROGRAMMES FOR THE PERIOD 1960–81

The following lists the plays given by each of the six repertory theatres examined in Chapter 8 during the seasons 1960–1 (where applicable), 1970–1, and 1980–1. Because taken at ten-year intervals these play lists cannot of course be considered necessarily typical of a theatre's work as a whole: as has been shown in Chapter 8, a change of director, of building or of financial circumstances can have a marked effect on policy. The intention here is simply to provide a detailed record of what six theatres were producing during three identical seasons; to demonstrate how the number of plays per season became reduced as more theatres from the sixties onwards began to run their shows for three to four weeks; and to suggest some of the ways in which the repertoire has broadened during this period and at the same time allowed for significant variations between one theatre and another. The lists should be read in the context of each theatre's general development as outlined in Chapter 8, and of its financial position for the years in question as summarised in Appendix 3, Table I.

[*An asterisk * indicates a première*]

Nottingham Playhouse

1960–1
Director of Productions: Val May

Rhinoceros	Eugene Ionesco	*Celebration*	
A Cry of Players	William Gibson		K. Waterhouse and W. Hall
The Merchant of Venice		*Richard III*	William Shakespeare
	William Shakespeare	*The Unexpected Guest*	
Roots	Arnold Wesker		Agatha Christie
The Survivors	Irwin Shaw	*The Winslow Boy*	Terence Rattigan
One Way Pendulum	N.F. Simpson	*Mam'zelle Nitouche*	
Oliver Twist	Charles Dickens,		D. Cotton and J. Stephens
	adapted by R. Protherough	*The Tiger and the Horse*	Robert Bolt
The Happiest Days of Your Life		*A Taste of Honey*	Shelagh Delaney
	John Dighton	*Lady Windermere's Fan*	Oscar Wilde
The School for Scandal	R.B. Sheridan	*The Aspern Papers*	Henry James,
A Passage to India	E.M. Forster,		adapted by Michael Redgrave
	adapted by Santha Ram Rau	*Second Post!*	[Revue]

1970–1
Artistic Director: Stuart Burge

The Misanthrope	Molière	*The Rivals*	R.B. Sheridan
Lulu	Wedekind,	*The Birthday Party*	Harold Pinter
	adapted by Peter Barnes	*The Amazons*	Sir A.W. Pinero;
Hamlet	William Shakespeare		musical adaptation by
Nicholas Nickleby	Charles Dickens,		Stewart, Henneken and Addison
	adapted by C. Brahms and N. Sherrin	*Lily White Lies*	Alun Richards
The Popcorn Man		*A Close Shave*	Georges Feydeau
	Dodi Rob and Pat Patterson	*Antigone*	Sophocles
Waiting for Godot	Samuel Beckett		

1980–1
Artistic Director: Richard Digby-Day

The Boyfriend	Sandy Wilson	*Fresh Fields*	Ivor Novello
Mrs Warren's Profession	G.B. Shaw	*The Little Foxes*	Lilian Hellmann
Stevie	Hugh Whitemore	*The Skin Game*	John Galsworthy
A View from the Bridge		*The Devil's Disciple*	G.B. Shaw
	Arthur Miller	*The Comedy of Errors*	
Under Milk Wood	Dylan Thomas		William Shakespeare
A Little Night Music		**Robin Hood*	
	Stephen Sondheim		David Wood and T. Arthur
Old King Cole	Ken Campbell	*Piaf*	Pam Gems
Godspell			
	J.M. Tebalak and S. Sondheim		

Citizens' Theatre, Glasgow

1960–1
General Manager: Reginald Birks

Romulus the Great		*Lysistrata*	Aristophanes,
	Frederick Durrenmatt		adapted by Dudley Fitts
The Enchanted	Jean Giraudoux	*Hedda Gabler*	Henrik Ibsen,
Hamlet	William Shakespeare		adapted by Max Faber
The Lesson, The New Tenant and		**Breakdown*	Stewart Conn
Maid to Marry	Eugene Ionesco	*Great Expectations*	Charles Dickens,
Rollo	Marcel Achard		adapted by Alec Guinness
Roots	Arnold Wesker	*Murder in the Cathedral*	T.S. Eliot
The Aspern Papers		*Under Milk Wood*	Dylan Thomas
	from Henry James,	*A Passage to India*	E.M. Forster,
	adapted by Michael Redgrave		adapted by Santha Rama Rau
*Gaggiegalorum		*Sixes an' Sevens*	
	[Christmas entertainment]		[Revue, second edition]

1970–1
Artistic Directors: Giles Havergal, Robert David MacDonald and Philip Prowse

Hamlet	William Shakespeare	*The Balcony*	Jean Genet
Rosencrantz and Guildenstern		*Twelfth Night*	William Shakespeare
are dead	Tom Stoppard		
Mother Courage	Bertold Brecht	At the Close Theatre Studio:	
Saint Joan	G.B. Shaw	*Landscape and Silence*	Harold Pinter
A Taste of Honey	Shelagh Delaney	*Stop, You're Killing Me*	
Aladdin Terry Jones, Michael Palin			James Herlily
	and John Gould	*What the Butler Saw*	Joe Orton
The Hostage	Brendan Behan	*The Madman and the Nun*	
Waiting for Godot	Samuel Beckett		Stanislaw Witkiewicz
A Streetcar Named Desire		*'Tis Pity She's a Whore*	John Ford
	Tennessee Williams	*Private Lives*	Noel Coward
She Stoops to Conquer		*Bread and Butter*	C.P. Taylor
	Oliver Goldsmith	*Early Morning*	Edward Bond

Close Theatre Studio (cont.)

Nana Emile Zola, adapted by Keith Hack	*Capone* Rob Walker
Titus Andronicus William Shakespeare	*The Life and Death of Marilyn Monroe* Gerlind Reinshagen

1980–1

Artistic Directors: Giles Havergal, Robert David Macdonald and Philip Prowse

The Battlefield Carlo Goldoni	*Desperado Corner* Shaun Lawton
The Caucasian Chalk Circle Bertold Brecht	*The Massacre at Paris* Christopher Marlowe
Don Juan R.D. MacDonald	*Madame Louise* Vernon Sylvaine
Babes in the Wood John Byrne	*Desperado Corner* Shaun Lawton

The Salisbury Playhouse

1960–1 (August–July)
General Manager: Reginald Salberg

The Grass in Greener
    Hugh and Margaret Williams
Five Finger Exercise   Peter Shaffer
The Constant Wife
    W. Somerset Maugham
The Complaisant Lover
    Graham Greene
The Cat and the Canary   John Willard
The French Mistress   Robert Munro
Roar Like a Dove   Lesley Storm
A Shred of Evidence   R.C. Sherriff
The Marriage Go Round
    Leslie Stevens
Laura
    Vera Caspary and George Sklaa
She Stoops to Conquer
    Oliver Goldsmith
Rollo   Marcel Richard
How Say You
    Harold Brooke and Kay Bannerman
An Inspector Calls   J.B. Priestley
Family Albums and *Brief Encounter*
    Noel Coward
The Wrong Side of the Park
    John Mortimer
The Long View   Lewis Grant Wallace
Larger Than Life   Guy Bolton
    and W. Somerset Maugham

Strike for Death   John Creasey
Jack and the Beanstalk
    Henry Marshall
The Boy Friend   Sandy Wilson
Arsenic and Old Lace
    Joseph Kesselring
A Taste of Honey   Shelagh Delaney
Death of a Salesman   Arthur Miller
Dial M for Murder   Frederick Knott
Master of Arts
    William Douglas Home
Revue   [Various]
Henry IV   William Shakespeare
The Happiest Days of Your Life
    John Dighton
The Brides of March   John Chapman
The Toff   John Creasey
Roots   Arnold Wesker
Orange Island   Margaret Luce
Shop at Sly Corner   Edward Percy
The Naked Island   Russell Braddon
The More the Merrier   Ronald Millar
Long Day's Journey into Night
    Eugene O'Neill
Your Obedient Servant
    Diana Morgan

1970–1 (August–June)
General Manager: Reginald Salberg

Forty Years On	Alan Bennett	*Cinderella*	Henry Marshall
The Cherry Orchard	Anton Chekhov	*Plaza Suite*	Neil Simon
What Every Woman Knows		*Hamlet* and *Rosencrantz and*	
	James Barrie	*Guildernstern are Dead*	
The Prize	Arthur Miller		William Shakespeare
Not Now Darling	Ray Cooney		and Tom Stoppard
Rattle of a Simple Man	Charles Dyer		

1980–1 (August–July)
Artistic Director: Roger Clissold

The Good Old Days	[Music Hall]	*Babes in the Wood*	Henry Marshall
Hay Fever	Noel Coward	*Outside Edge*	Richard Harris
What the Butler Saw	Joe Orton	*Othello*	William Shakespeare
Package Deal	Peter Robert Scott	*Rose*	Andrew Davies
Old Herbaceous	Alfred Shaughnessy	*The Circle*	W. Somerset Maugham
Ours	Tom Robertson	*Betrayal*	Harold Pinter
Parting Day	Alfred Shaughnessy	*84 Charing Cross Road*	
Old Tyme Music Hall	[Music Hall]		Helene Hanff,
Whose Life is it Anyway?	Brian Clark	adapted by James Roose Evans	

Victoria Theatre, Stoke

1970–1
Artistic Director: Peter Cheeseman

The Recruiting Officer		** Tess of the d'Urbervilles*	Thomas
	George Farquhar	Hardy, adapted by Bill Morrison	
The Daughter-in-Law		*Major Barbara*	G.B. Shaw
	D.H. Lawrence	** Conan Doyle Investigates*	
Eh?	Henry Livings		Roger Woddis
Hamlet	William Shakespeare	** The Samaritan*	Peter Terson
* The Affair at Bennett's Hill		** Hands Up – For You the War is*	
	Peter Terson	*Ended*	[Documentary]
Pinocchio		** The Time Travellers*	Bill Morrison
	Brian Way and Warren Jenkins		

[Plus two productions outside the Victoria Theatre]

1980–1
Artistic Director: Peter Cheeseman

* Plain Jos	[Documentary]	*Crown of Thorns*	Mystery Plays,
The Merchant of Venice			adapted by Nigel Bryant
	William Shakespeare	** Miner Dig the Coal*	[Documentary]
* The Pied Piper	Peter Terson	** Treasure Island*	R.L. Stevenson,
Joking Apart	Alan Ayckbourn		adapted by Rony Robinson
* Quiet Please	Arthur Berry		

[All plays were presented in 'true repertory']

Everyman Theatre, Liverpool

1970–1
Artistic Director: Alan Dossor

Stop It Whoever You Are
Henry Livings
*The Braddocks' Time Stephen Fagan
Waiting for Godot Samuel Beckett
The Wakefield Miracle Plays
Adapted/directed by P. Lover
and Alan Dosser

*Sweeney Todd Chris Bond
Toad of Toad Hall A.A. Milne
Entertaining Mr Sloane Joe Orton
Look Back in Anger John Osborne
*Unruly Elements John McGrath
Welfare Charles Wood
The Cleverness of Us C.P. Taylor

1980–1
Artistic Director: Ken Campbell

*The Warp, parts 1–10 Neil Oram
*Disco Queen Jimmy Oakes
*Lucky Strike H. Alienak
*Psychosis Unclassified
Christopher Fairbank
with **Sammy* Ken Hughes

*Hank Williams Colin Maynard
*The War with the Newts
Kenny Murray
*Charles Dexter Ward
Camilla Saunders

Royal Exchange Theatre, Manchester

1970–1: as the '69' Theatre company at the Manchester University Theatre (shared with University Departments and Student Union groups)
Artistic Directors: Casper Wrede, Jack Good, Michael Elliott, Richard Pilbrow, Braham Murray

A Midsummer Night's Dream
William Shakespeare
*Catch My Soul [a rock 'Othello']
Jack Good
Peer Gynt Henrik Ibsen

The Glass Menagerie
Tennessee Williams
Prick Up Your Ears [Entertainment]
Barry Humphries and Julian Chagrin
Green Julia Paul Abelman

1980–1
Artistic Directors: Michael Elliott, Braham Murray

The Duchess of Malfi John Webster
The Emperor Jones Eugene O'Neill
with *The Chairs* Eugene Ionesco
Waiting for Godot Samuel Beckett
Harvey Mary Chase
*Hello Socks! [Children's
entertainment (matinées)]

Rosmersholm Henrik Ibsen
The Corn is Green Emlyn Williams
Measure for Measure
William Shakespeare
The Misanthrope Molière
*Take Eight [Musical Entertainment]

There were in addition three contemporary plays performed during the season as late night or matinée shows.

The Funding of Repertory

SIX REPERTORY THEATRES: FACTS AND FIGURES FOR THREE SPECIMEN SEASONS

The purpose of the tables given below is to back up the descriptive–historical account of the theatres dealt with in Chapter 8 with some factual detail about audience figures and sources of income – e.g. to show how in the past fifteen to twenty-five years subsidy has become an established part of the financing of most reps, and to illustrate the variations from one theatre to another in the extent of subsidy, the proportions of Arts Council and local authority grant-aid, and audience size in relation to subsidy, size of theatre, catchment area, etc. The figures have been obtained from the individual theatres and double-checked with them for accuracy so far as existing records permit. Because different theatres often have different accounting methods these figures may not always be directly comparable. Also, records for the earlier years are often less detailed and in several cases have proved untraceable. The figures should therefore be taken as a *guide*, rather than an accurate-to-every-penny record, of each theatre's financial position during the years in question. Finally, it should be pointed out that the ten-year intervals employed may in some cases distort the actual trend in audience attendance that may have occurred in between the selected dates (e.g. the jump in attendance experienced by the Everyman in the years immediately following the 1970–1 season). The figures should be read therefore in the context of the accounts given in Chapter 8.

Table I *Theatre Audience Figures and Sources of Income*

Theatre	Year	No. of performances	Audience figures per season (and average percentage attendance where available)	Income			Box Office [* = including other earned income]
				Arts Council	Local Authorities	Other Sources	
Nottingham Playhouse [old theatre sat 460; new theatre, opened 1963, seats 754]	1960–1	212 (20 productions)	(63%)	£10000	[unavailable]	nil	£28131
	1970–1	236 (9 productions)	132740 (75.4%)	£65000	£42175	nil	£63695
	1980–1	229 (15 productions)	93736 (57.2%)	£322000	£150450	£2750 (sponsorship)	£207352
Glasgow Citizens' Theatre [main theatre seats 830; The Close sat 150 until closed in 1974]	1960–1	[numbers unavailable] (16 productions)		£5250	[unavailable]	nil	£31707*
	1970–1	233 (12 productions) (main theatre)	82500 (main theatre)	£44800 (+£11200 for The Close)	£12000	nil	£32368*
	1980–1	203 (8 productions)	112231	£219000	£104500	nil	£138733*
Salisbury Playhouse [old theatre sat 406; new playhouse,	1960–1	300 (38 productions)	c.75000 62%	£4000	£600	nil	[unavailable]
	1970–1	301	c.95000	£22950	£1760	nil	c.£39000*

						(sponsorship etc.)	
		(main stage) 115 (Studio) (16 productions)	8050 (81%)				
Stoke-on-Trent: Victoria Theatre [seats 389]	1970–1	300 (12 productions)	66833 (65%)	£20000	£12105	nil	£23900*
	1980–1	296 (8 productions)	63548 (55%)	£122150	£53170	£1500 (West Midlands Arts Assn)	£103526*
Liverpool: Everyman Theatre [old theatre sat approx. 400; new theatre, opened 1977, seats 432]	1970–1	194 (12 productions)	32362	£24848	[unavailable]	£7000 (Merseyside Arts Assn)	£12282
	1980–1	187 (7 productions)	35011 (49%)	£28300	£39500	£1400 (donations, grants)	£56209 (£74325*)
Manchester: 69 Theatre Company at the University Theatre [sat 285]	1970–1	142 (6 productions)	32469 (75%)	£31500	[unavailable]	nil	£19896
Royal Exchange [new theatre seats 733] N.B. The 69 Company became The Royal Exchange Co. n 1976	1980–1	344 (9 productions)	206508 (82%)	£285500	£243000	£12000 (sponsorship)	£534789

COMPARATIVE STATISTICS

Table II illustrates the dramatic increase in government grant-aid for the arts that has taken place over the twenty years from 1960–1 to 1980–1, though it does not include grant-aid administered via the Regional Arts Associations nor by local government. It shows in particular how that grant-aid increase has been reflected in the number of companies supported: it has been a real increase (up to the late seventies at least) and not merely an inflationary one. It should be noted that the Arts Council now distinguishes between 'building-based' and 'touring' companies, and the figures below follow that distinction. For the most part, building-based companies may be read as repertory theatres (both regional and London based), although there are several companies in that category that do not fully fit the repertory description (e.g. because they tour more than they perform in their own building).

The diagrams give a break-down of audience attendance figures for the regional repertory theatres in England (only) for the year 1981–2; they are based on the quarterly returns made to the Arts Council by its client repertory theatres outside London. The Arts Council's requests in recent years for an exhaustive supply of information from its client theatres, together with computerisation, has now made analyses of audience figures possible in a more detailed and reliable form than ever before. (It should be noted that 'Tours in' refers to work produced by outside companies and not by the resident repertory company.)

Table II *Arts Council of Great Britain: General Grants Made in 1960–1 and 1980–1*

	1960–1	1980–1
Parliamentary Grant-in-Aid received by the Arts Council	£1 500 000	£70 970 000
General expenditure on the arts (excluding operating costs)		
in England	£1 225 424	£54 679 613
in Scotland	£93 932	£8 075 748
in Wales	£52 187	£4 717 191
Drama expenditure: England	£154 341	£9 591 121 (excluding National Theatre, RSC and Touring)
Grants and guarantees to:		
National Theatre	[none]	£5 188 000
Royal Shakespeare Company	[none]	£2 535 934
Other building-based companies	£139 591 (28 companies)	£7 360 408 (61 companies)
and touring companies	£8115 (4 companies)	£1 763 759 (38 companies)
Other Drama touring companies financed from separate Touring allocation	[none]	£730 592 (17 companies)
Drama expenditure: Scotland	£23 975	£5 740 850
Building-based companies	£21 000 (including 5 reps)	£1 707 021 (including 5 reps)
Touring companies	[none]	£131 569
Drama expenditure: Wales		
Drama	£12 215 (no reps)	£1 415 504 (including 2 reps and various touring and community companies)

AUDIENCE ATTENDANCE AT REGIONAL REPERTORY THEATRES IN ENGLAND, 1981–2

1 Per cent of theatre capacity by type of production

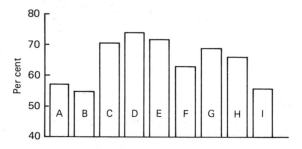

A   Drama, home-based
B   New work, home-based
C   Musicals, home-based
D   Pantomime, home-based
E   Children's theatre, home-based
F   Drama, tours in
G   Opera/dance, tours in
H   Children's theatre, tours in
I   Concerts/other, tours in

2   Share of total audience by production type

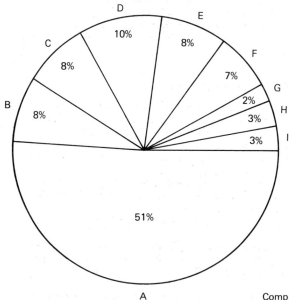

Compiled by Tim Baker
Reproduced by permission of the Arts Counci

Notes

2 The Nineteenth-Century Background

1 Reprinted in Allardyce Nicoll, *A History of English Drama 1660–1900*, vol. 4: *Early Nineteenth Century Drama 1800–1850*, 2nd edn (Cambridge, 1955), pp. 239–44.

2 See V.C. Clinton Baddeley, *All Right on the Night* (London, 1954),. p. 113.

3 Laurence Irving, *Henry Irving: The Actor and His World* (London, 1951), Appendix B, pp. 685–84.

4 Squire and Marie Bancroft, *The Bancrofts: Recollections of Sixty Years* (London, 1909), pp. 53–4.

5 *The Same Only Different* (London, 1969), pp. 203–4.

6 John Coleman, *Fifty Years of an Actor's Life* (London, 1904), vol. 2, pp. 146–7.

7 Quoted in Rennie Powell, *The Bristol Stage* (Bristol, 1919), p. 113.

8 John Coleman, *Memoirs of Samuel Phelps* (London, 1886), p. 67.

9 William Toynbee (ed.), *Diaries of William Charles Macready, 1833–1851* (London, 1912), vol. 1, p. 285.

10 Introduction, Christopher St John (ed.), *Ellen Terry and Bernard Shaw: A Correspondence* (London, 1949), p. xxiv.

11 *Seven Ages: an Autobiography 1888–1927* (London, 1970), p. 45.

12 Joseph Macleod, *The Actor's Right to Act* (London, 1981), p. 70.

13 Winifred F.C. Isaac, *Alfred Wareing: A Biography* (London, 1948), p. 35.

14 Prospectus reproduced in Michael Orme, *J.T. Grein: The Story of a Pioneer* (London, 1936), p. 76.

3 First Steps: The Beginnings of a Movement

1 See A. Jackson, 'Harley Granville Barker as Director at the Royal Court Theatre', in *Theatre Research/Recherches Theatrales*, vol. 12, no. 2 (1972), 26–33, from which in adapted form several sections of this chapter have been drawn.

2 From Granville Barker's speech at the Complimentary Dinner given to Vedrenne and Barker at the end of the Court venture to celebrate their achievement, 7 July 1970: the printed record of the proceedings, pp. 12–13.

3 Arnold, 'The French Play in London', in *The Nineteenth Century*, August 1879, p. 243; quoted in Archer and Granville Barker, *A National Theatre: Scheme and Estimates* (London, 1907), preceding their Preface.

4 Quoted in P.P. Howe, *The Repertory Theatre: A Record and a Criticism* (London, 1910), p. 37.

5 For a penetrating analysis of the Independent Theatre see J. Stokes, *Resistible Theatres: Enterprise and Experiment in the Late Nineteenth Century* (London, 1972). See also A. Miller, *The Independent Theatre in Europe* (London, 1931).

6 See Miller, p. 177.

7 Shaw, in *The Saturday Review*, 14 March 1896, reprinted in his *Our Theatres in the Nineties*, vol. 2, p. 70; quoted in Stokes, *Resistible Theatres*, p. 18.

8   Shaw, *The Saturday Review*, 21 March 1896, reprinted in *Our Theatres in the Nineties*, vol. 2, p. 81.
9   Speech given to the Social Science Congress, 4 October 1898. I am grateful to the staff of The Shakespeare Birthplace Trust, Stratford-upon-Avon, for their help in locating and transcribing the m.s. drafts of Irving's speech.
10 Pearson, *Beerbohm Tree* (London, 1956), p. 60.
11 *Ibid.*, p. 60.
12 J.C. Trewin, *The Edwardian Theatre* (Oxford, 1976), p. 24.
13 Letter dated 21 April 1903, quoted in Charles Archer, *William Archer: Life, Work and Friendships* (London, 1931), pp. 272–3.
14 W. Archer and H. Granville Barker, *A National Theatre: Scheme and Estimates* (London, 1907).
15 *Ibid.*, p. 33.
16 Complimentary Dinner speech (see n. 2).
17 Lillah McCarthy, *Myself and my Friends* (London, 1934), p. 90.
18 W. Archer, *A Record and Commentary of the Vedrenne–Barker Season, 1904–5* (London, 1906); quoted in Archibald Henderson, *Shaw: Man of the Century* (London, 1956), p. 509.
19 This point is made by Janet McDonald in a paper, 'The Promised Land of the London Stage – Acting Style at the Court Theatre, 1904–7', given at the International Federation for Theatre Research World Congress, Prague, 1973.
20 The play programmes for each of the ventures in question may be found in D. McCarthy, *The Court Theatre, 1904–1907: A Commentary and a Criticism* (London, 1907); R. Pogson, *Miss Horniman and the Gaiety Theatre, Manchester* (London, 1952); T.C. Kemp, *The Birmingham Repertory Theatre: The Playhouse and the Man* (Birmingham, 1943); and G. Wyndham Goldie, *The Liverpool Repertory Theatre, 1911–1934* (Liverpool and London, 1935).
21 Miller, *Independent Theatre*, p. 198.
22 Howe, *Repertory Theatre*, p. 53.
23 Shaw, 'Granville-Barker: Some Particulars', *Drama*, NS no. 3 (Winter 1946), reprinted in E.J. West (ed.), *Shaw on Theatre* (New York, 1959), p. 262.
24 Granville Barker, interview in the *Pall Mall Gazette*, 14 March 1908; quoted in C.B. Purdom, *Harley Granville Barker* (London, 1955), p. 80.
25 Archer and Barker, *A National Theatre*, p. xiv.
26 See Howe, *Repertory Theatre*, p. 217.
27 Archer and Barker, *A National Theatre*, p. xviii.
28 Granville Barker, 'The Theatre – The Next Phase', a lecture given on 9 July 1910; printed in *The Forum*, vol. 44 (August 1910), p. 640.
29 *Ibid.*, p. 638.
30 Quoted in Hugh Hunt, *The Abbey: Ireland's National Theatre, 1904–79* (London, 1979), p. 19.
31 Quoted in *ibid.*, p. 39.
32 Archer and Barker, *A National Theatre*, p. xi.

4   1907–1918: Manchester to Birmingham

1   Ben Iden Payne, *A Life in a Wooden O* (New Haven, 1977), p. 78.
2   *Ibid.*, p. 93.
3   *Ibid.*, p. 92.
4   Whitford Kane, *Are We All Met?* (London, 1931), p. 94.
5   Payne, *A Life in a Wooden O*, p. 89.
6   Rex Pogson, *Miss Horniman and the Gaiety Theatre, Manchester* (London, 1952), p. 29.
7   *Ibid.*, p. 71.
8   Kane, *Are We All Met?*, p. 92.

9   *Ibid.*, p. 91.
10 Pogson, *Miss Horniman*, pp. 36–7.
11 *Ibid.*, p. 162. See also Diana Devlin, *A Speaking Part: Lewis Casson and the Theatre of His Time* (London, 1982), pp. 101–2.
12 Kane, *Are We All Met?*, p. 105.
13 Grace Wyndham Goldie, *The Liverpool Repertory Theatre 1911–1934* (Liverpool and London, 1935), p. 51.
14 *Ibid.*, p. 83.
15 Basil Dean, *Seven Ages: An Autobiography 1888–1927* (London, 1970), p. 100.
16 Wyndham Goldie, *Liverpool Repertory Theatre*, p. 85.
17 Pogson, *Miss Horniman*, pp. 52–3.
18 Harold Brighouse, *What I Have Had* (London, 1953), p. 179.
19 Pogson, *Miss Horniman*, p. 183.
20 Brighouse, *What I Have Had*, p. 178.
21 David Hutchison, *The Modern Scottish Theatre* (Edinburgh, 1977), p. 18.
22 Foreword to Winifred F.E.C. Isaac, *Alfred Wareing: A Biography* (London, 1948), p. v.
23 *Glasgow Herald*, 16 February 1912.
24 *Ibid.*, 10 November 1911.
25 Isaac, *Alfred Wareing*, p. v.
26 Hutchison, *Modern Scottish Theatre*, p. 18.
27 *Ibid.*, p. 18.
28 Kathleen Barker, *The Theatre Royal, Bristol, 1766–1966. Two Centuries of Stage History* (London, 1974), p. 185.
29 Pogson, *Miss Horniman*, p. 175.

5   The Inter-War Years

1   J.C. Trewin, *The Birmingham Repertory Theatre, 1913–1963* (London, 1963), pp. 107–8.
2   *Ibid.*, p. 82.
3   John Parker (ed.), *Who's Who in the Theatre*, 8th edn (London, 1936), p. 351.
4   *Ibid.*, p. 1148.
5   Cedric Hardwicke, *A Victorian in Orbit* (London, 1961), p. 102.
6   T.C. Kemp, *The Birmingham Repertory Theatre. The Playhouse and the Man* (Birmingham, 1943), p. 35.
7   Wyndham Goldie, *The Liverpool Repertory Theatre 1911–1934* (Liverpool and London, 1935), p. 218.
8   Reproduced in the Souvenir to mark the Golden Jubilee of the Playhouse (Oxford, 1973).
9   'Thirty-three Years', by Louis Frewer, in *ibid.*
10 Souvenir (see n. 8).
11 *Oxford Magazine*, 17 October 1929.
12 T. Guthrie, *A Life in the Theatre* (London, 1960), p. 27.
13 N. Marshall, *The Other Theatre* (London, 1947), p. 24.
14 'Introduction to the Theory and Practice of Stagecraft', in Harold Downs (ed.), *Theatre and Stage*, vol. 1 (London, 1934), p. 7.
15 Richard Cave, *Terence Gray and the Cambridge Festival Theatre* (Cambridge, 1980), p. 22.
16 C.H. Ridge and F.S. Aldred, *Stage Lighting: Principles and Practice* (London, 1935), p. 89.
17 Downs (ed.), *Theatre and Stage*, p. 7.
18 *Ibid.*
19 *Ibid.*
20 Marshall, *The Other Theatre*, p. 68.

21 Cave, *Terence Gray*, p. 13.
22 See Graham Woodruff, ' "Down with the Boot-Faced". Public Relations at the Festival Theatre, Cambridge', in *Theatre Research International*, vol. 1, no. 2 (1976), p. 117.
23 *Ibid.*, p. 123.
24 Marshall, *The Other Theatre*, p. 68.
25 Foreword to Winifred Isaac, *Alfred Wareing: A Biography* (London, 1948), p. vii.
26 J.C. Trewin, *Portrait of Plymouth* (London, 1973), p. 189.
27 Lady Constance Malleson, *After Ten Years* (London, 1933), p. 174.
28 *The Stage Year Book 1928* (London, 1928), p. 15.
29 *A Short History of Bristol's Little Theatre* (Bristol, 1925), pp. 9–10.
30 *Ibid.*, p. 12.
31 *The Times*, 18 December 1928.
32 *Short History of Bristol's Little Theatre*, p. 26.
33 *Stage Year Book 1928*, p. 16.
34 *Ibid.*, p. 16.
35 *Ibid.*, p. 24.
36 *The Story of the Little Theatre, Bristol*, compiled and edited by the Rapier Players (Bristol [1948]), p. 24.
37 Trewin, *Birmingham Repertory Theatre*, p. 117.
38 Aubrey Dyas, *Adventure in Repertory. The Northampton Players* (Northampton, 1948), p. 82.
39 John Parker (ed.), *Who's Who in the Theatre*, 10th edn (London, 1947), p. 502.
40 J. Counsell, *Counsell's Opinion* (London, 1963), pp. 51–2.
41 *Oxford Magazine*, 23 April 1933.
42 Counsell, *Counsell's Opinion*, p. 37.

6 The War Years and After

1 Eric Walter White, *The Arts Council of Great Britain* (London, 1975), p. 33.
2 *The Repertory Movement in Great Britain* (London, 1968), p. 10.
3 For a detailed account of the negotiations see Kathleen Barker, *The Theatre Royal, Bristol, 1766–1966. Two Centuries of Stage History* (London, 1974), pp. 202–14.
4 Winifred Bannister, *James Bridie and his Theatre* (London, 1955), p. 211.
5 Charles Landstone, *Off-Stage. A Personal Record of the First Twelve Years of State Sponsored Drama in Great Britain* (London, 1953), pp. 126 and 158.
6 *Ibid.*, pp. 60–1.
7 Barker, *Theatre Royal*, p. 205.
8 Audrey Williamson and Charles Landstone, *The Bristol Old Vic. The First Ten Years* (London, 1957), p. 76.
9 Arts Council of Great Britain, *5th Annual Report, 1949–50* (London, 1950), p. 26.
10 *The Repertory Movement in Great Britain*, p. 13.
11 Figures supplied by Nancy Burman, Administrator, in conversation with A.R. Jackson, 6 August 1980.
12 White, *Arts Council*, p. 97.
13 A.W. Tolmie (compiler), *The Stage Guide* (London, 1946), p. 196.
14 *The Stage Year Book 1949* (London, 1949), p. 30.
15 Phyllis Leggett, 'The Repertory Movement in Great Britain', in *Who's Who in the Theatre*, 15th edn (London, 1972), pp. 1687–8.
16 Alec McCowen, *Young Gemini* (London, 1979), pp. 68–9.
17 John Osborne, *A Better Class of Person. An Autobiography 1929–1956* (London, 1982), p. 246.
18 *Ibid.*, p. 247.
19 *The Stage Year Book, 1950* (London, 1950), pp. 32–3.

20   *The Stage Year Book, 1954* (London, 1954), pp. 44–5.
21   *The Stage Year Book, 1955* (London, 1955), pp. 189–91.
22   *The Stage Year Book, 1956* (London, 1956), p. 16.
23   In conversation with the writer.
24   *The Repertory Movement in Great Britain*, p. 12.

7   *1958–1983: Renewal, Growth and Retrenchment*

1   The figures given for the numbers of buildings and companies are gleaned from various sources, the main ones being the *Annual Reports* of the Arts Council, the *Stage Year Books* (published up to 1969) and *The British Theatre Directory* (published annually since 1974).
2   Tynan, 'Curtain up in Coventry', in *The Observer*, 30 March 1958.
3   Statement in the commemorative brochure of the Belgrade Theatre issued to mark its opening in March 1958.
4   *The Theatre Today in England and Wales* (The Arts Council of Great Britain, 1970), p. 35.
5   See Gordon Vallins, 'The Beginnings of TIE', in T. Jackson (ed.), *Learning through Theatre: Essays and Casebooks on Theatre in Education* (Manchester, 1980). Further information on the growth and methodology of TIE is contained elsewhere in the book.
6   See Catherine Itzin, *Stages in the Revolution: Political Theatre in Britain since 1968* (London, 1980), p. xiv.
7   In 1977–8, for example, the National Theatre building cost well over one million pounds to run before anything was put on its stages, and this sum ate up nearly a third of its total subsidies. (From *The National Figures, 1976–8*, National Theatre pamphlet, 1978.)
8   Salberg, in an interview with the author, May 1982.
9   Havergal, in an interview with the author, September 1981.
10   Howard Goorney's *The Theatre Workshop Story* (London, 1981) is the major source of information on this subject.
11   Tynan, 'Curtain up in Coventry'.
12   Bailey, in the Belgrade Theatre commemorative brochure, March 1958.
13   Elliott, in an interview with the author, March 1982.
14   See Moro, 'A Flexible Design', in *The Stage Year Book, 1962, pp. 16–17*.
15   Joseph, Introduction to *Actor and Architect* ed. Joseph (Manchester, 1964), p. 6.
16   *Ibid.*, p. xi.
17   Comparative figures for the funding of theatres abroad in relation to the UK may be found in the Arts Council *Annual Report* for 1953–4; in the Report of the House of Commons' *Eighth Report from the Education, Science and Arts Committee – Public and Private Funding of the Arts* (London, 1982); and in John Allen, *Theatre in Europe* (Eastbourne, 1981).
18   See Peter Brigg, 'The New Birmingham Repertory Theatre: A Case Study in Marketing', in *Educational Theatre Journal*, vol. 29, no. 1 (March 1977), 95–107.
19   A notable exception is the Nuffield Theatre, Southampton (funded by Southern Arts Association).
20   *Theatre Today*, p. 35.
21   Arts Council *Annual Report* for 1975–6, p. 26.
22   See Arts Council *Annual Report* for 1980–1, p. 6.
23   In May 1981, the Council published a full list of the thirteen criteria which were to be employed in its assessment procedure, among which were:
    quality of artistic product, including, as appropriate, standards of presentation, performance, design, and direction and their relationship to the conception of the company's overall programme;

the extent to which stated aims and objects are realised;
the fullest practicable use of facilities and the widest provision of arts to the community;
education policy in relation to the artistic programme;
box office and attendance returns;
the company's success in raising local authority support and other income;
the balance of provision between London and other regions.

24   D. Austen-Smith, 'On the Impact of Revenue Subsidies on Repertory Theatre Policy', in *Journal of Cultural Economics*, vol. 4, no. 1 (1980), p. 15. The conclusions were based on an analysis of the programmes of thirty-four repertory theatres in England in 1974–5.

25   *Theatre Today*, p. 51.

26   Hedley, 'Still Writers' Theatres?' (an interview with D. Roper), in *Plays and Players*, December 1982, p. 12.

27   Cheeseman, 'Permanent Companies', in *Cue* (Greenwich Theatre Magazine), October 1972.

28   P. James, 'Hammersmith's Man' (an interview with D. Roper) in *Plays and Players*, February 1983, p. 12.

29   T. Browne, *Playwrights' Theatre: The English Stage Company at the Royal Court* (London, 1975), p. 75.

30   A.V. Williams, 'Our Two Theatres', in *Plays and Players*, March 1967, p. 64.

31   Theatre Writers' Union: *Playwrights – An Endangered Species?* (1982), p. 42.

32   R. Cushman in *The Observer*, 14 June 1981.

33   J. Elsom, 'A Policy for New Plays', in *Theatre Quarterly*, vol. 11 (July–Sept. 1973), 58–69.

34   Seventy-five new plays are recorded for 1980–1; Elsom noted 109 for 1971–2. These figures are necessarily approximate because of the notorious difficulty involved in compiling accurate statistics on the production of new plays: different theatres apply different criteria in determining what constitutes a 'new' play (e.g. when is a new play not really a new play but a translation or an adaptation?); and not all theatres keep a complete and accurate record of their past productions. It should be noted that the figure given for 1980–1 does not include TIE and touring productions but does include new plays given at studios attached to repertory theatres. The main source used has been theatres' returns to Arts Council offices in London, Cardiff, Edinburgh and Belfast.

35   *Playwrights*, p. 21.

36   From Arts Council reports compiled by George Darroch (Research officer) and Tim Baker (Statistician), based on an analysis of statistical returns from its subsidised companies for 1981–2. These figures relate specifically to the regional companies but figures for those in London are similar. See also *Playwrights*, pp. 20–2; 42–6.

37   Arts Council *Annual Report* for 1979–80, p. 13.

38   P. Cheeseman, 'The Victoria Theatre', in *The Stage – Municipal Theatre Supplement*, 9 May 1968.

39   See Select Committee Report for audience attendance figures for 1968–9 and 1981–2, which should be read in conjunction with the Arts Council Report, *Attendances for Subsidised Dance, Drama and Opera Performances in England, 1981–2*. The latter (probably more accurate) document claims that 'English drama repertory companies (including the National Theatre and the RSC) sold almost 6 800 000 tickets in 1981–2', of which 5 604 000 were for home-based performances.

40   Arts Council Research Report: 'The Audience for Subsidised Drama in Scotland and the North of England' (1975).

8 *1958–1983;: Six Reps in Focus*

1 Digby-Day, in an interview with the author, April 1982.
2 Neville, in an interview with Emrys Bryson in the *Nottingham Evening Post*, 2 June 1967.
3 *Ibid.*
4 *Ibid.*
5 Hodgkinson, 'The Bureaucrat and the Artist', in Pick (ed.), *The State and the Arts* (Eastbourne, 1980), p. 113.
6 Neville, 'On How Not to Run a Theatre', *The Sunday Times*, 3 September 1967. A detailed account of the whole affair, very supportive of Neville, was drawn up by members of the Nottingham Playhouse Club and published in 1968: *The Neville Affair – The Facts*, by G.R. Hibbard, published by the Nottingham Playhouse Action Group.
7 Burge, quoted in the *Nottingham Evening Post*, 5 December 1967.
8 Eyre, quoted in the *Nottingham Evening Post*, 6 March 1978.
9 Eyre, in an interview with the author, November 1981.
10 Eyre, in the *Nottingham Evening Post*, 6 March 1978.
11 Digby-Day, in an interview in the *Nottingham Evening Post*, 5 September 1980.
12 *Ibid.*
13 Digby-Day, in an interview with Frank Eggins, in *Plays and Players*, August 1982, p. 39.
14 Oliver, 'Citizens' Band', in *Plays and Players*, October 1979, p. 15.
15 For the early (pre 1970) history of the Citizens', see the informative booklet by Tony Paterson, *Citizens' Theatre: Its Story from the Beginning to the Present Day* (Glasgow, 1970).
16 'Mass Observation Report of In-Theatre Surveys at the Citizens' Theatre', February 1976.
17 'Citizens' Band', p. 15.
18 Havergal, in an interview with the author, September 1981.
19 'Citizens' Band', p. 16.
20 *The Times*, 3 March 1980.
21 R.D. MacDonald, quoted in Prof. Janet McDonald, 'The Citizens' Theatre, Glasgow: a House of Illusions' (unpublished paper read at the Conference of the International Federation for Theatre Research, Venice, September 1980), p. 14.
22 *The Financial Times*, 30 August 1979.
23 See McDonald, *Citizens' Theatre*, pp. 16–19, for a useful discussion of acting style at the Citizens'.
24 Cushman, in *The Observer*, 15 April 1979.
25 Havergal, in an interview with the author, September 1981.
26 For a useful summary of the early years of the Arts Theatre/Playhouse, see John Bavin, *Heart of the City: The Story of the Salisbury Playhouse* (Salisbury, 1976).
27 *Ibid.*, p. 20.
28 Bavin, *Heart of the City*, p. 22.
29 Findlater, 'Points from the Provinces', in *Time and Tide*, 7 December 1961, p. 2069.
30 Salberg and Clissold, both in interviews with the author, May 1982.
31 Salberg, in a Playhouse programme article, 6 October 1976.
32 See Ned Chaillet in *The Times*, 3 August 1981, and B.A. Young in *The Financial Times*, 8 August 1981.
33 Horlock, in *Plays and Players*, March 1983, p. 36.
34 'Salisbury Playhouse: Facts and Figures Incorporating an Audience Survey' (1980).
35 Preface by Theatre Chairman, Director and Manager, in *ibid.*
36 Cheeseman, 'The Victoria Theatre: The First Three Rounds' (August 1965) – a report on the theatre's first three seasons.

37   Cheeseman, in *Plays and Players*, September 1965, pp. 48, 50.
38   Joseph, in *Plays and Players*, March 1962, p. 38.
39   *Ibid.*
40   Cheeseman, Introduction to *The Knotty* (London, 1970), p. xiv.
41   For a full description of the theory and working method involved in the Stoke documentaries, see Cheeseman's Introduction to *The Knotty*.
42   From a lecture given by Cheeseman at the conference on Documentary Theatre, Milton Keynes, April 1980, organised by East Midlands Arts Association.
43   Introduction to *The Knotty*, p. xix.
44   Richard Howells, in *The Stage*, 8 April 1982.
45   Hands, quoted in *The Times*, 27 March 1971.
46   Tanner, *Everyman: The First Ten Years* (Liverpool, 1974), p. 11.
47   Quoted in *ibid.*, p. 43.
48   See McGrath, *A Good Night Out – Popular Theatre: Audience, Class and Form* (London, 1981), pp. 50–2.
49   Tanner, *Everyman*, p. 51.
50   Quoted in *ibid.*, p. 51.
51   Thornber, in *Plays and Players*, October 1981, p. 56.
52   See Robert Scott, *The Biggest Room in the World: A Short History of the Manchester Royal Exchange* (Manchester, 1976), p. 55.
53   Mayer, in *Plays and Players*, April 1980, p. 20.
54   Elliott, 'Exchange Experience', in *Architectural Review*, December 1976, p. 362.
55   Elliott, in an interview with the author, March 1982.
56   Robin Thornber, reviewing the new musical *Andy Capp* at the Exchange, in *The Guardian*, 30 June 1982.
57   Audience survey conducted for the North-West Arts Association (Manchester, 1981).

9   The Repertory movement: Summary, Assessment, Conclusion

1   Barker: from his speech at the Complimentary Dinner given to mark the end of the Vedrenne–Barker seasons at the Court. See Chapter 3, p. 16.
2   Barker, 'The Theatre: The Next Phase', *Forum*, 44 (August 1910), p. 162.
3   Barker, 'Two German Theatres', *Fortnightly Review*, N.S., 89 (Jan. 1911), p. 65.
4   See Barker, 'The Theatre: The Next Phase'.
5   St John Ervine, *The Organised Theatre* (London, 1924).
6   House of Commons, *Eighth Report from the Education, Science and Arts Committee – Public and Private Funding of the Arts* (London, 1982), vol. 1, p. lxxi.
7   *Ibid.*, pp. lxxi, lxxiii.
8   *Ibid.*, p. xcic.
9   Elsom, *Theatre Outside London* (London, 1971), p. 10.
10 Barker, 'The Theatre: The Next Phase', p. 164.
11 See especially John McGrath, 'The Theory and Practice of Political Theatre', *Theatre Quarterly*, 35 (Autumn 1979), 43–54; also Su Braden, *Artists and People* (London, 1978).
12 *Commons Committee Report*, p. lxxxix; see also the Arts Council discussion document, 'The Arts and Education' (July 1981).
13 Elliott, in an interview with the author, March 1982.

Select Bibliography

Allen, John. *Theatre in Europe*. Eastbourne, 1981

Archer, William. *The Old Drama and the New*. London, 1923

Archer, W. and Harley Granville Barker. *A National Theatre: Scheme and Estimates*. London, 1907

Arts Council of Great Britain. *The Theatre Today in England and Wales*. London, 1970

Bannister, Winifred. *James Bridie and His Theatre*. London, 1955

Barker, H. Granville. *A National Theatre*, rev. edn. London, 1930

    The Exemplary Theatre. London, 1922

    'The Theatre: The Next Phase', *Forum*, 44 (August 1910), 159–70

Barker, Kathleen. *The Theatre Royal, Bristol, 1766–1966. Two Centuries of Stage History*. London, 1974

Bavin, J. *Heart of the City: The Story of the Salisbury Playhouse*. Salisbury, 1976 [pamphlet]

Beauman, Sally. *The Royal Shakespeare Company: A History of Ten Decades*. Oxford, 1982

Bell, S.H. *The Theatre in Ulster*. Dublin, 1972

Bentham, F. *New Theatres in Britain*. London, 1970

Borsa, Mario. *The English Stage of Today*. London, 1908

Bradby, D. and J. McCormick, *People's Theatre*. London, 1978

Braun, Edward. *The Director and the Stage*. London, 1982

Bristol, Little Theatre. *A Short History of Bristol's Little Theatre*. Bristol, 1925

Browne, Terry. *Playwrights' Theatre: The English Stage Company at the Royal Court*. London, 1973

Cave, Richard. *Terence Gray and the Cambridge Festival Theatre* (Theatre in Focus series). Cambridge, 1980

Chambers, Colin. *Other Spaces: New Theatre and the RSC*. London, 1980

Chisholm, Cecil. *Repertory: An Outline of the Modern Theatre Movement*. London, 1934

Cook, Judith, *Directors' Theatre*. London, 1974

Council of Repertory Theatres. *The Repertory Movement in Great Britain*. London, 1968 [booklet]

Counsell, John. *Counsell's Opinion*. London, 1963

Craig, S, ed. *Dreams and Deconstructions: Alternative Theatre in Britain*. Ambergate, Derbyshire, 1980

Dean, Basil. *The Repertory Theatre*. Liverpool, 1911 [a lecture given at the Liverpool Playgoers' Society, 1911, in pamphlet form]

    Seven Ages: An Autobiography, 1888–1927. London, 1970

    The Theatre at War. London, 1956

Dyas, Aubrey. *Adventure in Repertory. The Northampton Players*. Northampton, 1948

Elsom, John. *Theatre Outside London*. London, 1971

    Postwar British Theatre. London, 1979

Elsom, John and Nicholas Tomalin. *The History of the National Theatre*. London, 1978
Ervine, St John. *The Organised Theatre*. London, 1924
Findlater, F. *The Unholy Trade*. London, 1952
    The Future of the Theatre. London, 1959 [Fabian Society pamphlet]
Flannery, J.W. *Miss Annie F. Horniman and the Abbey Theatre*. Dublin, 1970
Goldie, Grace Wyndham. *The Liverpool Repertory Theatre 1911–1934*. Liverpool and London, 1935
Goorney, Howard. *The Theatre Workshop Story*. London, 1981
Guthrie, Tyrone. *A Life in the Theatre*. London, 1960
Hayman, Ronald. *The Set-up: An Anatomy of British Theatre*. London, 1973
    British Theatre Since 1955. London, 1979
House of Commons. *Eighth Report from the Education, Science and Arts Committee – Public and Private Funding of the Arts*. London, 1982
Howe, P.P. *The Repertory Theatre: A Record and a Criticism*. London, 1910
Hunt, Hugh. *The Abbey: Ireland's National Theatre, 1904–79*. London, 1979
Hunt, Hugh, Kenneth Richards and J.R. Taylor. *Revels History of Drama in English*, vol. 7: *1880–Present*. London, 1978
Hutchison, Robert. *The Politics of the Arts Council*. London, 1982
Isaac, Winifred, F.E.C. *Alfred Wareing: A Biography*. London, 1948
Itzen, Catherine. *Stages in the Revolution: Political Theatre in Britain since 1968*. London, 1980
Joseph, Stephen. *New Theatre Forms*. London, 1968
    Theatre in the Round. London, 1967
    ed. *Actor and Architect*. Manchester, 1964
Kemp, T.C. *The Birmingham Repertory Theatre: The Playhouse and The Man*. Birmingham, 1943
Landstone, Charles. *Off-Stage: A Personal Record of the First Twelve Years of State Sponsored Drama in Great Britain*. London, 1953
Leggett, Phyllis. 'The Repertory Movement in Great Britain', in *Who's Who in the Theatre*, 15th edn. London, 1972
McCarthy, Desmond. *The Court Theatre, 1904–1907: A Commentary and A Criticism*. London, 1907
McGrath, John. *A Good Night Out – Popular Theatre: Audience, Class and Form*. London, 1981
Marshall, Norman. *The Other Theatre*. London, 1947
    The Producer and the Play. London, 1962
Matthews, W. Bache. *A History of the Birmingham Repertory Theatre*. Birmingham, 1924
Miller, Anna I. *The Independent Theatre in Europe*. New York, 1931
Nicoll, Allardyce. *A History of English Drama, 1660–1900*, vol. 5: *Late Nineteenth-Century Drama*. Cambridge, 1959
    English Drama 1900–1930: The Beginnings of the Modern Period. Cambridge, 1973
ÓhAodha, Micheál. *Theatre in Ireland*. Oxford, 1974
Paterson, Tony. *Citizens' Theatre: Its Story from the Beginning to the Present Day*. Glasgow, 1970 [pamphlet]
Payne, Ben Iden. *A Life in a Wooden O*. New Haven, 1977
Pick, J. ed. *The State and the Arts*. Eastbourne, 1980
Pogson, Rex. *Miss Horniman and the Gaiety Theatre, Manchester*. London, 1952
Priestley, J.B. *Theatre Outlook*. London, 1947
Purdom. C.B. *Harley Granville Barker*. London, 1955
Rapier Players, compilers and eds. *The Story of the Little Theatre, Bristol*. Bristol [1948]
Roberts, Peter. *The Old Vic Story*. London, 1976

Rowell, George. *Theatre in the Age of Irving.* Oxford, 1981
  The Victorian Theatre, rev. edn. Cambridge, 1978
Seed, T. Alec. *The Sheffield Repertory Theatre. A History.* Sheffield, 1959
Short, Ernest. *Sixty Years of Theatre.* London, 1951
Stokes, John. *Resistible Theatres: Enterprise and Experiment in the Late Nineteenth
  Century.* London, 1972
Sweeting, Elizabeth. *Theatre Administration.* London, 1969
Tanner, Doreen. *Everyman: The First Ten Years.* Liverpool, 1974 [booklet]
Trewin, J.C. *The Birmingham Repertory Theatre, 1913–63.* London, 1951
  The Edwardian Theatre. Oxford, 1976
  The Theatre Since 1900. London, 1951
Wareing, Alfred. 'The Little Theatre Movement', *The Stage Year Book: 1928.* London,
  1928, pp. 11–28
White, E.W. *The Arts Council of Great Britain.* London, 1975
Whitworth, Geoffrey. *The Making of a National Theatre.* London, 1951
Wilkie, R. and D. Bradley. *The Subsidised Theatre: Its Organisation and Audience.*
  Glasgow, 1970
Williamson, Audrey and Charles Landstone. *The Bristol Old Vic. The First Ten Years.*
  London, 1957
Wintour, Charles, *et al. Celebration: 25 Years of British Theatre.* London, 1980

OTHER USEFUL SOURCES OF INFORMATION

Arts Council of Great Britain. *Annual Reports.* London, 1946–present
The British Theatre Directory. Eastbourne, 1974–present [published annually]
The Stage Year Book. London, 1908–28, 1949–69

Index

London theatres are listed under their names. All other theatres are listed under their locations.

220